# CAMBRIDGE LIBRARY COLLECTION

*Books of enduring scholarly value*

## Classics

From the Renaissance to the nineteenth century, Latin and Greek were compulsory subjects in almost all European universities, and most early modern scholars published their research and conducted international correspondence in Latin. Latin had continued in use in Western Europe long after the fall of the Roman empire as the lingua franca of the educated classes and of law, diplomacy, religion and university teaching. The flight of Greek scholars to the West after the fall of Constantinople in 1453 gave impetus to the study of ancient Greek literature and the Greek New Testament. Eventually, just as nineteenth-century reforms of university curricula were beginning to erode this ascendancy, developments in textual criticism and linguistic analysis, and new ways of studying ancient societies, especially archaeology, led to renewed enthusiasm for the Classics. This collection offers works of criticism, interpretation and synthesis by the outstanding scholars of the nineteenth century.

## On Editing Aeschylus

This is an early publication (1891) by the highly regarded classical scholar and poet Walter George Headlam (1866–1908). Headlam, who taught at King's College, Cambridge, was deeply interested in textual criticism and dedicated much of his short life to translating and interpreting the works of Aeschylus, and even thirty years after his untimely death his notes formed the basis for an influential edition of the *Oresteia.* Although Headlam's subtitle does not name the target of his 'criticism', this book is in fact an impassioned attack on the style and method of editing employed by A. W. Verrall in *Seven Against Thebes* in 1887, and *Agamemnon* in 1889. Headlam condemns Verrall's 'rationalist' methods which in his view 'required outspoken criticism'. The young Headlam painstakingly dissects Verrall's work on Aeschylus, pointing out the errors, inconsistencies and shortcomings of the texts and proposing his own editorial methods. Also reissued in this volume is Verrall's riposte: *On Editing Aeschylus: A Reply*, of 1892.

Cambridge University Press has long been a pioneer in the reissuing of out-of-print titles from its own backlist, producing digital reprints of books that are still sought after by scholars and students but could not be reprinted economically using traditional technology. The Cambridge Library Collection extends this activity to a wider range of books which are still of importance to researchers and professionals, either for the source material they contain, or as landmarks in the history of their academic discipline.

Drawing from the world-renowned collections in the Cambridge University Library, and guided by the advice of experts in each subject area, Cambridge University Press is using state-of-the-art scanning machines in its own Printing House to capture the content of each book selected for inclusion. The files are processed to give a consistently clear, crisp image, and the books finished to the high quality standard for which the Press is recognised around the world. The latest print-on-demand technology ensures that the books will remain available indefinitely, and that orders for single or multiple copies can quickly be supplied.

The Cambridge Library Collection will bring back to life books of enduring scholarly value (including out-of-copyright works originally issued by other publishers) across a wide range of disciplines in the humanities and social sciences and in science and technology.

# On Editing Aeschylus

A Criticism,
*together with* A Reply

Walter Headlam
Arthur Woolgar Verrall

Cambridge
University Press

CAMBRIDGE UNIVERSITY PRESS

Cambridge, New York, Melbourne, Madrid, Cape Town, Singapore,
São Paolo, Delhi, Dubai, Tokyo

Published in the United States of America by Cambridge University Press, New York

www.cambridge.org
Information on this title: www.cambridge.org/9781108009645



This edition first published 1891
This digitally printed version 2010

ISBN 978-1-108-00964-5 Paperback

# ON EDITING AESCHYLUS

# ON EDITING AESCHYLUS

## A Criticism

BY

WALTER HEADLAM M.A.

FELLOW OF KING'S COLLEGE, CAMBRIDGE

London

DAVID NUTT 270 AND 271 STRAND

1891

*Πεῖρά τοι μαθήσιος ἀρχά.*

ALCMAN.

*Δόξα μὲν ἀνθρώποισι κακὸν μέγα, πεῖρα δ' ἄριστον·*
*πολλοὶ ἀπείρητοι δόξαν ἔχουσ' ἀγαθῶν.*

THEOGNIS.

*Τὸ διδάξασθαι δέ τοι*
*εἰδότι ῥᾴτερον· ἄγνωμον δὲ τὸ μὴ προμαθεῖν·*
*κουφότεραι γὰρ ἀπειράτων φρένες·*

PINDAR.

## CORRIGENDUM.

P. 69 note: *for* "Diphilus *fr.* 10" *read* "Diphilus *fr.* 86."

Of the editions by which I have quoted it is necessary to mention the following:

Aeschylus: Wecklein, 1885.

" for the readings of later MSS., Hermann.

Euripides: Kirchhoff, 1855 (text and apparatus).

Pindar etc.: Bergk, *Poetae Lyrici Graeci.*

Fragments of Tragedy: Nauck, 1889.

" " Attic Comedy: Kock, 1880—1888.

Callimachus: Schneider, 1870—1873.

Theocritus, Bion, Moschus: H. L. Ahrens, 1884.

---

Where I refer to pages, the references (unless otherwise indicated) are to the pages of this book. I have added an Index of the chief matters.

# ON EDITING AESCHYLUS.

The *Seven against Thebes* of Aeschylus, with an Introduction, Commentary, and Translation by A. W. VERRALL, M.A., Fellow of Trinity College, Cambridge. London: Macmillan and Co. 1887.

The *Agamemnon* of Aeschylus, with an Introduction, Commentary, and Translation by A. W. VERRALL, Litt. D., Fellow of Trinity College, Cambridge. London: Macmillan and Co. 1889.

IT will be admitted that the aim of a serious student should be to ascertain some part of truth; and that if he undertakes to produce general editions of a Greek classic, such as those we are now to consider, his chief business must be really to discover what his author wrote and meant. In the preface to the *Seven against Thebes*, Dr. Verrall informs his readers that 'the Introduction and explanatory notes are in the main the product of independent work.' The nature of the independent work we shall examine by-and-bye; but we may allow that as a plan of study independent work is admirable enough. Only we have a right to expect the student, before presenting an edition, to have consulted and weighed the views of previous workers in his field. Else we must demand that he shall by his own labour have made himself master at least of all the materials that previous workers brought to bear.

To the materials that may serve for elucidation and emendation of Aeschylus a limit could hardly be defined. There is no Greek of any age that may not be useful for the purpose. It is only by knowledge of prose that we can know what is poetical in language; it is only by knowledge of late prose that we can judge what may or may not be glosses. The chief material of that too much neglected study is of course the language of the ancient lexicons and scholia. So we have this paradox, that one of the chief qualifications for editing Aeschylus is familiarity with what is baldest and most prosaic in Greek. That qualification, though necessary for a sound method of criticism, few critics have appreciated the necessity of possessing. But no one will be hardy enough to deny that a competent editor of Aeschylus must possess knowledge at least of Homer, Hesiod, Solon, Theognis, Pindar and the lyric poets, Sophocles, Euripides, Herodotus. No one will assert that an editor is competent if ignorant of ordinary[1] scholiastic phrases.

Students to-day in this part of learning have great advantages over their predecessors, inasmuch as they have at hand materials for scientific work. To speak of such as most nearly concern the student of Aeschylus, he has Ellendt's admirable Lexicon to Sophocles; he has the Lexicon to Homer compiled under the editorship of Dr. Ebeling, a boon past estimation; it is impossible to see how it could in any way have been improved. For orthography, &c., he has a work of the highest importance, Dr. Meisterhans' *Grammatik der Attischen Inschriften.*

Scholars will never sneer at the labours of a lexicographer, for the information he collects enables them to form conclusions that are more than guesses. The glossaries appended by Blomfield to the five plays he edited retain their value still. Such work is not superseded, for facts are never out of date. Again, we possess much fuller and more accurate MSS. apparatus. The value of this is chiefly indirect; we may profit by finding similar variations continually repeated, and it is possible that we may discover causes of error and arrive

[1] See p. 76.

at wide-reaching results. The deeper an editor of Aeschylus goes into this subject the better; but he cannot be considered competent unless he knows something of palaeography in general and has mastered the elements of textual criticism.

When Dr. Verrall says that the Introduction and explanatory notes to the *Seven against Thebes* are in the main the product of independent work, what does he mean by the phrase? If he means that from the materials collected by others he has been independent in the conclusions that he draws, the statement is entirely superfluous, for, successfully or not, he has only done what every editor is bound to do. But if he means what his remark suggests, that the materials used have been in the main collected by his own reading in the ancient authors, then the statement becomes very strange indeed. For not only is the Introduction based on passages nearly all of which are cited for the basis of articles in Grote's *History of Greece* and Smith's *Dictionary of Geography*, but the quotations given in the commentary are again and again exactly those adduced by Paley,[1] or by Liddell and Scott. Further, this criticism will show that Dr. Verrall brings to his task nothing deserving the name of independent reading. Not only is he unfamiliar even with the authors mentioned above as most immediately necessary, but he does not know what is in Aeschylus himself. An editor should have read through these and other authors for the illustration of his own. Nothing can make up for lack of reading. But if anything can serve at all to remedy the defect, it is the consultation of Lexicons and Indices. Yet Dr. Verrall has omitted even this. Paley's edition he supplements by Liddell and Scott's Lexicon. If his were elementary editions for schools, he might of course refer to that lexicon as the most accessible. It is not so; he refers to it continually as though the most exhaustive. The very existence of the Paris *Thesaurus* appears to be unknown to him. Of lexicons to particular

[1] "... Doubtless however I am much more indebted than I am aware, particularly to Professor Paley, whose work was my sole 'Aeschylus' for many years."

authors, including that to Aeschylus, he has yet to learn the use.

If such be the amount of Dr. Verrall's reading, it is natural that his knowledge both of Greek thought and of Greek language should be unsound; but there is room even then for astonishment at the extent of their unsoundness.

His text is based upon Wecklein's edition, 'with occasional references to earlier collations in cases of doubt.' Wecklein gives Prof. Vitelli's collation of M, and in the lacunae of M the readings of the copies, elsewhere recording only such few readings of later MSS. as may tend to immediate emendation of M's text. Dr. Verrall has been content with this information (on his two plays only) without any general study of MS. errors. He seems to be bent on defending through all improbabilities the readings of M in every place. Were this a task undertaken for a wager, one might applaud the unfailing cleverness with which a *tour de force* is carried through. But the object of a student should be to find out truth. Dr. Verrall's constant opposition to accepted views, his constant effusion of new theories and interpretations, lead one to think that this continual defence of M is but one manifestation of an overmastering cleverness, too fertile in resource, that persuades him ever to prefer his own ingenious novelty to the truth which others have deduced. Scepticism is indeed a necessary habit in a critic; but scepticism does not mean a determination to reject existing views. Cleverness is a quality valuable enough; but cleverness alone, however fertile, will never make a scholar. There is but one method for a scholar's work, the scientific; which requires that he shall reason from the evidence. To this Dr. Verrall's method shows everything that is most opposed; recklessness of assertion without care to verify; arguments invented to serve a present turn; citation of such evidence as may seem to bear out a proposition, and omission of the rest.

It is time that I should support the statements I have made. I have tried to group the notes criticised as closely as possible, but many of them contain error in so many different forms that without much repetition this grouping could not be strictly carried out. The index at the end will facilitate reference: but the criticism is meant to be read consecutively; and I hope that the remarks on metre may not be passed over.

We will deal with metre first.

The iambic trimeter:—

*Theb.* 565. δίς τ' ἐν τελευτῇ τοὔνομ' ἐνδατούμενος
καλεῖ· λέγει δὲ τοῦτ' ἔπος διὰ στόμα.

The second line is bracketed, for one reason because

> the effect of the stop after the first foot (a rare thing in polished iambic verse where the sense is continued from the previous line) is to throw more emphasis upon the word so placed; . . . but καλεῖ, so far from admitting emphasis is useless, . . .

'Rare' is of course a relative term; but I shall not call 'rare in polished iambic verse' a stop of which I find in Aeschylus more than 110 examples distributed equally enough throughout all the plays. Whether the effect of it is to throw more emphasis upon the word so placed the following[1] instances may serve to show:—

Aesch. *Supp.* 392. εἴ τοι κρατοῦσι παῖδες Αἰγύπτου σέθεν
νόμῳ πόλεως, φάσκοντες ἐγγύτατα γένους
εἶναι, τίς ἂν τοῖσδ' ἀντιωθῆναι θέλοι;

„ „ 461. θέλω δ' ἄιδρις μᾶλλον ἢ σοφὸς κακῶν
εἶναι·

„ „ 768. ἀλλ' ἔστι φήμη κρείσσονας λύκους κυνῶν
εἶναι·

„ *Cho.* 872. ὅπως δοκῶμεν τῶνδ' ἀναίτιαι κακῶν
εἶναι·

„ „ 1028. χρήσαντ' ἐμοὶ
πράξαντι μὲν ταῦτ' ἐκτὸς αἰτίας κακῆς
εἶναι, παρέντα δ'. . .

Soph. *O. T.* 402. εἰ δὲ μὴ 'δόκεις γέρων
εἶναι, παθὼν ἔγνως ἄν. . .

[1] Punctuation is a matter of editorial judgment. The examples from Aeschylus I have punctuated according to Wecklein.

Soph. *O.C.* 260. εἰ τάς γ' Ἀθήνας φασὶ θεοσεβεστάτας
εἶναι, μόνας δὲ. . .

Eur. *Alc.* 774. οὐ χρὴ σκυθρωπὸν τοῖς ξένοις τὸν πρόσπολον
εἶναι, δέχεσθαι δ' εὐπροσηγόρῳ φρενί.

Doubtless Dr. Verrall could contrive to discover emphasis in these as he does in the following :—

*Ag.* 1078. ἔοικεν εὖρις ἡ ξένη κυνὸς δίκην
εἶναι, ματεύει δ' ὧν ἀνευρήσει φόνον.

εἶναι; note the emphasis; 'The strange woman *is indeed*, it seems, keen at a scent.

There has been no reference of any kind to her keenness of scent.

*Ag.* 1122. οὐ κομπάσαιμ' ἂν θεσφάτων γνώμων ἄκρος
εἶναι, κακῷ δέ τῳ προσεικάζω τάδε.

εἶναι; with emphasis, exactly as we should give it in English, 'A very good judge of the oracular I cannot boast that I am.'

That would be expressed by

γνώμων μὲν ἄκρος θεσφάτων οὐ κομπάσαιμ' ἂν εἶναι.

*P. V.* 700. εὐθὺς δὲ μορφὴ καὶ φρένες διάστροφοι
ἦσαν, κεραστὶς δ'. . .

Eur. *fr.* 382, 9. λοξαὶ δ' ἐπ' αὐτῆς τρεῖς κατεστηριγμέναι
εἰσίν· τὸ πέμπτον δ'. . .

„ *Alc.* 1054. καὶ πῶς ἀκραιφνὴς ἐν νέοις στρωφωμένη
ἔσται;

Therefore at

*Ag.* 1083. ἦμην κλέος σου μαντικὸν πεπυσμένοι
ἦμεν προφήτας δ' οὔτινας ματεύομεν

which is the reading of M, there would be no objection to

. . . . . . πεπυσμένοι
ἦμεν·

(Dr. Verrall's edition has '1084 ἦμην (ἦμεν written above)'; but that this is not a misprint for '1083' &c, the remark upon it shows:—

ἦμεν: this, as the accentuation shows was the word wrongly written at first in M as ἤμην, and in my judgment may well be right, as an emphatic repetition of the verb.)

*Ag.* 1230. τοιάδε τόλμα θῆλυς ἄρσενος φονεὺς
ἔστιν. τί νιν καλοῦσα δυσφιλὲς δάκος
τύχοιμ' ἄν;

[1230. τόλμα H. L. Ahrens: τολμᾶ (τολμᾷ) libri.]

With the punctuation θῆλυς . . . ἔστιν., the division of the rhythm is bad and ἔστιν not correct.

Now I know that Elmsley proposed ἔσται, and I know why. I know also that Wecklein places Elmsley's ἔσται in his margin, without however adopting it either in 1885 or in 1889. But I should be glad to know why ἔστιν is (so vaguely) 'not correct.'

*P. V.* 479. ὅπως θνητοῖς μεγίστων διάδοχοι μοχθημάτων
γένοινθ',

*Supp.* 206. καὶ μὴ πρόλεσχος μηδ' ἐφολκὸς ἐν λόγῳ
γένῃ·

*Cho.* 1003. τοιάδ' ἐμοὶ ξύνοικος ἐν δόμοισι μὴ
γένοιτ'· ὀλοίμην πρόσθεν

So Eur. *Hec.* 1136. ὡς πρόσω πατρὸς
γένοιντο,

(at another time it will be possible to show that, for emphasis, this pause after a foot and a half has as much value as that after a foot, and as little).

Aesch. *P. V.* 279. ἐλαφρὸν ὅστις πημάτων ἔξω πόδα
ἔχει παραινεῖν νουθετεῖν τε τὸν κακῶς
πράσσοντ'· ἐγὼ δὲ . .

Eur. *Med.* 38. οὐδ' ἀνέξεται κακῶς
πάσχουσ'· ἐγᾦδα τήνδε

Soph. *O. C.* 758. τήνδε τὴν πόλιν φίλως
εἰπών· ἐπαξία γάρ·

" *El.* 252. εἰ δὲ μὴ καλῶς
λέγω, σὺ νίκα·

Soph. *El.* 1503. μὴ μὲν οὖν καθ' ἡδονὴν
θάνῃς· φυλάξαι δεῖ με τοῦτό σοι πικρόν.

Aesch. *P. V.* 1068. ἡμῖν μὲν Ἑρμῆς οὐκ ἄκαιρα φαίνεται
λέγειν·

„ *Supp.* 506. Νεῖλος γὰρ οὐχ ὅμοιον Ἰνάχῳ γένος
τρέφει.

„ *Pers.* 323. Ἀμφιστρεύς τε πολύπονον δόρυ
νωμῶν, ὅ τ' ἐσθλὸς Ἀριόμαρδος . .

„ *Cho.* 752. εἰ λιμὸς ἢ δίψη τις ἢ λιψουρία
ἔχει, νέα δὲ νηδὺς αὐτάρκης τέκνων.

„ *Theb.* 633. Δίκη δ' ἄρ' εἶναί φησιν, ὡς τὰ γράμματα
λέγει· κατάξω δ' ἄνδρα τόνδε καὶ πόλιν
ἕξει . . .

[634. λέγει recc.: λέξει (ε in ras. scripsit m) M.]

λέξει of M is probably a mistaken alteration induced by ἕξει below. For the only meaning it could bear would be 'as the inscription will (presently) say'; and that seems as inappropriate here as it is appropriate in an epitaph (Kaibel, 679):

Μαρκέλλης τάφος εἰμί· τίς αὐτὴ γράμματα λέξει.

Dr. Verrall however reads λέξει:

λέξει: emphasized by the rhythm and pause (see on *v.* 566)—*as the inscriptions will declare,* if they are to be believed.

*Ag.* 832. μόνος δ' Ὀδυσσεύς, ὅσπερ οὐχ ἑκὼν ἔπλει
ζευχθεὶς ἕτοιμος ἦν ἐμοὶ σειραφορος·
εἶτ' οὖν θανόντος εἴτε καὶ ζῶντος πέρι
λέγω.

Note the emphasis given by the rhythm to λέγω, which is properly a separate clause in itself; with εἶτ' οὖν . . . πέρι another λέγω is supplied; *that I will say for him living or dead.*—Another most unhappy remark . . .

There is no emphasis whatever on λέγω. The clause means no more than 'whether he of whom I am speaking is alive or dead.'

Soph. *Ant.* 1077. καὶ ταῦτ' ἄθρησον εἰ κατηργυρωμένος
λέγω· φανεῖ γὰρ . .

Soph. *fr.* 25. τοιαῦτά τοί σοι πρὸς χάριν τε κοὺ βίᾳ
λέγω·

Eur. *Ion.* 811. καὶ σὸν οὐ στυγῶν πόσιν
λέγω, σὲ μέντοι μᾶλλον ἢ κεῖνον φιλῶν.

*Ag.* 1046. ἑρμηνέως ἔοικεν ἡ ξένη τοροῦ
δεῖσθαι·

Note the emphasis on δεῖσθαι: 'An interpreter, and a plain one, she *does*, it seems, want.

Soph. *O. T.* 1292. ῥώμης γε μέντοι καὶ προηγητοῦ τινος
δεῖται·

Eur. *Tro.* 87. ἔσται τάδ'· ἡ χάρις γὰρ οὐ μακρῶν λόγων
δεῖται·

*Ag.* 912. μηδ' εἵμασι στρώσασ' ἐπίφθονον πόρον
τίθει·

τίθει with emphasis, do not *invite* jealousy at a time when it is specially to be shunned.

The verb is no more emphatic than it is, for example, at

Aesch. *Eum.* 460. σὺν ᾧ σὺ Τροίαν ἄπολιν Ἰλίου πόλιν
ἔθηκας.

" " 773. ὁδοὺς ἀθύμους καὶ παρόρνιθας πόρους
τιθέντες,

Eur. *Med.* 569. τὰ λῷστα καὶ κάλλιστα πολεμιώτατα
τίθεσθε.

" " 1198. τίς τὸν γέροντα τύμβον ὀρφανὸν σέθεν
τίθησιν;

" *Rhes.* 573. σώζει γὰρ αὐτὸν ὅστις εὐτυχῆ θεῶν
τίθησιν·

In many cases, of course, a word so placed is emphatic; but it would be equally emphatic if the sentence were prose.

*Ag.* 536. τίεσθαι δ' ἀξιώτατος βροτῶν
τῶν νῦν·

The words τῶν νῦν are emphasized by the irregular pause after the first foot.

The emphasis is independent of the rhythm: so *e.g.*:

Soph. *El.* 462. τῷ τε φιλτάτῳ βροτῶν
πάντων, ἐν Ἅιδου κειμένῳ κοινῷ πατρί.

Aesch. *Ag.* 12. εὖτ' ἂν δὲ νυκτίπλαγκτον ἔνδροσόν τ' ἔχω
εὐνὴν ὀνείροις οὐκ ἐπισκοπουμένην
ἐμήν·

εὐνὴν . . . ἐμήν, 'the couch where no dream visits *me*.' ἐμήν, emphatic in itself, is here emphasized strongly by position in the sentence and the verse, importing a contrast between the speaker and some one else, whom dreams *do* visit.

If ἐμήν is genuine, it is doubtless emphatic; but by position in the sentence, not in the verse. In the following[1] passages I do not judge the possessive pronoun to have any such emphasis as Dr. Verrall should discover :—

*P. V.* 1048. πρῶτα μὲν γὰρ ὀκρίδα
φάραγγα βροντῇ καὶ κεραυνίᾳ φλογὶ
πατὴρ σπαράξει τήνδε, καὶ κρύψει δέμας
τὸ σόν· πετραία δ' ἀγκάλη σε βαστάσει.

*Eum.* 440. λέξας δὲ χώραν καὶ γένος καὶ ξυμφορὰς
τὰς σάς, ἔπειτα τόνδ' ἀμυναθοῦ ψόγον.

,, 652. τούτων ἐπῳδὰς οὐκ ἐποιήσεν πατὴρ
οὑμός, τὰ δ' ἄλλα . . .

Eur. *Hec.* 225. γίγνωσκε δ' ἀλκὴν καὶ παρουσίαν κακῶν
τῶν σῶν.

,, ,, 544. μή τις ἅψηται χροὸς
τοῦ 'μοῦ·

,, *Ion.* 1273. ἐν συμμάχοις γὰρ ἀνεμετρησάμην φρένας
τὰς σάς, ὅσον μοι πῆμα δυσμενής τ' ἔφυς.

,, *El.* 364. ὅδ' ἀνὴρ ὃς συνεκκλέπτει γάμους
τοὺς σούς, 'Ορέστην οὐ καταισχύνειν θέλων;

[1] At *P.V.* 1039
λέγων ἔοικα πολλὰ καὶ μάτην ἐρεῖν·
τέγγῃ γὰρ οὐδὲν οὐδὲ μαλθάσσῃ λιταῖς
ἐμαῖς· δακὼν δὲ στόμιον . . .
is given by all MSS. Robortello's edition gives, with a superfluous foot,
τέγγῃ γὰρ οὐδὲν οὐδὲ μαλθάσσῃ κέαρ λιταῖς
ἐμαῖς·
whence τέγγει γὰρ οὐδὲν οὐδὲ μαλθάσσει κέαρ
λιταῖς·
was read by Porson, who is followed by Blomfield, Dindorf, Hermann, Weil, Paley. But ἐμαῖς need not be emphatic, and Robortello's reading is due, I have little doubt, merely to recollection of 395 ἐάν τις ἐν καιρῷ γε μαλθάσσῃ κέαρ.

So with an equivalent for a possessive pronoun:

*Theb.* 1003. οὕτω μὲν ἀμφὶ τοῦδ' ἐπέσταλται λέγειν·
τούτου δ' ἀδελφὸν τόνδε Πολυνείκους νεκρὸν
ἔξω βαλεῖν ἄθαπτον, ἁρπαγὴν κυσίν,
ὡς ὄντ' ἀναστατῆρα Καδμείων χθονός,
εἰ μὴ θεῶν τις ἐμποδὼν ἔστη δορὶ
„ 1008. τῷ τοῦδ' ἄγος δὲ καὶ θανὼν κεκτήσεται
θεῶν πατρῴων, οὓς ἀτιμάσας ὅδε
στράτευμ' ἐπακτὸν ἐμβαλὼν ᾕρει πόλιν.
οὕτω πετηνῶν τόνδ' ὑπ' οἰωνῶν δοκεῖ
ταφέντ' ἀτίμως τοὐπιτίμιον λαβεῖν, . .

The passage is not carefully constructed, and the addition of ὅδε in 1009 is doubtless awkward. τῷ τοῦδ' in 1008 is added for clearness, and supplies a nominative to κεκτήσεται. For the pause, cf.:

Soph. *Phil.* 1350. οἴμοι, τί δράσω; πῶς ἀπιστήσω λόγοις
τοῖς τοῦδ', ὃς εὔνους ὢν ἐμοὶ παρῄνεσεν;
„ *Aj.* 961. οἱ δ' οὖν γελώντων κἀπιχαιρόντων κακοῖς
τοῖς τοῦδ'.
„ „ 983. φεῦ τάλας· τί γὰρ τέκνον
τὸ τοῦδε, ποῦ μοι γῆς κυρεῖ . . . ;
„ *O. C.* 636. ἁγὼ σεβισθεὶς οὔποτ' ἐκβαλῶ χάριν
τὴν τοῦδε, χώρᾳ δ' ἔμπολιν κατοικιῶ.

ὅδε is constantly used in Tragedy as an unemphatic pronoun, with little or no deictic force:

Aesch. *P. V.* 1089. τί γὰρ ἐλλείπει μὴ οὐ παραπαίειν
ἡ τοῦδ' εὐχή; τί χαλᾷ μανιῶν;
ἀλλ' οὖν ὑμεῖς αἱ πημοσύναις
συγκάμνουσαι ταῖς τοῦδε . .
Eur. *Tro.* 883. αἰνῶ σε, Μενέλα', εἰ κτενεῖς δάμαρτα σήν.
ὁρῶν δὲ τήνδε φεῦγε μή σ' ἕλῃ πόθῳ.
„ *Rhes.* 955. οὐκ εἶσι γαίας ἐς μελάγχιμον πέδον·
τοσόνδε νύμφην τὴν ἔνερθ' αἰτήσομαι
τῆς καρποποιοῦ παῖδα Δήμητρος θεᾶς,
ψυχὴν ἀνεῖναι τοῦδ'.

I will now give, without further comment, Dr. Verrall's text and interpretation:

οὕτω μὲν ἀμφὶ τοῦδ' ἐπέσταλται λέγειν·
τούτου δ' ἀδελφὸν τόνδε Πολυνείκους νεκρὸν
ἔξω βαλεῖν ἄθαπτον, ἁρπαγὴν κυσίν,
ὡς ὄντ' ἀναστατῆρα Καδμείων χθονός,
εἰ μὴ θεῶν τις ἐμποδὼν ἔστη δορὶ—
τῷ τοῦδ'· ἄγος δὲ καὶ θανὼν κεκτήσεται·—
θεῶν πατρῴων οὓς ἀτιμάσας ὅδε
στράτευμ' ἐπακτὸν ἐμβαλὼν ᾕρει πόλιν.
οὕτω πετηνῶν τόνδ' ὑπ' οἰωνῶν . .

had not some one of our gods thwarted his spear—by the spear of his brother here, who, though he died, shall be worshipped for his deed—one of those ancestral gods in whose dishonour this Polynices brought in a host. . . (Transl. p. 167). 1008. τῷ τοῦδε, *i.e.* τῷ τοῦ Ἐτεόκλους δορί, instrumental dative,—*had not a higher power prevented his* (Polynices') *spear by means of the spear of Eteocles*. . . If τῷ τοῦδε be taken with δορί in the sense τῷ Πολυνείκους, it is superfluous and not Greek, especially as the rhythm throws an emphasis upon it. The sense and the situation also require that Eteocles, the instrument of heaven, should not be ignored. In the next clause (v. 1009) ὅδε is added to mark the return from Eteocles to Polynices. But for this it would be out of place. . . ἄγος δὲ κεκτήσεται *who* (Eteocles) *though he lost his life will have the worship* (*of his deed*). The clause is in form a parenthesis. The object of it is to satisfy the religious feeling by showing that the champion of gods will not go unrewarded . . . it is just possible, reading ἄγος, to join the clause with ὡς ὄντ' ἀναστατῆρα—*and though he* (Polynices) *died, he shall still bear his sin*. But then ὅδε would have been inserted here instead of in the following verse . . .

1011. Τόνδε implying an ἐκεῖνον, is inserted here to mark the contrast between the οἰωνοί of Polynices and the ὄρνεα of Eteocles.

It should be interesting another time to compare the use of Comedy with respect to this pause, and similar pauses in dactylic verse.

2. The pause after the second foot.

*Theb.* 254. ὀλολυγμὸν . . . παιάνισον,
Ἑλληνικὸν νόμισμα θυστάδος βοῆς,
θάρσος φίλοις, λύουσα πολέμιον φόβον.

is the accepted punctuation. Dr. Verrall reads—

θάρσος φίλοις λύουσα, πολέμιον φόβον.

Discharging the good Greek custom of the religious note, which cheers the friend and scares the foe.

That view is certainly tenable (see the note); but according to the received interpretation, we are told, the form of expression 'would be unnatural,' while Dr. Verrall's is 'superior both in simplicity of construction and in rhythm, a pause after the second foot being so rare that it does not occur once in the play.'

This is not correct, for it occurs at

*Theb.* 6. Ἐτεοκλέης ἂν . . .
ὑμνοῖθ' ὑπ' ἀστῶν φροιμίοις πολυρρόθοις
οἰμώγμασιν θ', ὧν Ζεὺς ἀλεξητήριος
ἐπώνυμος γένοιτο. . .

A construction like that of Aesch. *Theb.* 256 is retained at

*Ag.* 566. δρόσοι κατεψέκαζον, ἔμπεδον σίνος
ἐσθημάτων, τιθέντες ἔνθηρον τρίχα,

and no remark is made upon the pause either there or at 525. But we find at

*Ag.* 1443. ναυτίλων δὲ σελμάτων
ἱστοτριβής. [ἰσοτριβής Pauw].

It may be added that the practice of Aeschylus is strongly against running on the sentence from line to line and then stopping it at the second foot. Even when the sense is not run on, this very rare pause produces a quite sufficient rhythmical dislocation; which however is here justified, the torrent of invective being broken by a new thought.

*Ag.* 935. ἀλλ' εἰ δοκεῖ σοι ταῦθ' ὑπαί τις ἀρβύλας
λύοι τάχος, πρόδουλον ἔμβασιν ποδός.

Note the pause after the second foot, almost unknown to Aeschylus' iambic verse, and always significant to the ear. It here adds abruptness to the abrupt command. The king is impatient to have done.

Now this rhythm is not common in Aeschylus; but so far from being 'almost unknown,' there are fifteen instances of it in the *P. V.*, of which ten are in continuation of the previous line:

*P. V.* 357. ἄταρ | μηδὲν πόνει·
„ 376. ὃς αὐτὸν ἐξέπληξε τῶν ὑψηγόρων
κομπασμάτων.
„ 710. εἰ δ' ἔχεις εἰπεῖν ὅ τι | λοιπὸν πόνων, σήμαινε

*P. V.* 759. βόσπορος δ' ἐπώνυμος | κεκλήσεται.
" 775. ὅπως πέδοι σκήψασα τῶν πάντων πόνων ἀπηλλάγην;
" 879. πέμπτη δ' ἀπ' αὐτοῦ γέννα πεντηκοντάπαις πάλιν πρὸς Ἄργος οὐχ ἑκοῦσ' ἐλεύσεται θηλύσπορος, φεύγουσα συγγενῆ γάμον ἀνεψιῶν·
" 940. οἷον ἐξαρτύεται | γάμον γαμεῖν,
" 971. κρατείτω τόνδε τὸν βραχὺν χρόνον | ὅπως θέλει·
" 1053. Διὸς δέ τοι | πτηνὸς κύων,

The others are 46 τί νιν στυγεῖς; 74 χώρει κατω, 275 δόξει δὲ πῶς; 624 κεἰ μὴ θέλοι, 789 ποίῳ τρόπῳ;

*Pers.* 354. τίνες κατῆρξαν πότερον Ἕλληνες μάχης ἢ παῖς ἐμός,
" 404. καὶ παρῆν ὁμοῦ κλύειν | πολλὴν βοήν·
" 421. ὑπτιοῦτο δὲ | σκάφη νεῶν,
*Supp.* 392. εἴ τοι κρατοῦσι παῖδες Αἰγύπτου σέθεν νόμῳ πόλεως,
" 404. μή καί ποτε | εἴπῃ λεώς,
*Cho.* 232. ἔνδον γενοῦ,
" 1020. ἡνιοστρόφου δρόμου | ἐξωτέρω·

That instances should be more frequent in one play than in another is no great wonder, for a particular rhythm tends to possess the mind and to repeat itself at a particular time. In Sophocles this pause is commoner than in Aeschylus; rarer, I should say, in Euripides.

3. Caesura by elision.

*Theb.* 394. ἐγὼ δὲ Τυδεῖ κεδνὸν Ἀστακοῦ τόκον
τόνδ' ἀντιτάξω προστάτην πυλωμάτων,
μάλ' εὐγενῆ τε καὶ τὸν Αἰσχύνης θρόνον.
" 397. τιμῶντα καὶ στυγοῦνθ' ὑπέρφρονας λόγους·

397. Suspicious from the metre, in this play almost unknown, and not defended by the context. Without this line the context would mean that Melannipus was known in the legends by some name or description importing 'one in whom sits modesty,' Αἰσχύνης θρόνος. Cited as a known title, it would of course take the article. The metaphor implied in it is illustrated by *Eum.* 520 τὸ δεινὸν ἐπίσκοπον φρενῶν καθήμενον.

For the text cf. Aesch. *Eum.* 542 βωμὸν αἴδεσαι δίκας (Paley), and

Ar. *Nub.* 994. καὶ μὴ περὶ τοὺς σαυτοῦ γονέας σκαιουργεῖν ἄλλο τε μηδὲν
αἰσχρὸν ποιεῖν ὅ τι τῆς Αἰδοῦς μέλλει τἄγαλμ' ἀναπλήσειν.

In view of Dr. Verrall's repudiation of the ordinary unemphatic article in Aeschylus (see p. 59) one may doubt whether the remark upon the article here does not betray a truer reason for his objection to this line. We must deal, however, with this caesura. It occurs

*Theb.* 238. οὐκ ἐς φθόρον σιγῶσ' ἀνασχήσει τάδε; (no remark).

„ 371. τοιαῦτ' ἀυτῶν τρεῖς κατασκίους λόφους
σείει, κράνους χαίτωμ', ὑπ' ἀσπίδος δ' ἔσω . .

[δ' ἐσώ M γρ. τῶ m'.]
372. That there is error here appears . . . from the uncouth metre for, if the punctuation be allowed for, there is no caesura at all . . .

„ 622. ἁλώσιμον παιᾶν' ἐπεξιακχάσας (no remark).

„ 524. γοργὸν δ' ὄμμ' ἔχων προσίσταται.
οὐ μὴν ἀκόμπαστός γ' ἐφίσταται πύλαις.

Note the subtle device by which the contrast of προσίσταται and ἐφ-ίσταται is enforced. The rhythm of the line in verse so regular as this, compels the division of the word, and thus gives prominence to the preposition.

(See p. 17).

„ 996. δοκοῦντα καὶ δόξαντ' ἀπαγγέλλειν με χρή.

The redundance of expression . . . The effect of it is happily aided by the stiff and peculiar rhythm of the verse (with only the quasi-caesura after the preposition ἀπ-αγγέλλειν), in this place artistic and quite justifiable.

*Ag.* 1378. ἕστηκα δ' ἔνθ' ἔπαισ' ἐπ' ἐξειργασμένοις.

Note the harsh and striking rhythm of this verse, which, as ἐπ' ἐξειργασμένοις belongs to ἕστηκα, has in effect no caesura.

That is the only remark on this caesura in the *Agamemnon*; and in that play there are fourteen other examples (20, 610, 824, 912, 920, 937, 946, 1033, 1052, 1253, 1269, 1393, 1420, 1599). In the *P. V.* there are two (641, 736); *Persae* six (182,

496, 809, 823, 833, 847); *Supp.* four (373, 474, 719, 942); *Cho.* six (257, 514, 543, 748, 918, 990); *Eum.* two (710, 907).

Now in the *Theb.* we have six, of which four are admitted by Dr. Verrall. Of the other six plays, only one has more than six, while three have not more than four. It is idle therefore because this rhythm is 'almost unknown' in the *Theb.*, to call 372, 392 suspicious on account of that rhythm. And to apply the epithets 'uncouth,' 'stiff and peculiar,' 'harsh and striking' to a rhythm which occurs forty times in Aeschylus and is frequent both in Sophocles and Euripides, seems to belong to other than sound criticism. See Elmsley, Eur. *Med.* 214.

4. Lines 'without caesura.'

*Theb.* 444. *καὶ μὴν τὸν ἐντεῦθεν λαχόντα πρὸς πύλαις λεξω.*

444. Almost all the examples in Aeschylus of a line without caesura are open to suspic on on independent grounds; and such a license is especially improbable in the strict versification of this play.

Now in the pause at the first foot, which was called 'a rare thing in polished iambic verse,' the *Theb.* has a full share (thirteen instances); and it has a full share (six instances) in the 'harsh,' 'uncouth' caesura by elision. There were no grounds therefore for speaking of the 'regular metre' and 'strict versification' of this play. Lines without caesura are found even in Euripides, and in Sophocles there are many indubitable examples. The 'independent ground' on which 'almost all' the examples in Aeschylus are open to suspicion seems to me to consist in the absence of caesura. I perceive no other ground for suspecting *Pers.* 254, 355, 468, 472, 492, 506, 512, 522; *P. V.* 667; *Supp.* 406, 920, 958, 1027; *Cho.* 150, 491; *Eum.* 26. And these are 'almost all the examples.' The only example in the *Agam.* (which I do not defend as it stands) is defended thus:

*Ag.* 1251. *ἦ κάρτ' ἄρ' ἂν παρεσκόπεις χρησμῶν ἐμῶν.*

[παρεσκοπεις (η) f. κάρτα τἄρα παρεκόπης Hartung.]
There is apparently no reason to doubt this reading. . . Note that by the caesural division of παρ-εσκόπεις an emphasis is thrown upon

παρά (an adverb), and cf. *Theb.* 525. In fact παρεσκόπεις is not one word but two.

For this theory of a 'quasi-caesura' (see *Theb.* 525, 996 above), though not [1] first conceived by him, Dr. Verrall as a metrical critic will accept the responsibility. It is simply disproved by the evidence. That a preposition comes in that place is merely an accident. The preposition does not affect the caesura, nor does the caesura affect the preposition.

To Dr. Verrall, however, must always belong the credit for origination of the following view:

*Ag.* 533. καὶ σπέρμα πάσης ἐξαπόλλυται χθονός.

σπέρμα πάσης, i e. αὐτῆς, τῆς Τροίας . . . That πάσης is constructed with σπέρμα, not with χθονός, is shown both by the natural division of the rhythm and by the sense.

I will only remark that this statement and the word 'shown' are correctly quoted.

*Ag.* 503. ἀλλ' ἢ τὸ χαίρειν μᾶλλον ἐκβάξει λέγων—
τὸν ἀντίον δὲ τοῖσδ' ἀποστέγω λόγον·

ἀποστέργω MSS.
τοῖσδε 'out of respect for these,' *i.e.* τοῖς θεοῖς, the gods who stand as usual before the palace and to whom the herald addresses himself below (*vv.* 514, 524). The pronoun is explained by a reverend gesture towards the images, a 'deictic' use common in the poets. . . That τοῖσδε should be so taken and not as neuter with ἀντίον, 'the opposite of this,' may be seen (1) from the rhythm; to divide the line after τοῖσδ' spoils the caesura, and (2) because superfluous pronouns, such as τοῖσδε is if taken with ἀντίον, are offensive to Greek habit and above all in poetry. It is an additional argument for ἀποστέγω that it provides an acceptable construction for τοῖσδε.

For the 'superfluous pronoun' so offensive especially in poetry, cf.

Aesch. *Pers.* 225. ἐσθλά . . , τἄμπαλιν δὲ τῶνδε.
Eur. *Hel.* 309. καὶ τἄμπαλίν γε τῶνδ'. . .
„ *Supp.* 200. ἐγὼ δὲ τούτοις ἀντίαν γνώμην ἔχω.
„ *El.* 690. θνήσκοντος δὲ σοῦ τἀναντί' ἔσται τῶνδε.
„ *Tr.* 381. τὰ δ' οἴκοι τοῖσδ' ὅμοι' ἐγίγνετο.
Meleag. *A. P.* xii. 165. λευκάνθης Κλεόβουλος· ὁ δ' ἄντια τοῦδε μελίχρους | Σώπολις·

[1] It is stated by Mr J. B. Bury in the *Journal of Philology*, xxix. p. 76 (1886).

*Theb.* 203. ἀλλ᾽ οὖν θεοὺς
τοὺς τῆς ἁλούσης πόλεος ἐκλείπειν λόγος.

πόλεος recc.: πόλεως M. ἐκλιπεῖν ante correcturam M.

The poetical genitive in -ος is almost invariably changed in MSS. to the ordinary prose form in -ως. I could easily give a dozen instances from iambic verse alone of πόλεος thus corrupted to πόλεως. The constant confusion, again, of ι and ει is especially noticeable in the words λείπειν, λιπεῖν. It may be said that hardly ever does one of these occur without the other being found as a variant in MSS.

But Dr. Verrall, as usual, keeps exactly all the errors of M; transposing, however, the words:

τοὺς τῆς ἁλούσης ἐκλιπεῖν πόλεως λόγος.

*But as for gods, those of a taken town desert her citadel, 'tis said* . . . πόλεως belongs strictly to ἐκλιπεῖν, with ἁλούσης we must supply πόλεως, or rather γῆς: . . . ἐκλιπεῖν (gnomic aorist) with allusion to the military use of the word (see *Lex. s.v.*).

The very common word ἐκλείπω is used either with an accusative or absolutely, the origin of the absolute construction being ellipse of an accusative. Construction with a genitive is unknown to any author *probae aetatis*.[1] The military use, ἐ. χώραν, τάξιν, &c., is extremely frequent, but ἐ. χώρας, τάξεως is never said. Supposing however that Aeschylus could ever have used so abnormal a construction, it is inconceivable that he should have done so in this place, when πόλιν would have made the meaning clear, while πόλεως could not fail entirely to obscure it.

Dr. Verrall's knowledge of the anapaestic dimeter is of the same kind:

*Theb.* 808. δαίμονες οἳ δὴ Κάδμου πύργους
τούσδε ῥύεσθε,
πότερον χαίρω κἀπολολύξω

[1] The Thesaurus quotes only Pseudoplut. *Mor.* p. 851, A χορηγίαν ἀνδράσιν ἐπιδόντι, ὅτε ἐκλειπόντων τῶν Πανδιονιδῶν τοῦ χορηγεῖν ἐπέδωκεν. L. and S. also give only one reference: Plut. *Vit. Marcell.* xvii. 25 ἐλέληστο καὶ σίτου, καὶ θεραπείας σώματος ἐξέλειπε.

811. ἢ τοὺς μογεροὺς καὶ δυσδαίμονας
812. ἀτέκνους κλαύσω πολεμάρχους ;

Twice in these few lines is broken the rule deduced from the classical poets by Bentley, that in this metre there is no division of lines, the whole being metrically continuous (*synaphea*) : in 809—10 ῥύεσθε πότερον, and again in 811—12 δυσδαίμονας ἀτέκνους (for if these lines are scanned continuously we have a concurrence of four short syllables).

As to ῥύεσθε, well enough. Bentley's discovery, first briefly stated in his Latin dissertation on John of Antioch (Malalas), was that in the anapaestic dimeter the Greeks did not admit a common syllable at the end of the line : '...there was no License allowed by the Ancients to the last Syllable of *Anapæsts ;* but the *Anapæst* Feet run on to the *Paræmiac,* that is, to the end of the Sett, as if the whole had been a single Verse.' Boyle challenged this conclusion, and is refuted at large in the dissertation on the Epistles of Phalaris. Such scansions as

παῦρον δὴ γένος ἐν πολλαῖσιν
εὕροις ἂν ἴσως (Eur. *Med.* 1075.)

or καὶ νῦν ἐλαφρῷ ποδὶ κραιπνόσσυτον
θῶκον προλιποῦσ' (*P. V.* 295.)

or εἶτ' ἐπὶ χρηστοῖς μοχθοῦσι τόδε
ἔστιν ἄδηλον (Eur. *Med.* 1092.)

Bentley shows to be wrong. Each foot, taken in relation to its successor, must be pure and perfect, whether anapaest, dactyl, or spondee. But that a 'concurrence of four short syllables' when the feet are pure and perfect breaks the rule deduced by Bentley is a strange error : in neither dissertation did Bentley say or imply anything of the sort ; nor, as we shall see, was it likely that he should. What we have here is an anapaest immediately succeeding a dactyl—a rare thing. Dr. Verrall imagines it has escaped notice in this place, and calls it an 'inadmissible flaw' :

'. . . it has not apparently been observed that we have another, less obvious but still inadmissible flaw of metre in 812 . . .'

With what justice in either case I proceed to show. Porson,[1] the first to touch this matter, said merely: 'rarissime etiam dactylo anapaestum subjiciunt.' The statement is repeated by Gaisford,[2] who gives examples of the consecution from both tragedy and comedy. Hermann[3] went further: 'Dactylo anapaesti locum tenenti fere aut alius dactylus aut spondeus, raro anapaestus succedit. Et, si anapaestus, apud tragicos hoc non fit in eadem dipodia...sed ita, ut dipodiam finitam sequatur dipodia ab anapaesto incipiens. Ita apud Aeschylum in Sept. ad Th. 833' (*our passage*) . . . Comici vero et hoc modo anapaestum dactylo interdum subiciunt . . .

H. L. Ahrens[4] in a well-known treatise remarks: 'Quod in anapaestis Euripideis non rarum est, ut dactylum anapaestus sequatur initio dipodiae cf. Herm. El. D. M. p. 376, apud Aeschylum quatuor tantum locis reperitur Sept. v. 809 (*our passage*), 849; Eum. v. 909; Suppl. v. 8,' all which passages, he proceeds to show, may be altered with probability:

At *Theb.* 853. τὸν δυσκέλαδόν θ' ὕμνον 'Ερινύος
ἰαχεῖν . . .

ἀχεῖν is generally read (after Elmsley, Eur. *Heracl.* 752) here as in other places.

At *Supp.* 8. ἀλλ' αὐτογένητον φυλαξάνοραν (in marg. γρ. φυξάνοραν)
γάμον Αἰγύπτου . . .

is the reading of M.

*Eum.* 950. ἦ τάδ' ἀκούετε, πόλεως φρούριον,

'facile corrigas ἀκούεσθε,' H. L. Ahrens. 'ἀκούεις,' Meineke. 'Malim χώρας φρούριον,' Weil, retaining, however, πόλεως, as does Wecklein. Paley's notion, 'the metre suggests that πόλεως is here a spondee,' I consider most improbable. But it is very likely that here, as elsewhere, πόλεως is a gloss on χώρας, or some other word of that quantity.

[1] Euripides, Supplement. ad praef. p. 33 (ed. Scholef.)
[2] Hephaestion. Oxon. 1810. (p. 279.)
[3] *Elementa Doctrinae Metricae.* Lips. 1816. (p. 239.)
[4] *De causis quibusdam Aeschyli nondum satis emendati.* Gottingen, n. d.

We are justified then in thinking it improbable that Aeschylus admitted this metrical consecution; but we are not justified in calling it inadmissible with him, and to speak of it absolutely as inadmissible is simply wrong. It may be made inadmissible for a school-boy versifier; it was not so with Euripides, whose examples in strict anapaests are here collected:

1 *Hec.* 143. *ἴζ' Ἀγαμέμνονος ἱκέτις γονάτων*
2 *El.* 1315. *θάρσει· Παλλάδος ὁσίαν ἥξεις*
3 „ 1318. *σύγγονε φίλτατε·*
*διὰ γὰρ ζευγνῦσ' ἡμᾶς πατρῴων*
4 *Hipp.* 1356. *ὅδ' ὁ σωφροσύνῃ πάντας ὑπερέχων*
5 *Tro.* 101. *μεταβαλλομένου δαίμονος ἀνέχου*
6 „ 1242. *ἐλπίδας ἐπὶ σοὶ κατέγναψε βίου.*

In 1 and 2 we have a proper name. On 4 Valckenaer says: 'In vs. 1365...si quis ita velit, servari poterit *ὑπερέχων·* quia tamen *σχὼν, σχὲς* et similia tragicis frequenti sunt in usu, hic accommodatius videtur *πάντας ὑπερσχών·*...' Certainly the error *ἔχειν* for *σχεῖν* is common, and may warrant Paley's *ἄνσχου* in 5. In 6 also the text is doubtful (*κατέκαμψε*, Seidler). 3 remains a certain instance.

Such being the knowledge possessed by Dr. Verrall of these simple metres, it cannot be with any anticipation of profit that one approaches his treatment of choric rhythms. In the range of classical studies there is perhaps no more difficult branch than this. The investigation can be conducted only upon most careful scientific method, and with the help of other subsidiary studies. Were the text of every chorus sound and sure, there would be little difficulty in the metrical enquiry; but since this is very far from being the case, the student of choric metres must first be well acquainted with the phenomena of MS. corruption and understand their causes, in order to know what to accept as certain and what to suspect impaired. In this respect Dr. Verrall shows himself to be entirely deficient; nor is there any respect in which he is prepared for the investigation. I know well that this is a subject which interests but few; and none but those whom it interests are likely to understand it. I shall confine myself therefore to exhibiting Dr. Verrall's metrical knowledge by such examples as will show its nature to metricians, and illustrate the remarks already made; but I hope to succeed in making clear, even to those who are not metricians, the nature of Dr. Verrall's metrical knowledge.

His dealing with choric metre is in harmony with his determination to keep at all costs exactly the text of M. This is now accomplished by maintaining that *in all choric rhythms alike, and in any place,* a syncopated foot may answer to a complete foot (♩. = ♩♪), a cyclic dactyl to a trochee, and a long syllable in thesis to a short syllable. This was stated in the *Seven against Thebes;* and in the *Agamemnon* Dr. Verrall says that he has 'reason to believe that the evidence for it has been found satisfactory.'

> To a very large extent the supposed proof of deep corruption rests on the assumption that in the rhythmic correspondence of *strophe* and *antistrophe* there was always a correspondence of syllables and quantities. This proposition can by no means be assumed *a priori;* it cannot be assumed to be true to the same extent of all poets, or of the same poet writing at different times; it is known not to be absolutely true; the precise limits of it have never been properly investigated: but it has been freely used as a principle of criticism wherever it appears to be easy of application. (*Theb.* Introd. p. xxxv.)

Most of this is true enough; and certainly it is true that the precise limits of strophic correspondence have not yet been properly investigated. One may suppose that Dr. Verrall considers his own to be the proper method of investigation. It consists in taking one play by itself, collecting the variations from strict strophic correspondence, and showing that if (without regard to the kind of rhythm or to place in the rhythmical phrase) we adopt the metrical equivalents as stated above, there is hardly ever any need to alter anything for the sake of the sense. In the course of the exposition, no distinction is allowed between one rhythm and another; trochaics, iambics, dochmiacs, glyconics are all indiscriminately compared. The whole horror of this method can only be seen in the articles themselves; but the specimens that I give will perhaps be horrible enough. Aeschylus' favourite rhythm is the syncopated trochaic. The following are typical phrases:

τὰ | μὲν κατ' | οἰκ- | ους ἐφ' | ἑστί- | ας ἄχ- | η

τέχ- | ναι δὲ | Κάλ- | χαντος | οὐκ ἄ- | κραντ- | οι

This is how Dr. Verrall expresses the last line in musical notation:

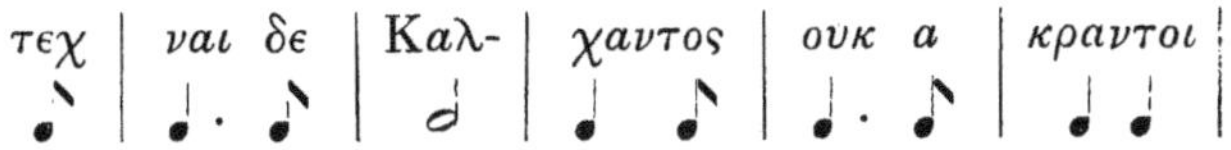
τεχ | ναι δε | Καλ- | χαντος | ουκ α | κραντοι

Here is a passage in this rhythm:

*Theb.* 274. μέλει, φόβῳ δ' οὐχ ὑπνώσσει κέαρ
γείτονες δὲ καρδίας
μέριμναι ζωπυροῦσι τάρβος
τὸν ἀμφιτειχῆ λεών·
δράκοντα δ' ὥς τις τέκνων
ὕπερ δέδοικεν λεχέ-
ων δυσευνάτορας ἁ
πάντρομος πελειάς.

279. δέδοικ* λεχέων M. 280. δυσευνήτορας ἀπάν M.

where I have given Dr. Verrall's text. His note is:

280—281 = 297—298. The rhythm of these lines is continuous and except for convenience they might be printed as one verse. The division in the MS. is as often arbitrary; 280–81 are divided at πάν- | τρομος. The rhythm is -ων δυσ- | ευ- | νάτορας | ἁ | πάντρομ- | ος πελ- | ειάς, answering to -δᾶν ὁ | γαι- | άο | χος | Τηθύ | ος τε | παῖδες. For the variation — ⏑⏑ = — ⏑ see 153. For the scansion of the second syllable of λεχέ-ων (treated as common at the 'end of the verse' or rhythmical break) cf. ῥύτορες in 305 and see 162, 225, etc.

Most metres admit a common syllable at the end of a rhythmical phrase, as in the examples cited; but that such a syllable may be common *in the middle of a word* is a proposition with which metricians will at once decide Dr. Verrall's competence.

Further, there is of course no rhythmical break at the point mentioned. The rhythm runs thus :

| | | | | | | | | | | |
|---|---|---|---|---|---|---|---|---|---|---|
| | | ♩ ♪ | ♩. | ♩ ♪ | ♩ ♪ | ♩ ♪ | ♩. | ♩ ♪ | | |
| | | –– ⏑ | ⌞ | –– ⏑ | — ⏑ | — ⏑ | ⌞ | –– ⏑ | — | |
| 277. | τὸν | ἀμφι- | τει- | χῆ λε- | ών, δρά- | κοντας | ὥς | τις τέκ- | νων | |
| 294. | ὕ- | δωρ τε | Διρ- | καῖον | εὔτρα- | φέστα- | τὸν | πωμά- | των | |

| | | | | | | | | | | |
|---|---|---|---|---|---|---|---|---|---|---|
| | | ♩ ♪ | ♩. | ♩ ♪ | ♩. | ♩ ♪ | ♩. | ♩ ♪ | | |
| | | — ⏑ | ⌞ | — ⏑ | ⌞ | — ⏑ | ⌞ | — ⏑ | — | |
| 279. | ὑ- | περδέ- | δοι- | κεν λε- | χαί- | ων δυσ- | ευ- | νάτορ | ας | |
| 296. | ὅ- | σων ἵ- | η- | σιν Πο- | σει- | δᾶν ὁ | γαι- | άο- | χος | |

I have given here the text adopted by Wecklein, with the two conjectures, δράκοντας (Bothe) which mends the sense, and λεχαίων (Lachmann), which mends both sense and metre. Dr. Verrall, as we have seen, rejects even this easy and certain alteration, while Bothe's suggestion only

requires mention because it is adopted in almost all modern texts.

His objections to their readings and defence of his own are oo long to be quoted. But this is how his text is to be taken :

*And as one fears a snake for her young, so doth it, poor trembling dove, fear the ravishers of our bed*, literally, *fear for our bed the ravishers*. Both τέκνων and λεχέων depend on ὑπέρ. . . The subject of δέδοικεν is καρδία. . .

There are a few lines in the *Agamemnon* of the *Ionic a minore* metre (⏑⏑ ⁝ – – ⏑⏑ | – – ⏑⏑) :

743. παρακλίνασ' ἐπέκρανεν
δὲ γάμου πικροῦ τελευτάς
δύσεδρος καὶ δυσόμιλος
συμένα Πριαμίδαισιν

The rhythm here would be unvaried if for the iambus πικροῦ we had a trochee, as τοῦδε; but this equivalent variation, – ⏑ – ⏑ for – – ⏑⏑, is characteristic of the metre. According to the MSS. this variation does not occur in the antistrophe, where we have τὸ | γὰρ δυσσεβὲς | ἔργον. This fact is the occasion of remarks by Dr. Verrall to which I ask attention :

| | | | | | |
|---|---|---|---|---|---|
| 743. | παρα | κλι- | νας επε | κρα- | νεν δε γαμ |
| | | | ου πικ | ρου τε | λευτας. |
| 754. | διχα δ | αλλ- | ων μονο | φρων- | ειμι το |
| | | | γαρ- | δυσσεβες | εργον. |

Here exact correspondence may be restored by changing the order of the words (τὸ δυσσεβὲς γὰρ Pauw) ; and though mistakes of this kind are not nearly so common in the MSS. of verse as they are sometimes said to be, still the case is doubtful. We should notice however that the antistrophe (not the strophe) has the rhythm which we should expect ; the metre is the so-called *Ionic a minore*, one of the many forms of the lyric trochaic.

What is one to say ? Or what might one not be excused for saying ? The final statement, that this metre is one of the many forms of the lyric trochaic, would be unintelligible had not Dr. Verrall by the figure given above shown how he conceives the feet to be divided. From this we discover that the phrase 'the so-called *Ionic a minore*,' is not a bull (like the 'so-called nineteenth century'), but implies that there is no such metre as the *Ionic a minore* ; that what is called by that name is merely one of the many forms of the lyric trochaic. What is meant by 'the many forms' I do not know ; but it will be seen from the figure that, according to the scansion given, no difference is made between this and the syncopated trochaic. Thus κρα- is a syncopated trochee, νεν δε γαμ is a cyclic dactyl, ου πικ is a trochee, all these being equivalent to one another ; while ου πικ corresponds to γαρ- a syncopated trochee, and ρου τε to δυσσεβες a cyclic dactyl. Having stated these propositions, I may be pardoned, I trust, for adding nothing to the statement.

But I will add a word upon the reading. –⏑–⏑, as I have said, occurs very frequently in the *Ionic a minore* as an equivalent variation for ––⏑⏑. But Aeschylus, who uses this metre largely (*P. V.* 413–430, *Persae* 66–116, *Supplices* 1029–1072), never elsewhere has the one *corresponding* to the other ; –⏑–⏑, where it occurs, occurs both in strophe and antistrophe (*P. V.* 417, 418, 419 = 426, 427, 428, *Pers.* 87=93, *Supp.* 1036=

1044, 1053 = 1062). If then exact correspondence here requires only a very easy change of order, the evidence warrants us in making the change. Now nothing is easier than the change we have here to make, as will be sufficiently explained at p. 114, where also may be estimated the value of Dr. Verrall's opinion on the point.

One of the cases on which Dr. Verrall relies most strongly for his theory of irregular correspondence is:

*Theb.* 723. καὶ χθονία κόνις πίῃ.
= 730. αἰῶνα δ' ἐς τρίτον μένει.

The use of χθονίος here is peculiar, but it must be the genuine word. The emendations which have been suggested (νερτέρα Weil, γαΐα Hermann etc.) are all open to the objection that no copyist who found them would have been likely to substitute χθονία, either as an interpretation or otherwise. (p. 136.)

In respect of γαΐα this is true. χθονία would not have been adscribed in the sense 'of the land.' Heimsoeth[1] is doubtless right[2] in saying: Der Artikel bei Hesychius: γαῖα, ἡ κόνις, καὶ ἡ γῆ welchen Hermann in γαΐα κόνις, ἡ γῆ ändern will, ist ohne Anstoss: γαῖα ἡ κόνις ist die homerische Glosse zu: θανόντι χυτὴν ἐπὶ γαῖαν ἔχευαν und τεθνηῶτα χυτὴ κατὰ γαῖα καλύπτοι. Weil referring to Hermann's suggestion says: Malim νερτέρα quae vox ut χθονία ad deos inferos alludit: an allusion which Dr. Verrall (note, p. 88) also discerns in χθονία. Now it happens that χθόνιος (like καταχθόνιος) is used in scholiastic language with the sense 'infernal,' and is so found explaining νέρτερος: see Hesych. *s.v.* νέρτεροι καὶ νερτέριοι, sch. Eur. *Or.* 613 and (on ἐνέρων) sch. Soph. *El.* 1391; νέρτερος explained by καταχθόνιος, Hesych., sch. Eur. *Or.* 956, *Med.* 1047, *Phoen.* 1023. (For νερτέρα χθὼν see Eur. *Alc.* 47, *H.F.* 335, *fr.* 450.) There is strong reason therefore for suspecting χθονία here to have supplanted νερτέρα: but whether so or not, this instance will serve to point what was said above, that for judging what may or may not be a gloss it is necessary to study the language of lexicons and scholia.

[1] *Die Wiederherstellung der Dramen des Aeschylus.* Bonn, 1861. (p. 345.)
[2] Cf. sch. Soph. *Ant.* 247, sch. Eur. *Phoen.* 1664.

Neither ⏑⏑‒‒⏑‒ nor ⏑⏑‒⏑⏑‒‒ is an admissible form of dochmiac verse. The extremely few cases that MSS. present of dochmiac verses in this form are overset by the comparison of certain MS. mistakes:

*Theb.* 219. *διὰ θεῶν πόλιν νεμόμεσθ' ἀδάμαντον*

is given by M; the true readings, *νεμόμεθ'* by *recc.*, *ἀδάματον* by Pauw. Dr. Verrall (p. 133) thinks

> it is quite possible that the MS. *νεμόμεσθ' ἀδάμαντον* is right. The examples in tragedy tend, as far as they go, to show that *ἀδάματος* was the form used by the Attic poets . . . ; but they are not numerous enough for a certain induction. In form there is nothing against *ἀδάμαντος*, and the rhythm *νεμόμεσθ'* | *ἀδάμαντ-* | *ον* is a quite conceivable variation of the *dochmius*.

*νεμόμεσθ'* shall be considered first. The mistake -*εθα* for -*εσθα* is, of course, very common; but there are also not a few examples of the contrary mistake, -*εσθα* for -*εθα*, as:

Eur. *Or.* 686. *δυναίμεθ', ἐνταῦθ' ἐλπίδος* . .
*δυναίμεσθ'* B

Eur. *Andr.* 1150. *οἰχόμεθ'· οὐκέτι μοι γένος,*
*ὀχόμεθ'* (*ᾠχόμεσθ'* *a m. sec.*) B

Eur. *Ion.* 210. *ὧδε δερκόμεσθ' ὦ φίλοι*
sic codd.; corr. Dobree.

Eur. *H. F.* 1174. *οἰχόμέσθ' οἰχόμεσθα πτανοὶ* cod.

With this evidence in view, how could any one resist the belief that *νεμόμεσθ'* is but a similar mistake? As for *ἀδάμαντον*, Ellendt (*Lex. Soph.*) states the case thus: ...cum nullo loco non conveniat *ἀδάματος*, multis noceat *ἀδάμαστος* (v. praeter Sophoclea Aesch. *Sept.* 215. *Choeph.* 53), cum Elmsleio ad O R 196 (=208) et Reisigio Comm. in O C p. 385 hoc ex tragicis exsulare iubemus. The form *ἀδάματος* has been restored with certainty according to the requirements of metre in

Aesch. *Cho.* 53 (=42). *σέβας δ' ἄμαχον, ἀδάμαντον, ἀπόλεμον τὸ πρὶν*

by Hermann, in

Soph. *O. T.* 205 (=191). *βέλεα θέλοιμ' ἂν ἀδάμαστ' ἐνδατεῖσθαι* by Erfurdt, these being lyric iambic lines, and in

Soph. *O. T.* 1315 (=1323) ἀδάμαστόν τε καὶ,

a dochmiac verse like ours, by Hermann. This is but one among innumerable cases of error in verbal forms. Thus for δυσεκπέρατον several MSS. have δυσεκπέραντον at Eur. *Med.* 643, *Hipp.* 674, 880; at *Rhes.* 124, ἐκ κόπων ἀρειφάτων, cod. *B* has ἀρειφάντων; the MSS. both of Aristides and of Aristotle *Athen. Pol.* (the new treatise), where Solon *fr.* 36 is quoted, have πατρίδ' εἰς θεόκτιστον for θεόκτιτον. Like error causes the same fault in dochmiacs at

*Ag.* 1105. ἀκόρεστος γενει [=1119 ἐν ἐνύδρῳ τεύχει]
=1137. νόμον ἄνομον οἷά τις ξουθὰ
ἀκόρεστος βοᾶς

ἀκόρετος is rightly read by the Aldine edition in 1138, and rightly restored by Bothe in 1105. But Dr. Verrall refuses ‘to substitute the supposed equivalent form ἀκόρετος’:

1105. I do not venture to write ἀκόρετος (Bothe): for making ἀκόρετος from the stem of κορέννυμι there appears to be no satisfactory analogy: -αινετος, -αιρετος, -δετος, etc. are different, and see on the other hand ἄσβεστος, ἀκέραστος, σκεδαστός.

Such philology as this deserves no more than to be quoted. Is Dr. Verrall unaware that besides ἀκέραστος there exists the form ἄκρατος? That besides ἀκόρεστος the form ἀκόρητος exists beyond disproof? Yet his philology impugns the existence equally of ἀκόρητος. This obvious refutation is contained briefly in Ellendt's note, *Lex. Soph.* s.vv.: ‘Has formas sola metri necessitate pendendas docet Aesch. Ag. 1003, 1331, 1483. Nec sane ἀκόρετος in ullam regulam peccat: primum si ἀδάματος compares, dein si memineris Homero ἀκόρητος dici (v. Eust. p. 957, 31), unde ἀκόρετος ita distat ut ἀδαμάτος ab ἄδμητος.’

Further illustration of MS. error in verbal forms I reserve for *Ag.* 82 and 464. Neither here nor there does Dr. Verrall discover any knowledge of it.

Of the inconsistencies displayed in the proposition of his theory more might be said than it is worth while to say.

But specimens may be given. Speaking of dochmiacs, he says:

118. πύλαις ἑβδόμαις = 132 στόνων αὐτάς. This is another variation upon the same principle, ⏑ –́ ⏑ –́ –́ for ⏑ –́ –́ ⏑ –́. (*Theb.* p. 137.)

Allowing this, he might equally have allowed

*Theb.* 770. τέκνοις δ' ἀραίας (⏑ –́ ⏑ –́ –́)
=763. ἐπεὶ δ' ἀρτίφρων (⏑ –́ –́ ⏑ –́)

to be equivalent upon the same principle. Instead of which he scans:

⏑ — ⏑ –́ –́
τεκν- | οις δ αρ- | αιας
⏑ — > –́ –́
= επ- | ει δ αρτ- | ιφρων (*Theb.* p. 137.)

making of the last line such a monstrosity of scansion as no Attic poet could have committed.

Again, according to his theory, the following are perfectly equivalent as they stand:

*Theb.* 993. ἰὼ | ποῦ σφε | θήσο- | μεν χθον | ός ;
= 994. ἰὼ ὅ | που | τιμι- | ωτα- | τον

but he places in his text Weckleín's[1] suggestion, 993, ἰώ σφε ποῦ . .

It will have occurred to readers that if Dr. Verrall's equivalents be accepted, there are hardly any two lines of at all the same length that may not be made out to be metrically equal. The following, however, give him pause:

*Theb.* 468. ἐπεύχομαι δὴ τάδε μὲν εὐτυχεῖν ἰὼ
= 508. πέποιθα τὸν Διὸς ἀντίτυπον ἔχοντα

But here, by a significant coincidence, it happens that

there is some slight reason, independent of metre, to doubt the reading. . . It is also difficult to see how the rhythms can have been divided so as to be equal . . . (p. 135.)

468. Regularity of antithesis would require either ἢ λὶν μὲν τάδε in the first clause, or κεῖνα for τοῖσι in the second. (p. 50.)

---

[1] The true reading, I have no doubt, is ἔνθα τιμιώ-ατον, ὅπου being a gloss. Support of this I reserve for another time.

But he himself admits that

the grammatical variation is scarcely worth notice.

This is the last piece of metrical method I shall give. I shall end this subject with the remark on

*Theb.* 898. τάφων πατρῴων λαχαί.
= 909. πολυφθόρους ἐν δαΐ

which, as will be seen, are identically equal. The remark is

δᾱΐ. See 215.

An editor of Aeschylus might be expected, at any rate, to remember the Epic phrases, ἐν δαΐ λυγρῇ, ἐν δ. λευγαλέῃ.

Let us turn now to examine Dr. Verrall's knowledge of Greek language:

*Theb.* 137. ἔλακον ἀξόνων βριθομένων χνόαι

βριθομένων, note the tense. *The naves cried as the axles felt the weight*, literally *were being loaded*.

Schoolboys might indeed be justly warned to 'note the tense' and observe that βρίθω does not mean 'I load,' nor βρίθομαι 'I am being loaded,' but that both βρίθω and βρίθομαι mean 'I am laden.' The following instances are all of the present tense:

With dative or genitive (βρίθω):

Hom. Σ 561. σταφυλῇσι μέγα βρίθουσαν ἀλωήν.

Pind. *Nem.* iii. 40, Soph. *fr.* 264, Eur. *Tro.* 218, *Phoen.* 1557, Theocr. xv. 119, &c.

With dative or genitive (βρίθομαι):

Hom. Θ 306. μήκων καρπῷ βριθομένη νοτίῃσί τε εἰαρινῇσι.

Hes. *Scut.* 290, 295, 300, Bacchyl. *fr.* 13, *Lyr. fr. adesp.* 98, Theocr. xii. 23, *Anth. Plan.* 335, *A. P.* v. 94, ix. 78, xiv. 3, &c.

Aesch. *fr.* 116. λευκοῖς τε γὰρ μόροισι καὶ μελαγχίμοις
καὶ μιλτοπρέπτοις βρίθεται ταὐτῷ χρόνῳ.

Eur. *fr.* 467. τί γὰρ ποθεῖ τράπεζα; τῷ δ' οὐ βρίθεται;

So Pherecrates *fr.* 190.

Absolutely (βρίθω):

Hom. *h.* xxx. 9. βρίθει μέν σφιν ἄρουρα φερέσβιος.

Hes. *Op.* 465. εὔχεσθαι δὲ Διὶ χθονίῳ Δημήτερί θ ἁγνῇ
ἐκτελέα βρίθειν Δημήτερος ἱερὸν ἀκτήν.

*Lyr. fr. adesp.* 138, Nicander *Alex.* 210, Aratus *Diosem.* 350.

Absolutely (βρίθομαι):

Leonid. *A. P.* vii. 67. εἰ καί σοι μέγα βρίθεται ὀκρυόεσσα βᾶρις

and so here. In the aorist and future the word is not uncommonly transitive; in the present tense, only in late authors (unless Hes. *Op.* 465, quoted above, be an example; against which the evidence is strong). But even if it were frequently so used, Dr. Verrall's remark would of course be equally erroneous.

*Theb.* 226. τοιαῦτ' ἐπεύχου μὴ φιλοστόνως θεοῖς
μηδ' ἐν ματαίοις κἀγρίοις ποιφύγμασιν
οὐ γάρ τι μᾶλλον μὴ φύγῃς τὸ μόρσιμον.

268. '*ἄλλων (fuerat κάλλων) mut. in μᾶλλον M.' W.

Dr. Verrall accordingly reads κἄλλων:

κἄλλων, i.e. καὶ ἄλλων, or as a prose writer would have said καὶ τῶν ἄλλων, 'the fate of others also' or *the general fate*, cf. *v.* 249 σὺν ἄλλοις πείσομαι τὸ μόρσιμον. This, which is said to be the original reading of M, is more to the point than μᾶλλον and less likely to have been an arbitrary correction.

According to this, τὸ μόρσιμόν μου, or τὸ ἐμὸν μόρσιμον is a correct expression for 'my fate'; a notion not supported by Greek, for τὸ μόρσιμον is always used absolutely:

Pind. *P.* xii. 30. τό γε μ. οὐ παρφυκτόν.
*Nem.* iv. 61, vii. 44.
Aesch. *Cho.* 102. τὸ μ. γὰρ τόν τ' ἐλεύθερον μένει
καὶ τὸν πρὸς ἄλλης δεσποτούμενον χερός.
" " 462. τὸ μ. μένει πάλαι.
Soph. *Ant.* 236. τὸ μὴ παθεῖν ἂν ἄλλο πλὴν τὸ μ.
*fr.* 867, Eur. *Alc.* 945, *Heracl.* 1030, *Hel.* 613;
and so τὰ μόρσιμα, Solon 13, 55.

The chorus can indeed say σὺν ἄλλοις πείσομαι τὸ μ., 'I will endure with others what is fated'; but not in their extremest agitation would they say πείσομαι τὸ μ. ἄλλων. οὔ τι μᾶλλον I find quite enough to the point, here as at

Aesch. *fr.* 362. οὔτ' ἐν στέγῃ τις ἥμενος παρ' ἑστίᾳ
φεύγει τι μᾶλλον τὸν πεπρωμένον μόρον.

*Theb.* 165. ET. ὑμᾶς ἐρωτῶ, θρέμματ' οὐκ ἀνασχετά
ἦ ταῦτ' ἄριστα καὶ πόλει σωτήρια. . .
αὔειν, λακάζειν, . . ;

ὑμᾶς. Note the emphasis. He appeals to their own reason.

The meaning is quite misapprehended. The pronoun is so placed constantly in calls, appeals, addresses, summons:

Aesch. *Cho.* 454. σέ τοί λέγω, συγγενοῦ, πάτερ, φίλοις.
Soph. *O. C.* 1578. σέ τοί κικλήσκω τὸν αἰένυπνον.
Eur. *Ion* 222, 464, *Helena* 1106, *Rhes.* 633.
„ *I. A.* 854. μεῖνον, ὦ σέ τοι λέγω.
Ar. *Av.* 405. ἰὼ ἔποψ, σέ τοι καλῶ.
„ „ 275. οὗτος, ὦ σέ τοι.[1]

Often it expresses contempt or impatience:

Aesch. *P. V.* 976. σὲ τὸν σοφιστήν, τὸν πικρῶς ὑπέρπικρον,
τὸν ἐξαμαρτόντ' εἰς θεοὺς ἐφημέροις
πορόντα τιμάς, τὸν πυρὸς κλέπτην λέγω.
Soph. *Aj.* 71, 1221, *El.* 1445, *Ant.* 441.
Eur. *Med.* 272, *Hel.* 547, *H. F.* 1201.

So here it indicates a peremptory summons, just as in

Eur. *Andr.* 536. ὑμᾶς ἐρωτῶ τόν τ' ἐφεστῶτα σφαγῇ,
τί ταῦτα καὶ πῶς; ἐκ τίνος λόγου νοσεῖ
δόμος; τί πράσσετ' ἄκριτα μηχανώμενοι;

*Theb.* 358. σπουδῇ διώκων πομπίμους χνόας ποδῶν.

*Urging for haste the axles of his returning feet.* σπουδῇ causal.

Since σπουδῇ is used again and again with the sense 'in haste,' it would in any case be a strange error of judgment to suppose it in this single place to mean 'for haste'; but σπουδῇ τι ποιεῖν can no more mean 'to do anything *for*

[1] The verb is omitted also at Soph. *Ant.* 441, Eur. *Hel.* 547.

*speed*' (σπουδῆς ἕνεκα, χάριν) than ἦλθε δρόμῳ can mean 'he went for a run.'

*Theb.* 640. ὦ θεομανές. [τε καὶ θεῶν μέγα στύγος].

So Dr. Verrall prints:

Paley observes truly, that Aeschylus hardly ever commences the iambic senarius with a dactyl except in proper names, though the MS. gives an example in *Cho.* 215 . . . and thinks the present verse probably spurious. As it stands, it can scarcely be correct: θεῶν μέγα στύγος must be intended for θεοῖς μέγα στυγούμενον deeply hated of the gods; but where is such a use of μέγας to be found? . . .

It is found in this very phrase at

Ap. Rhod. iv. 445. σχέτλι' Ἔρως, μέγα πῆμα, μέγα στύγος ἀνθρώποισι

and that is quoted in the Thesaurus *s.v.* στύγος. (στύγος θεῶν occurs in this sense *Cho.* 1026, στύγη θ. *Eum.* 647.) Paley says:—

Perhaps . . . it was here pronounced θευμανές. But the verse is a weak one, meaning θεομανὲς and θεοστυγὲς, and for the reason given in the preceding note it is possibly spurious—

(not 'probably,' as Dr. Verrall represents), the 'reason given' being the probability that this speech like the preceding contained twenty verses.

*Ag.* 288. ἀλλ' ἦ σ' ἐπίανέν τις ἄπτερος φάτις;

ἐπίανεν, *has cheered* or *encouraged thee*, from ἐπ-ιαίνω, where ἐπί has the same force (*up to* a certain point) as in ἐπαίρω, and ἰαίνω its usual meaning (see L. and Sc. *s.v.* ἰαίνω).—By an oversight this aorist is commonly referred to πιαίνω *to fatten*, taken in the sense of *puffing up*. The use of πιαίνω and the connected words lends no support whatever to this supposed metaphor.

To avoid one error it was necessary only to consult Blomfield:

Πιαίνω. *Pinguefacio. Laetum reddo.* Fortior metaphora aliquatenus defenditur a v. 1659. Πρᾶσσε, πιαίνου, μιαίνων τὴν δίκην. ἐπεὶ πάρα. [1]Toup. in Hesych. iv. p. 103, ἐπίανεν ducit ab ἐπιαίνω, optime quod ad sensum attinet; sed nusquam inveni hoc compositum ex ἰαίνω.

---

[1] Hesych. ἐπιανέω: ἐπιτρέπω. '. . . Legere poteris, Ἐπιαίνω, ἐπιτέρπω. Sic Aeschylus Agamemnon, v. 284. Ἐπίανεν. Beavit . . .' Toup. Meineke would read ἐπιάλλω, or ἐπιαλέω· ἐπιτρέψω.

So much for the oversight. The metaphorical uses of *πιαίνω* may be studied from the following:

Lycophr. *Alex.* 1200. *οὐδ' ἐπίανεν βορᾷ νηδύν* (so Babrius cvii.).

Xenophanes 2, 22. *οὐ γὰρ πιαίνει ταῦτα μυχοὺς πόλεως* (cf. Hesych. *πιῆναι: ὠφελῆσαι, αὐξῆσαι*).

Agathias *A.P.* v. 294. *μάστακα πιαίνων χείλεος εὐαφίῃ.*

Opp. *Hal.* v. 372. *ἑὴν φρένα πιαίνοντες.*[1]

„ „ „ 620. *πιαίνων ἐς ἄεθλα λιγυφθόγγου μέλος αὐδῆς.*[1]

Pind. *P.* ii. 55. *βαρυλόγοις ἔχθεσι πιαινόμενον.*

Themist. *Or.* vii. 90 D. *θρήνων ἐρῶντες καὶ στεναγμῶν, οἰμωγῆς ἀκορεῖς, δάκρυσι πιαινόμενοι.*[2]

Lex. Seguer. *ἐκ τῶν Φρυνίχου* (Anecd. Bekker, p. 51) *λόγοις πιαίνειν: οἷον παραμυθεῖσθαι.*[2]

What is the exact connotation of the word in our passage I will not venture to determine; but it may be judged from these quotations whether an appropriate metaphorical sense is so little supported by the evidence that we must assume a compound *ἐπ-ιαίνω* elsewhere quite unknown.

*Theb.* 344. *παντοδαπὸς δὲ καρπὸς*
*χαμάδις πεσὼν ἀλγύνει κυρήσας.*

*σῖτος, κριθή, κέγχρος, πάνθ' ὁμοῦ χρήματα,* says schol. B. But no longer may we translate *παντοδαπὸς* 'various,' 'of all kinds,' or here understand 'all manner of store':

*παντοδαπός of all soils* (from all places). A Schol. might have noted an 'anachronism,' for the epithet is suggested rather by the household stores of the age of commerce, than by the age 'of Eteocles.' (Note that *παντοδαπὸς* is not for *παντοῖος*, of which use there is no evidence.)

*Ipse dixit.* And with what an authoritative air is this negation made! The following, then, is not evidence:

Epicharm. Ἥβ. γάμ. *fr.* 1. *ἄγει δὲ παντοδαπὰ κογχύλια.*
Pherecr. 108. *τεμάχη καταχυσματίοισι π. εὐτρεπῆ.*
Antiphan. 174. *γέμουσαν πέμμασι π.*

[1] L. and Sc. [2] Thesaurus, *s.v.*

Nicostr. 26. κόσμησον αὐτὴν π. τραγήμασιν.
Menand. 462. ἰχθυδίοις π.
Xen. *Mem.* iii. 14. π. ἡδύσματα.
,, *Cyrop.* i. 3. π. ἐμβάμματα καὶ βρώματα.
,, *Hiero.* 1, 25. τῶν σίτων ὁ μὲν ἔχων παντοδαπὰ ἀεὶ. . . .
,, *Ages.* 1, 26. ἥ τε γὰρ ἀγορὰ μεστὴ ἦν παντοδαπῶν καὶ ὅπλων καὶ ἵππων ὠνίων.
,, *Cyneg.* x. 3. τὰ δὲ ἀκόντια ἔστω π., . .
Plat. *Rep.* vii. 515 A. σκεύη τε π. . . . καὶ ἄλλα ζῶα λίθινά τε καὶ ξύλινα καὶ παντοῖα εἰργασμένα.
,, *Phaed.* 109 B. πολλὰ κοῖλα καὶ π. καὶ τὰς ἰδέας καὶ τὰ μεγέθη.
,, *Tim.* 87 A. π. νοσήματα ψυχῆς ἐμποιοῦσι, μᾶλλον καὶ ἧττον καὶ ἐλάττω καὶ πλείω.
,, ,, 91 C. νόσους π. ἄλλας παρέχεται.
Ar. *Plut.* 667. ἕτεροι δὲ πολλοὶ π. νοσήματα ἔχοντες.
Pind. *P.* iii. 6. τέκτονα νωδυνίας ἅμερον γυιαρκέος
'Ασκλάπιον,
ἥρωα παντοδαπᾶν ἀλκτῆρα νούσων.
,, *I.* i. 45. κούφα δόσις ἀνδρὶ σοφῷ
ἀντὶ μόχθων π., ἔπος εἰπόντ' ἀγαθὸν
ξυνὸν ὀρθῶσαι καλόν.
Alexis 135. συγγράμματα π.
Ibycus 2. Ἔρος . . . κηλήμασι παντοδαποῖς ἐς ἄπειρα δίκτυα Κύπριδος με βάλλει.
Philoxenus 1, 5. παντοδαποῖσι τέχνας εὑρήμασι.
Xenarchus 8. εὕρηκα π. τέχνας.
Sophocles (?) *ap.* Stob. *ecl.* i. 5, 11. παντοδαπᾶν βουλᾶν.
Aristot. περὶ ζῴων γενέσ. p. 756ᵃ 3 τὰς διαφορὰς . . . π. οὔσας.
Plat. *Leg.* vi. 782 A. πόλεων συστάσεις καὶ ἐπιτηδεύματα παντοῖα τάξεώς τε καὶ ἀταξίας καὶ βρώσεως καὶ πωμάτων τε ἅμα καὶ βρωμάτων ἐπιθυμήματα παντοδαπὰ πάντως καὶ περὶ πᾶσαν τὴν γῆν ἆρ' οὐκ οἰόμεθα γεγονέναι καὶ στροφὰς ὡρῶν παντοίας, . . .

Ar. *Nub.* 310. παντοδαπαῖς ἐν ὥραις.
Xen. *de re eq.* ii. 5. π. μὲν ὄψεσι π. δὲ ψόφοις πλησιάζειν.
Plat. *Theaet.* 156 B. τὸ δ' αὖ αἰσθητὸν γένος τούτων ἑκάσταις ὁμόγονον, ὄψεσι μὲν χρώματα παντοδαπαῖς παντοδαπά, . . .
„ *Tim.* 80 E. π. μὲν χρώματα ἴσχει.
„ *Lys.* 222 B. ὁ δὲ Ἱπποθάλης ὑπο τῆς ἡδονῆς π. ἠφίει χρώματα.
Arist. μετεωρ. p. 342$^b$ 5. π. χρόας, *ib.* 342$^b$ 7. π. χρώματα, so Plutarch, &c.
Sappho 20. παντοδαπαῖς μεμιγμένα χροΐαισιν.
Pherecr. 46. τῶν ἐρίων καὶ τῶν ἀνθῶν τῶν π.
* Hom. *h. Cer.* 401. ὁππότε δ' ἄνθεσι γαῖ' εὐώδεσιν εἰαρινοῖσιν
παντοδαποῖς θάλλει.
Ar. *Vesp.* 709. ἔζων ἐν πᾶσι λαγῴοις καὶ στεφάνοισιν π.
Archestratus (Ath. iii. 101 c) στεφάνοισι π. So *Anth. Pal.* xv. 46, Athenaeus xv. 678 c.
Sotades 1. τριμμάτιον ἄνθινον π.
(as Hdt. iii. 24. παντοίη ἐγίνετο μὴ ἀποδημῆσαι τὸν Π.
„ vii. 10. παντοῖοι ἐγένοντο Σκύθαι δεόμενοι Ἰώνων λῦσαι τὸν πόρον.
„ ix. 109. Ξέρξης δὲ παντοῖος ἐγίνετο οὐ βουλόμενος δοῦναι.
and Lucian, &c., so)
Dio. Chr. vol. i. p. 164. παντοδαπὸς ἦν ἱκετεύων.[1]
Plat.* *Rep.* iii. 398. ἄνδρα . . . δυνάμενον ὑπὸ σοφίας παντοδαπὸν γίγνεσθαι καὶ μιμεῖσθαι πάντα χρήματα.
„ „ ii. 381 E. αὐτοὶ μὲν οἱ θεοί εἰσιν οἷοι μὴ μεταβάλλειν ἡμῖν δὲ ποιοῦσι δοκεῖν σφᾶς παντοδαποὺς φαίνεσθαι.
„ **Ion.* 541 E. ἀλλ' ἀτεχνῶς ὥσπερ ὁ Πρωτεὺς παντοδαπὸς γίγνῃ στρεφόμενος ἄνω καὶ κάτω.

[1] Thesaurus *s.v.*

*Ar. *Ran.* 289 (of Ἔμπουσα) παντοδαπὸν γοῦν γίγνεται, ποτὲ μέν γε βοῦς, νυνὶ δ' ὀρεύς, ποτὲ δ' αὖ γυνὴ ὡραιοτάτη τίς (Cf. Hes. *Theog.* 830 sqq., *fr.* 30).
Plat. *Rep.* ix. 588 E. τὸ παντοδαπὸν θηρίον.
Pind. *fr.* 96 (of Pan). ὦ μάκαρ ὅντε μεγαλᾶς θεοῦ
κύνα παντοδαπὸν καλέοισιν Ὀλύμπιοι.

(See however Rutherford, *New Phrynichus,* p. 130.)

Xen. *de re eq.* x. 7. οἷόν τε γὰρ καὶ τὸν τραχὺν π. ποιεῖν.
Orph. *fr.* (Macrob. *Sat.* I. 18). ἀλλαχθεὶς δ' ὄνομ' ἔσχε
προσωνυμίας τε ἕκαστον
παντοδαπὰς κατὰ καιρόν.
Macho (Ath. xii. 577 e). γένη μύρων παντοδαπῶν.
*Batrachom.* 31, 41.
Ion. *eleg.* I. 2. αὕτη γὰρ πρόφασις παντοδαπῶν λογίων.[1]
Plat. *Tim.* 52 D. παντοδαπὴν μὲν ἰδεῖν φαίνεσθαι.
„ *Symp.* 193 E. διὰ τὸ πολλὰ καὶ π. εἰρῆσθαι.
Isocr. *Nic.* 16. πολλαῖς καὶ π. διανοίαις.
„ *Busir.* 26. πολλὰς γὰρ αὐτοῖς καὶ π. ἀσκήσεις τῆς ὁσιότητος ἐκεῖνος κατέστησεν.
„ 284 c. παντοδαπῆς μεστὸς ποικιλίας καὶ ψευδολογίας.
Plat.* *Soph.* 228 E. τὸ τῆς πολλῆς καὶ π. ἀγνοίας πάθος.
„ *Prot.* 334 B. οὕτω δὲ ποικίλον[2] τί ἐστι τὸ ἀγαθὸν καὶ π.
„ *Rep.* vii. 559 D. π. ἡδονὰς καὶ ποικίλας καὶ παντοίως ἐχούσας δυναμένοις σκευάζειν.
comparative: *Arist. περὶ ζῴων γενέσ. p. 786$^b$2 αἱ ποικίλαι τροφαὶ παντοδαπωτέρας ποιοῦσι τὰς κινήσεις.
superlative: Isocr. *Antid.* 315. γυμνάσια πλεῖστα καὶ π. παρέχουσα . .
adverb: *Plat. *Parm.* 129 E. τὴν αὐτὴν ταύτην ἀπορίαν ἐν αὐτοῖς τοῖς εἴδεσι παντοδαπῶς πλεκομένην.
*Poeta *ap.* Aristot. *Eth. Nic.* II. 5. ἐσθλοὶ μὲν γὰρ ἁπλῶς π. δὲ κακοί.

[1] Ath. x. 447 d. λόγων cod. C. λογίοις should be read, or possibly ἐπέων.
[2] The word is very commonly combined with ποικίλος.

Such is some of the evidence which Dr. Verrall's independent work finds not to exist. In this catalogue are recorded very nearly all the examples I have found in verse; but throughout prose, beginning with Xenophon, examples are abundant. The word is in fact rarely used in any other sense. There was no need then, it seems, for the schol. to note an anachronism; and Hesychius, who himself of course uses the word in its ordinary sense (*s. vv.* ὄμπια, πανδαισίαν, ῥικνοῦσθαι), may be excused for giving

παντοδαποῖς : διαφόροις
παντοδαπός : παντοῖος σύμμικτος
παντοδα[πῶν] : παντοίων. καὶ διαφόρων.

and we for understanding the words of our text as καρπὸν σύμμικτον in Hes. *Op.* 563. Liddell and Scott, it may be mentioned, have but a very meagre article upon the word: of all the examples above quoted they refer only to those I have marked with an asterisk.

Here is another assertion of like character:

*Theb.* 664. μή, φίλτατ' ἀνδρῶν, Οἰδίπου τέκος, γένῃ
ὀργὴν ὁμοῖος τῷ κάκιστ' αὐδωμένῳ.

HERMANN.

In M. hoc scholion adscriptum est, τὸν τρόπον τῷ ἀδελφῷ σου βλασφημούμενος,[1] et in altera parte ὑπὸ σοῦ. Alter scholiastes interpretatur τῷ κακωνύμῳ Πολυνείκῃ. Glossa in G λέγοντι, in Vit. κακίστως λεγομένῳ. Praestat active intelligere αὐδωμένῳ, ut spectentur quae dixisse Polynicen rettulerat nuntius, velle illum cum fratre congredi.

PALEY.

Hermann understands it actively for λέγοντι, in allusion to the bloodthirsty wish in 630 seqq. The middle voice occurs *Eum.* 358, *Cho.* 144, but one can hardly think this interpretation more probable in the present instance.

DR. VERRALL.

τῷ κάκιστ' αὐδωμένῳ *him called by the dreadful name*, Πολυνείκει, as in *v.* 566 etc.: αὐδωμένῳ is an imperfect participle. This interpretation divides the scholiasts and later commentators with τῳ ὑπὸ σοῦ βλασφημουμένῳ. But the words ὑπὸ σοῦ can scarcely be supplied.—'Praestat active intelligere αὐδωμένῳ' Hermann; but there is no authority for a deponent αὐδῶμαι.

Paley, rejecting it here, cites for it *Eum.* 383 καὶ δυοφεράν τιν' ἀχλὺν κατὰ δώματος αὐδᾶται πολύστονος φάτις (where αὐδᾶται is passive, ἀχλὺν being an 'accusative in apposition to the sentence') and *Cho.* 151 παιᾶνα τοῦ θανόντος ἐξαυδωμένας, a very obscure and doubtful passage.

[1] Sch. rec. βλασφημουμένῳ.

Let it be observed first that, though quoting from Hermann's note, Dr. Verrall, in stating that two interpretations divide the scholiasts and later commentators, omits to mention the third interpretation λέγοντι, recorded by Hermann as a gloss in cod. G. Yet λέγοντι, of course, is active.

Paley refers to two passages as sufficient illustration of an active sense for *αὐδῶμαι*. Dr. Verrall proceeds as though these two were the only instances that could be cited; as though to dispose of these were to dispose of all authority for a deponent *αὐδῶμαι*. Of these indeed he does immediately dispose:

1. *Eum.* 380. τοῖον ἐπὶ
κνέφας ἀνδρὶ μύσος πεπόταται
καὶ δνοφεράν τιν' ἀχλὺν κατὰ δώματος
αὐδᾶται πολύστονος φάτις.

Schol. M. says *κακὴ δὲ φήμη περὶ τοῦ οἴκου αὐτοῦ λέγεται*: but the natural and the accepted interpretation regards *φάτις* as the subject and *ἀχλὺν* as the object of *αὐδᾶται*.

2. *Cho.* 149. τοιαῖσδ' ἐπ' εὐχαῖς τάσδ' ἐπισπένδω χοάς.
ὑμᾶς δὲ κωκυτοῖς ἐπανθίζειν νόμος
παιᾶνα τοῦ θανόντος ἐξαυδωμένας.

'A very obscure and doubtful passage.' Now the only possible obscurity is in the exact meaning of *ἐπανθίζειν*. Schol. M. explains it by *στέφειν ὡς ἄνθεσιν*, *i.e.* 'to strew with lamentations as with flowers' (the libations poured on the tomb). So we have

*Pers.* 622. ἀλλ', ὦ φίλοι, χοαῖσι ταῖσδε νερτέρων
ὕμνους ἐπευφημεῖτε.

According to this, which seems certainly the right interpretation, *ἐξαυδωμένας* is active, governing *παιᾶνα*. But even if *παιᾶνα* were taken as the object of *ἐπανθίζειν*, *ἐξαυδωμένας* would still be active; as to that there is neither doubt nor obscurity. Yet it is with the meaning of *ἐξαυδωμένας* that we are concerned.

It must be assumed in courtesy that Dr. Verrall knew of

no other instances. But that assumption compels us to suppose that he was unacquainted with the following:—

3. Aesch. *Cho.* 268. οὔτοι προδώσει Λοξίου μεγασθενὴς
χρησμὸς κελεύων τόνδε κίνδυνον περᾶν
κἀξορθιάζων πολλὰ καὶ δυσχειμέρους
ἄτας ὑφ' ἧπαρ θερμὸν ἐξαυδώμενος,
εἰ μὴ μέτειμι τοῦ πατρὸς τοὺς αἰτίους.

Is this, too, 'a very obscure and doubtful passage'?

On Hom K 300, ἄμυδις κικλήσκετο πάντας ἀρίστους, [1]Eustathius (806. 54) expressly says: πολλὰ καὶ ἕτερα οὕτω δέδεικται διφορούμενα ὧν ἐστι καὶ τὸ αὐδᾶν λεγόμενόν ποτε καὶ παθητικῶς οἷον ποικίλως αὐδωμένου . . . alluding to

4. Soph. *Phil.* 127. καὶ δεῦρο . . . αὖθις ἐκπέμψω πάλιν
τοῦτον τὸν αὐτὸν ἄνδρα, . . .
οὗ δῆτα, τέκνον, ποικίλως αὐδωμένου
δέχου τὰ συμφέροντα τῶν ἀεὶ λόγων.

Schol. L τοῦ Φιλοκτήτου ἀπατωμένου ἢ τοῦ ναυκλήρου δόλιά σοι διαλεγομένου καὶ ἀσυμφανῆ: and σοφιζομένου· διαλεγομένου (Gl.).

5. Soph. *Phil.* 850. κεῖνο λάθρᾳ
ἐξιδοῦ ὅπᾳ πράξεις·
οἶσθα γὰρ ὧν αὐδῶμαι·
εἰ ταὐτὰν τούτῳ γνώμαν ἴσχεις.

852. So L. Above ὧν L[2] has written .ον. Schol. L δι' ὃν λέγω ἀντὶ τὸν Φιλοκτήτην. Brunck read ὅν γ': Hermann (Jebb) ἂν (γνώμαν).

However the passage be read there can be little doubt that αὐδῶμαι is active, 'I speak.' Still, the text being in many respects uncertain, this place shall not be urged. But there is no uncertainty at

6. Soph. *Aj.* 770. τοσόνδ' ἐκόμπει μῦθον. εἶτα δεύτερον
δίας 'Αθάνας, ἡνίκ' ὀτρύνουσά νιν
ηὐδᾶτ' ἐπ' ἐχθροῖς χεῖρα φοινίαν τρέπειν
τότ' ἀντιφωνεῖ δεινὸν ἄρρητόν τ' ἔπος.

for ηὐδᾶτο can mean only 'she charged him to .'

7. Soph. *Phil.* 395. σὲ κἀκεῖ, μᾶτερ πότν', ἐπηυδώμαν.

Sch. L ἐπεκαλούμην.

[1] Ellendt *Lex. Sophocl.* *s.v.* αὐδάω.

8. Pind. *O.* II. 90. ἐπί τοι
'Ακράγαντι τανύσαις
αὐδάσομαι ἐνόρκιον λόγον ἀλαθεῖ νόῳ.

V. 91 . . *τανύσαις* vel *τανύσσαις* plurimi, *τανύσας* ΗΙΓΞΠΣ, *τάνυσον* (*τάνυσσον*) $N_1Q_2U_2$. Vulgo hic stigme ponitur, sed schol. *τείνας* interpretatur et cum seq. iungit, quem praeeunte Hartungo secutus sum.
V. 92 *αὐδάσομαι*, $B_1$ Ω *αὐδάσομεν*. Bergk.

To be unacquainted with this matter of *αὐδᾶσθαι*, in connexion with which all these passages are well known, is a strange thing in an editor of Aeschylus. But further, the examples are so near to hand that any enquiry must have discovered them: therefore the statement that 'there is no authority for a deponent *αὐδῶμαι*' is made not only without truth, but without any attempt at truth.

Who, again, could have believed a Greek scholar capable of the following declaration:

*Theb.* 100. κτύπον δέδορκα· πάταγος οὐχ ἑνὸς δορός.

The MS. appears to me impossible; *not one* is no synonym for *many*.

So says Dr. Verrall, reading οὐ κενὸς δ.

*οὐχ εἷς* is used constantly throughout Greek for *οὐχ εἷς μόνον*. The following passages will show the various forms of this *meiosis*:

Hom. *h. Merc.* 284. ἦ σε μάλ' οἴω
. . . οὐχ ἕνα μοῦνον ἐπ' οὔδει φῶτα καθίσσαι.

Soph. *O. T.* 122. οὐ μιᾷ ῥώμῃ . . . ἀλλὰ σὺν πλήθει χερῶν.

" *O. C.* 737. οὐκ ἐξ ἑνὸς στείλαντος ἀλλ' ἀνδρῶν ὑπὸ πάντων . .

Eur. *Med.* 939. εὐδαιμονήσει δ' οὐχ ἓν ἀλλὰ μυρία.

" *Andr.* 96. πάρεστι δ' οὐχ ἓν ἀλλὰ πολλά μοι στένειν.

" " 550. οὐ γὰρ μιᾶς σε κληδόνος προθυμίᾳ
μετῆλθον ἀλλὰ μυρίων ὑπ' ἀγγέλων,

Eur. *fr.* 547. ἑνὸς δ' ἔρωτος ὄντος οὐ μί' ἡδονή.
„ *Supp.* 96. οὐχ ἕνα ῥυθμὸν κακῶν ἐχούσας.
„ *Cycl.* 513. στεφάνων οὐ μία χροιά.
Hdt. v. 78. δηλοῖ δὲ οὐ κατ' ἓν μόνον ἀλλὰ πανταχῇ.
Pherecr. (?) 248. πανταχῇ λυπηρόν, οὐ καθ' ἓν μόνον.
Plat. *Crito* 44. ὡς ἐμοί, ἐὰν σὺ ἀποθάνῃς, οὐ μία ξυμφορά ἐστιν, ἀλλὰ . .
Eur. *fr.* 271. τῆς τύχης δ' οὐχ εἷς τρόπος.
Philem. *fr.* 10. νῦν δ' οἶδ' ἀκριβῶς τὴν τύχην ὡς οὐ μία.
„ „ 28. οὐχ εἰς ἡμέραν
χειμάζομαι μίαν γὰρ εἰς τὸ ζῆν δ' ὅλον.
Com. *fr.* 1330. ἵνα . . σκευασία μὴ μί' ᾖ τῆς μουσικῆς.
Crates *fr.* 22 (Bergk). οὐχ εἷς πάτρας μοι πύργος, οὐ μία στέγη.
*Trag. fr. adesp.* 392. Ἀργεῖος ἢ Θηβαῖος· οὐ γὰρ εὔχομαι
μιᾶς.
Callim. *h. Dian.* 33. τρὶς δέκα σοι πτολίεθρα καὶ οὐχ ἕνα πύργον ὀπάσσω.
„ *h. Del.* 192. πόδες δέ οἱ οὐχ ἑνὶ χώρῳ (v. Schneider).
see also *h. Jov.* 89. οἳ δὲ τὰ μὲν πλειῶνι, τὰ δ' οὐχ ἑνί.
Ap. Rhod. iv. 498. ἔλπομαι οὐχ ἕνα μῦθον . . τοὺς πεισέμεν.
Nicaenet. *A. P.* xii. 29. ἔπνεεν οὐχ ἑνὸς ἀσκοῦ
Κρατῖνος ἀλλὰ παντὸς ὠδώδει πίθου.
Nicander, *Ther.* 147. χροιὴν ἀλλόφατόν τε καὶ οὐ μίαν οἴαδον ἴσχει.
Nonnus xxv. 472. οὐ γὰρ ἕνα πρήνιζεν ὁδοιπόρον οὐδὲ νομῆα.
„ xl. 53. ἐγὼ δ' ἐμὸν ἆορ ἑλίσσω
θῆρσι πολυσπερέεσσι καὶ οὐχ ἕνα θῆρα δαμάζω.

so xxviii. 184, xxxiv. 8. The use is common also in prose.

So in Latin:

Hor. *Carm.* iv. 9. 39. consulque non unius anni.

Persius v. 53. uelle suum cuique est nec uoto uiuitur uno.

Juvenal iii. 150. crassum atque recens linum ostendit non una cicatrix.

Juvenal vi. 218. non unus tibi rivalis dictabitur heres.

„ viii. 213. cuius supplicio non debuit una parari simia nec serpens unus nec culeus unus.

Lucan i. 478. agmine non uno densisque incedere castris.

Martial xii. 51. et non unius balnea solus habes.

Auson. *Epitaph.* iv. non una Aeaciden tellus habet; ossa teguntur
litore Sigeo, crinem Larissa cremauit.

*Catalect.*[1] p. 197. et quidquid Libyco secatur aruo
non una positum tenere cella.

and also in prose.

So with *οὐχ ἅπαξ*:

Aesch. *P. V.* 225. *ἐμοὶ δὲ μητὴρ οὐχ ἅπαξ μόνον . . προὐτεθεσπίκει.*

Soph. *O. T.* 689. *εἶπον μὲν οὐχ ἅπαξ μόνον.*

„ „ 1275. *τοιαῦτ᾽ ἐφυμνῶν πολλάκις τε κοὐχ ἅπαξ*
*ἤρασσ᾽ ἐπαίρων βλέφαρα.*

„ *Phil.* 443. *ὃς οὐκ ἂν εἵλετ᾽ εἰσάπαξ εἰπεῖν.*

Eur. *Andr.* 81. *ἔπεμψ᾽ ἐπ᾽ αὐτὸν οὐχ ἅπαξ μόνον.*

„ „ 923. *ἀλλ᾽ οὔποτ᾽ οὔποτ᾽· οὐ γὰρ εἰσάπαξ ἐρῶ.*

so Hdt. ii. 59, vii. 46.

In Latin:

Plaut. *Poen.* 1. 2. 148. Iurauisti haud semel sed centies.

Horace *Carm.* iv. ii. 49. io Triumphe,
non semel dicemus, io Triumphe.

Nepos *Epam.* 7. neque uero hoc semel fecit sed saepius.

[1] Blomfield on *Theb.* 100.

Many similar forms of expression might be given, *e.g.* Hom. π. 245, where in answer to Odysseus' question :

> *ἀλλ' ἄγε μοι μνηστῆρας ἀριθμήσας κατάλεξον*
> *ὄφρ' ἰδέω ὅσσοι τε καὶ οἵτινες ἀνέρες εἰσίν·*

Telemachus answers :

> *μνηστήρων δ' οὔτ' ἂρ δεκὰς ἀτρεκὲς, οὔτε δύ' οἶαι,*
> *ἀλλὰ πολὺ πλέονες.*

Lucian ii. 876. *ῥήτορας δὲ καὶ φιλοσόφους εὕροι τις ἂν οὐ τινάς, ἀλλὰ πάντας ὑπό τύφου καὶ δόξης τριβέντας.*

It is quite true that in English we cannot use 'not one,' 'not once' *simply*, in this way; but there are many Greek idioms which are not also English.

Another use of *εἷς* may be considered here :

*Theb.* 526. *ἐν σάκει*
*Σφίγγ' ὠμόσιτον προσμεμηχανημένην*
*γόμφοις ἐνώμα, . .*
530. *φέρει δ' ὑφ' αὑτῇ φῶτα Καδμείων ἕνα*
*ὡς πλεῖστ' ἐπ' ἀνδρὶ τῷδ' ἰάπτεσθαι βέλη.*

*τῷ διαπτέσθαι*, Dr. Verrall :

*The Sphinx beneath her carries a Cadmean man and never for any* one *before did she fly through such a cloud of spears.*

The equivalent in prose terms for *v.* 531 would be ὥστε πλεῖστα ἐφ' ἑνὶ ἀνδρὶ τούτῳ βέλη διαπτέσθαι.

I shall concern myself only with Dr. Verrall's remarks. First those on *εἷς* :

It should be observed that εἷς is not found as a mere equivalent for τις : in the apparent examples it generally signifies nearly *quivis* 'any one, equal to one, merely one'; see Eur. *Med.* 945, *Or.* 264, *Bacch* 917, Soph. *El.* 1342. In Soph. *Ant.* 269 λέγει τις εἷς ὃς πάντας κ.τ.λ. there is an antithesis between εἷς and πάντας, and so elsewhere.

Dr. Verrall is indeed careful to say 'generally'; but the statement that '*εἷς* is not found as a mere equivalent for *τις*' is absolute. It would be supposed, I conceive, that the passages mentioned are those showing, if not the only, at any rate the most apparent examples of εἷς in such a sense. We will see. The passages are:

Eur. *Med.* 931. καὶ πείσειν γε δοξάζω σφ' ἐγώ,
εἴπερ γυναικῶν ἐστι τῶν ἄλλων μία.
„ *Or.* 254. μέθες· μί' οὖσα τῶν ἐμῶν Ἐρινύων
μέσον μ' ὀχμάζεις ὡς βάλῃς ἐς Τάρταρον.
*Bacch.* 905. ΔΙ. σὲ τὸν πρόθυμον ὄνθ' ἃ μὴ χρεὼν ὁρᾶν
σπεύδοντά τ' ἀσπούδαστα, Πενθέα λέγω,
ἔξιθι πάροιθε δωμάτων, ὄφθητί μοι,
σκευὴν γυναικὸς μαινάδος βάκχης ἔχων
μητρός τε τῆς σῆς καὶ λόχου κατάσκοπος·
πρέπεις δε Κάδμου θυγατέρων μορφῇ μιᾷ.
Soph. *El.* 1342. εἷς τῶν ἐν Ἅιδου μάνθαν' ἐνθάδ' ὢν ἀνήρ.

In these examples the signification assigned by Dr. Verrall does make sense. It happens however that just those examples which do not admit that signification are not selected for reference:

Soph. *Ant.* 1066. τῶν σῶν αὐτὸς ἐκ σπλάγχνων ἕνα
νέκυν νεκρῶν ἀμοιβὸν ἀντιδοὺς ἔσει.
Eur. *Ion* 1. Ἄτλας . . θεῶν | μιᾶς ἔφυσε Μαῖαν.
„ *Rhes.* 382. παῖ τῆς μελῳδοῦ μητέρος, Μουσῶν μιᾶς.
„ „ 883. ἡ γὰρ ἐν σοφοῖς
τιμὰς ἔχουσα Μοῦσα, συγγόνων μία,
πάρειμι.
„ *Hel.* 6. ὃς τῶν κατ' οἶδμα παρθένων μίαν γαμεῖ,
Ψαμάθην.
„ *Cycl.* 21. ἵν' οἱ μονῶπες ποντίου παῖδες θεοῦ
Κύκλωπες οἰκοῦσ' ἄντρ' ἔρημ' ἀνδροκτόνοι.
τούτων ἑνὸς ληφθέντες ἐσμὲν ἐν δόμοις.

The following instance admits Dr. Verrall's signification:

Eur. *Phoen.* 1677. νὺξ ἆρ' ἐκείνη Δαναΐδων μ' ἕξει μίαν.

and so, with a difference, might

Eur. *I. A* 68. δίδωσ' ἑλέσθαι θυγατρὶ μνηστήρων ἕνα
ὅτου πνοαὶ φέροιεν Ἀφροδίτης φίλαι.

But in the other examples I have quoted that signification is excluded. And yet, if I have not erred, they are all the other instances in tragedy of εἷς with a partitive genitive in which a numeral force cannot be urged; and all, except Eur. *Cycl.* 23, are, equally with the examples selected by Dr. Verrall, to be found in the Indices *s.v.* εἷς.

So Hom. Ξ. 275. *ἦ μὲν ἐμοὶ δώσειν Χαρίτων μίαν ὁπλοτεράων Πασιθέην* (as 267).

Pind. *N.* iv. 65. *ἔγαμεν ὑψιθρόνων μίαν Νηρεΐδων.*

Ar. *Eq.* 1300. *φασὶν ἀλλήλαις ξυνελθεῖν τὰς τριήρεις εἰς λόγον,*
*καὶ μίαν λέξαι τιν' αὐτῶν ἥτις ἦν γεραιτέρα, . . .*

„ *Vesp.* 1165. *πάνυ μισολάκων αὐτοῦ 'στιν εἷς τῶν δακτύλων.*

Ap. Rhod. iv. 896. *Τερψιχόρη, Μουσέων μία.*

„ „ „ 1016. *εἴ νυ καὶ αὐτὴ*
*ἀνθρώπων γενεῆς μία φέρβεται.*

The same use is common in prose from Herodotus downward. The distinction of meaning which Dr. Verrall with his peculiar method endeavours to establish is without any value in truth. With a partitive genitive εἷς may be used in Greek just as 'one of . .' in English. Therefore

*φέρει δ' ὑφ' αὐτῇ φῶτα, Καδμείων ἕνα,*

would be perfectly good Greek.

I come now to ἐπὶ with the dative:

'Never before for a single prey did she fly through.' (Transl p. 158.)
For ἐπὶ with the dative of the cause or object of an action, cf. ἐπὶ τυραννίδι (to gain despotic power) τι ποιεῖν and other examples in the *Lex. s.v.* ἐπὶ.

Of the main ideas expressed by the dative with ἐπί, one, the *aim of one's action*, the *object of one's bent*, belongs to many cases. ἐπὶ τυραννίδι is one in which the essential notion is clear. Proud possessor of this instance, Dr. Verrall must needs have that essential notion applicable in all its purity, or not at all. As though the original notion were not the parent of more definite senses:

*aiming at*:

Hom. E. 97. ἐπὶ Τυδείδῃ ἐτιταίνετο καμπύλα τόξα. Λ. 370.
„ Λ. 583. τόξον ἕλκετ' ἐπ' Εὐρυπύλῳ.
„ O. 464. (νευρὴν) ἐπὶ τῷ ἐρύοντι.
„ χ. 8. ἐπ' Ἀντινόῳ ἰθύνετο πικρὸν ὀιστόν.
Pind. *O.* II. 90. ἐπί τοι Ἀκράγαντι τανύσαις.
Soph. *Phil.* 197. ἐπὶ Τροίᾳ
τεῖναι τὰ θεῶν ἀμάχητα βέλη.
Rufin. *A.P.* v. 97. εἰ μὲν ἐπ' ἀμφοτέροισιν, Ἔρως, ἴσα τόξα τιταίνεις.

*Ag.* 374. Δία τοι ξένιον μέγαν αἰδοῦμαι
τὸν τάδε πράξαντ' ἐπ' Ἀλεξάνδρῳ
τείνοντα πάλαι τόξον,

*i.e.* τάδε πράξαντ', ἐπ' Ἀ. τείνοντα τόξον. But hear Dr. Verrall:

who hath wrought this vengeance for Paris' sin, though long he bent his bow, . . . (Transl. p. 237.)

*hurling*, or *shooting at*:

Hom. A. 382. ἧκε δ' ἐπ' Ἀργείοισι βέλος.
„ Π. 358. ἐφ' Ἕκτορι . . . ἀκοντίσσαι.
„ „ 608. ἐπὶ Μηριόνῃ δόρυ χάλκεον ἧκεν. X. 206.
Hes. *Theog.* 684. ἐπ' ἀλλήλοις ἵεσαν βέλεα στονόεντα.
Aesch. *P. V.* 1043. πρὸς ταῦτ' ἐπ' ἐμοὶ ῥιπτέσθω μὲν
πυρὸς ἀμφήκης βόστρυχος.
„ *Supp.* 1003. παρθένων χλιδαῖσιν εὐμόρφοις ἔπι
πᾶς τις . . . τόξευμ' ἔπεμψεν.
Eur. *Ph.* 1254. ἐπ' ἀλλήλοισιν ἱέναι δόρυ.
„ *Med.* 629. μήποτ', ὦ δέσποιν', ἐπ' ἐμοὶ
χρυσέων τόξων ἀφείης
. . . ἄφυκτον οἰστόν.
Ap. Rhod. II. 1036. ἧκ' ἐπί οἱ πτερὸν ὀξύ. III. 234, *Anth. Pal.* v. 194, xii. 19.

Nonnus xxviii. 248. πέτρην ῥῖψεν ἐπ' ἀντιβίοισιν.
*Theb.* 298. τοὶ δ' ἐπ' ἀμφιβόλοισιν
ἰάπτουσι πολίταις
χερμάδ' ὀκριόεσσαν.

It is the besieging party who are throwing *at* the defenders of the town. But even here Dr. Verrall avoids that rendering:

Shower upon our men the flinty stone. (Transl. p. 153.)

So with any notion of hostility

*against, at*:

Hom. Λ. 293. ὡς ἐπ' Ἀχαιοῖσιν σεῦε Τρῶας.
„ „ 460, N 332. ἐπ' αὐτῷ πάντες ἔβησαν.
„ Π. 751. ἐπὶ Κεβριόνῃ ἥρωϊ βεβήκει.
„ Κ. 214. ὡρμήθησαν ἐπ' ἀνδράσιν.
„ Ρ. 725. οἵτ' ἐπὶ κάπρῳ . . . ἀίξωσι.
Eur. *Ph.* 1384. ᾖξαν δρόμημα δεινὸν ἀλλήλοις ἔπι.
Hom. δ. 822. ἐπ' αὐτῷ μηχανόωνται.

Similarly Aesch. *Cho.* 989, *P. V.* 95, Soph. *Aj.* 44, *Phil.* 1137, Hdt. iv. 154 *bis*, Eur. *I. A.* 743, *fr.* 918, *Rhes.* 568, Ap. Rh. iii. 743, *Anth. Pal.* ix. 339, xii. 127.

Aesch. *P. V.* 952. τοῖον παλαιστὴν νῦν παρασκευάζεται ἐπ' αὐτὸς αὑτῷ.
Soph. *Aj.* 18. ἐπ' ἀνδρὶ δυσμενεῖ βάσιν κυκλοῦντα.
„ „ 451. ἐπ' αὐτοῖς χεῖρ' ἐπευτύνοντα.
Eur. *Rhes.* 84. ἐπ' ἐχθροῖς . . . ὁπλίζειν χέρα
„ „ 565. Ἕκτορος κοίτας ἐφ' ᾧπερ ἔγχος εἵλκυσται τόδε.
Ar. *Lys.* 50. ἐπ' ἀλλήλοισιν αἴρεσθαι δόρυ.
„ *Av.* 338, Meleag. *A. P.* v. 152.
Eur. *Heracl.* 837. ἀνὴρ δ' ἐπ' ἀνδρὶ στὰς ἐκαρτέρει μάχῃ.
„ *H. F.* 827. μανίας τ' ἐπ' ἀνδρὶ τῷδε καὶ παιδοκτόνους φρενῶν ταραγμοὺς καὶ ποδῶν σκιρτήματα ἔλαυνε κίνει.
Patrocles *fr.* 1. δεινοὺς ἐπ' ἀλλήλοισι πέμποντες λόγους.

Eur. *H.F.* 897. μελάθρων τάραγμα Ταρτάρειον, ὡς
ἐπ' Ἐγκελάδῳ ποτε Παλλάς, εἰς δόμους
πέμπεις ;

Antip. Thess. *A.P.* ix. 77. Ἄρσεν πῦρ ἔτεκεν Τροία Διΐ·
τοιγὰρ ἐγὼ πῦρ
πέμψω ἐπὶ Τροίᾳ, πῆμα
φέροντα Πάριν.

*Ag.* 57. ἢ Πὰν ἢ Ζεὺς . . ὑστερόποινον
πέμπει παραβᾶσιν Ἐρινύν·
οὕτω δ' Ἀτρέως παῖδας ὁ κρείσσων
ἐπ' Ἀλεξάνδρῳ πέμπει ξένιος Ζεύς,

'sends against Alexander': but Dr. Verrall:

Even such ministers are the sons of Atreus, sent to punish the triumph of Paris by their mightier Zeus. (Transl. p. 232.)

*Theb.* 434. ἀνὴρ δ' ἐπ' αὐτῷ, κεἰ στόμαργός ἐστ' ἄγαν,
αἴθων τέτακται λῆμα, Πολυφόντου βία.

The use of ἐπ' αὐτῷ is precisely like that in *v.* 607 . . . , where see note. It is literally 'on the top of that itself,' or more simply *over and above that*, ἐπί having the same sense as in τρίτος ἐπὶ δέκα, ἄτην ἐπ' ἄτῃ, etc.—That αὐτῷ does not mean *against him* may be proved, apart from the question of emphasis, by the considerations, (1) that ἐπ' αὐτῷ τέτακται could only mean 'is appointed *over* him,' or 'ranged *behind* him,' not 'against him,' which is ἀντιτέτακται αὐτῷ (see *Lex. s.v.* ἐπιτάσσω) ; (2) that the occurrence of ἐπ' αὐτῷ here and in *v.* 607 only among the seven parallel passages, taken with the close logical resemblance of these two, is itself strong evidence of a sense common to these two and peculiar to them.

*Theb.* 602. δοκῶ μὲν οὖν σφε μηδὲ προσβαλεῖν πύλαις, . .
607. ὅμως δ' ἐπ' αὐτῷ φῶτα, Λασθένους βίαν,
ἐχθρόξενον πυλωρὸν ἀντιτάξομεν, . .

ἐπ' αὐτῷ, neuter, for ἐπ' αὐτῷ τούτῳ *over and above*, lit. 'above the thing itself,' *i.e.* as a security in addition to the improbability of an attack ; not 'against him' ; if the pronoun were expressed at all, which according to Aeschylus' manner of writing it should not be, the simple dative αὐτῷ would be the correct construction with ἀντιτάξομεν.

With the pronoun and the 'question of emphasis' I will deal presently (p 54). Meantime, observe how, for proof that ἀνὴρ τέτακται ἐπ' αὐτῷ could not mean 'against him,' we are told to see what Liddell and Scott have to say on the meaning of ἐπιτάσσω! At this rate, in

Soph. *Aj.* 772. ἐπ' ἐχθροῖς χεῖρα φοινίαν τρέπειν

we may disprove the meaning 'turn his hand against the foe,' by saying 'see *Lex. s.v.* ἐπιτρέπω.'
So we have:

Eur. *Phoen.* 1100. λόχους ἔνειμεν ἑπτὰ καὶ λοχαγέτας
πύλας ἐφ' ἑπτὰ, φύλακας Ἀργείου δορός,
σὸς παῖς, ἐφέδρους θ' ἱππότας μὲν ἱππόταις [θ' addidit Valckenaer]
ἔταξ', ὁπλίτας δ' ἀσπιδηφόροις ἔπι, . .

Again, under the same general idea, the dative with ἐπὶ may signify *for, in the direction of, towards one's destination*:

Hom. Δ. 251. ἦλθε δ' ἐπὶ Κρήτεσσι.
" " 273. ἦλθε δ' ἐπ' Αἰάντεσσι.
" Λ. 274. νηυσὶν ἐπὶ γλαφυρῇσιν ἐλαυνέμεν. O. 259.
" O. 743. κοίλης ἐπὶ νηυσὶ φέροιτο. X. 392. ἐπὶ ν. νεώμεθα.
" P. 574. βῆ δ' ἐπὶ Πατρόκλῳ.
" " 706. αὐτὸς δ' αὖτ' ἐπὶ Πατρόκλῳ ἥρωι βεβήκει.
Pind. *O.* viii. 49. ἐπ' Ἰσθμῷ ποντίᾳ ἅρμα θοὸν τανύεν.
*Theb.* 701. XO. μὴ 'λθῃς ὁδοὺς σὺ τάσδ' ἐφ' ἑβδόμαις πύλαις.

ἐφ' ἑβδόμαις πύλαις: *for* (*the defence of*) *the seventh gate* or *to defend, etc.*; the dative with ἐπὶ expresses the object of any action, the relation of the object to the action being determined by the context; see on *v.* 531. Not of course '*to*' the gate.

Having ὁδοὺς τάσδ', it is improbable that we should read ἐφ' ἑβδόμας πύλας. And in this passage the notion of *destination* seems well to justify the use of the dative in the sense 'to.' But in any case we shall not say "not of course 'to' the gate."

In a stationary sense, for 'at the gate' we can have ἐπὶ πύλαις, ἐν π., πρὸς π.:

ἐπὶ πύλαις: Hom. Γ. 149, Aesch. *P.V.* 755, Soph. *Aj.* 49, Ar. *Eq.* 1245, 1246, 1398.

ἐν πύλαις: Hom. M. 127, Π. 712, X. 360, Pind. *O.* ix. 86, *N.* x. 27, Aesch. *Theb.* 146, 198, 235, 938, Soph. *fr.* 324, *O.C.* 1569, Eur. *Or.* 1278, 1483, *Ph.* 1074, *I.T.* 1273, *I.A.* 802, *Supp.* 106, *Bacch.* 163, *El.* 341, *Cycl.* 660, *fr.* 623, Eubulus 15.

πρὸς πύλαις: Aesch. *Theb.* 487, Soph. *El.* 818, Eur. *Med.* 50, *Hel.* 438 (*bis*), Ar. *Lys.* 281.

ἐπὶ θύραις: Hom. B. 788, H. 346, Λ. 644, α. 120, Pind. *N.* i. 19, Ar. *Nub.* 466, *Eccl.* 865, 997, 1114, Eubulus 53, Theocr. xxiii. 39.

ἐν θ.: Hom. ι. 417, κ. 220, 310, μ. 256.

πρὸς θ.: Phoenix Coloph. (Athen. viii. 360), Hdt. v. 92 δ, vi. 134, Menand. 420, 830, Theocr. ii. 41.

ἐπ' ἐξόδοις:

Eur. *Hel.* 1164. ἐπ' ἐ. γὰρ
ἔθαψα, Πρωτεῦ, σ' . . .

„ *Rhes.* 503. ζῶντα συλλαβὼν ἐγὼ
πυλῶν ἐπ' ἐ. ἀμπείρας ῥάχιν
στήσω πετεινοῖς γυψὶ θοινατήριον.

πρὸς ἐ.:

Soph. *El.* 328. τίν' αὖ σὺ τήνδε πρὸς θυρῶνος ἐ.
ἐλθοῦσα φωνεῖς . . φάτιν;

*Theb.* 33. πληροῦτε θωρακεῖα κἀπὶ σέλμασιν
πύργων στάθητε καὶ πυλῶν ἐπ' ἐξόδοις
μίμνοντες εὖ θαρσεῖτε, . . .

So enamoured, however, is Dr. Verrall of ἐπὶ expressing the object of an action that this is translated

man the breast-works, post yourselves on the platforms, and await the moment of sally with a good courage. (Transl. p. 147.)

*Theb.* 57. πρὸς ταῦτ' ἀρίστους ἄνδρας ἐκκρίτους πόλεως
πυλῶν ἐπ' ἐξόδοισι τάγευσαι τάχος.

Therefore let thy bravest soldiers, chosen from all the folk, be placed with all speed to sally forth from the gates. (Transl. p. 148.)

These renderings are fortified by a note on

*Theb.* 269. ἐγὼ δ᾽ . . ἀντηρέτας ἐχθροῖσι . .
εἰς ἑπτατειχεῖς ἐξόδους τάξω μολών.

εἰς ἐξόδους is strictly εἰς τὸ ἐξιέναι rather than εἰς πύλας.

ἔξοδοι does, of course, sometimes mean 'outgoing'; and of course, in all these three places it means 'portals.'

So of soldiers posted at a gate:

ἐν:

Pind. *P.* viii. 45. θαέομαι σαφὲς
δράκοντα ποικίλον αἰθᾶς Ἀλκμᾶν᾽ ἐπ᾽ ἀσπίδος
νωμῶντα πρῶτον ἐν Κάδμου πύλαις.

Eur. *Ph.* 1141. ταῖς δ᾽ ἑβδόμαις Ἄδραστος ἐν πύλαισιν ἦν.

πρός:

Aesch. *Theb.* 557. Ὁμολωίσιν δὲ πρὸς πύλαις τεταγμένος.

Eur. *Ph.* 750. ET. τάξω λοχαγοὺς πρὸς πύλαισιν (defenders).

" " 1126. Ὁμολωίσιν δὲ τάξιν εἶχε πρὸς πύλαις Τυδεὺς . .

ἐπί:

Soph. *Ant.* 148. ἑπτὰ λοχαγοὶ γὰρ ἐφ᾽ ἑπτὰ πύλαις.
ταχθέντες ἴσοι πρὸς ἴσους ἄνδρας . .

Aesch. *Theb.* 57. πυλῶν ἐπ᾽ ἐξόδοισι τάγευσαι (defenders).

*Theb.* 618. τὸν ἕβδομον δὴ τόνδ᾽ ἐφ᾽ ἑβδόμαις πύλαις λέξω.

Now am I come to the seventh champion for the *Seventh* gate. (Transl. p. 159.)

(1) *Theb.* 362. ΑΓ. λέγοιμ᾽ ἂν εἰδὼς εὖ τὰ τῶν ἐναντίων.
ὥς τ᾽ ἐν πύλαις ἕκαστος εἴληχεν πάλον.

(2) " 410. ΑΓ. Καπανεὺς δ᾽ ἐπ᾽ Ἠλέκτραισιν εἴληχεν πάλον.

(3) " 438. ET. λέγ᾽ ἄλλον ἄλλαις ἐν πύλαις εἰληχότα.

(4) *Theb.* 444. ΑΓ. καὶ μὴν τὸν ἐντεῦθεν λαχόντα πρὸς πύλαις
λέξω.

These four passages all refer to the assignment by lot of the seven gates each to one of the attacking chiefs: they are all similar in expression, though differing in the prepositions ἐν, ἐπί, πρός; and we have seen that with πύλαις these may be used synonymously. We should infer that they are so used here; and since with πύλαις the only sense common to the three prepositions is '*at*,' we should render in each case 'has drawn (a lot) at . .'; a brief expression easily intelligible. But not so easily will Dr. Verrall resign ἐπὶ expressing the object of an action:

(2) 410. ἐπ' . . . εἴληχεν *hath drawn (his lot) for.*

With this rendering Dr. Verrall could hardly venture in the other three passages to translate 'at the gates': so the results are these:

(1) 363. ἐν πύλαις literally 'in the matter of the gates'; . . .

which leads necessarily to this:

(3) 438. ἄλλαις εἰληχότα, a very doubtful construction. For ἐν πύλαις *in the (allotting of the) gates* see *v.* 363.—ἄλλας (πύλας) ἐν πύλαις εἰληχότα would be more clear, if not more correct.

On *Ag.* 533. καὶ σπέρμα πάσης ἐξαπόλλυται χθονός.
the note (see p. 17) says:

σπέρμα πάσης, *i.e.* αὐτῆς, τῆς Τροίας. . . That πάσης is constructed with σπέρμα, not with χθονός, is shown both by the natural division of the rhythm and by the sense.

So, I suppose, here, that ἄλλαις is constructed, not with ἐν πύλαις, but with another πύλαις understood, is 'shown' by the natural division of the rhythm as well as by the sense!

On the last of our four passages the note says:

(4) 444. Almost all the examples in Aeschylus of a line without caesura are open to suspicion on independent grounds; and such a license is especially improbable in the strict versification of this play. This verse (omitted by H. Wolf) is unnecessary and injurious, λέξω being better explained by the λέγε of 438, to which it replies, and inattention to this accounts for the insertion. It is also ungrammatical.

Thus, by different methods, Dr. Verrall disposes of the three parallels to ἐπ' Ἠλέκτραισιν εἴληχεν πύλαις, which he is then free to render 'for the gate.'

On the statement about lines without caesura I have already spoken (p. 16). Let it be noticed that the only reference (and that not explicit) to what was inferred to be the true construction in all these passages lies in the final remark on 444, that the line is ungrammatical.

We are now quit of ἐπὶ with the dative. Only, however, to be plunged in the oblique cases of αὐτὸς in Aeschylus. The notes on 434, 607 have been already quoted (p. 49). Dr. Verrall's doctrine will be seen in the following:

*Theb.* 55. κληρουμένους δ' ἔλειπον ὡς πάλῳ λαχὼν
ἕκαστος αὐτῶν πρὸς πύλας ἄγοι λόχον.

I left them casting lots, how they should themselves lead each his band against an appointed gate. (Transl. p. 148.)

*Theb.* 178. κεἰ μή τίς ἀρχῆς τῆς ἐμῆς ἀκούσεται,
ἀνὴρ γυνή τε χὤ τι τῶν μεταίχμιον,
ψῆφος κατ' αὐτῶν ὀλεθρία βουλεύσεται.

κατ' αὐτῶν, i.e. κατ' αὐτῶν τῶν βουλευομένων. αὐτός is emphatic, as almost always in Aeschylus.

*Theb.* 431. πέποιθα δ' αὐτῷ ξὺν δίκῃ τὸν πυρφόρον
ἥξειν κεραυνόν, . .

The construction, of course, is ἥξειν αὐτῷ, as

*P.V.* 359. ἀλλ' ἦλθεν αὐτῷ Ζηνὸς ἄγρυπνον βέλος, etc.
But

αὐτῷ, to be joined with πέποιθα. Note that this word is emphatic both here and in *v.* 434. It has been already observed, that except with emphasis αὐτός in Aeschylus is exceedingly rare. Here the emphasis is all-important to the sense . . . αὐτῷ may be either masculine or neuter. If masculine, we may understand either (1) τῷ Διί, or (2) τῷ Καπανεῖ, *I rely on the man himself, that the thunderbolt will come*, meaning 'his behaviour is enough to call it.' If neuter, which I think better Greek, αὐτό *the thing itself* refers to the whole preceding description and the meaning is 'I take assurance from the very facts.'

*Theb.* 1026. τούτῳ δὲ σάρκας οὐδὲ κοιλογάστορες
λύκοι σπάσονται· μὴ δοκησάτω τινί.
τάφον γὰρ αὐτῷ καὶ κατασκαφὰς ἐγώ,

*γυνή περ οὖσα, τῷδε μηχανήσομαι*
*κόλπῳ φέρουσα βυσσίνου πεπλώματος·*
*καὐτὴ καλύψω.*

'1026. *τούτου* recc. *τούτω* M.' '1028. *αὐτῶ* M.' W.

The note is too long to give: but I cannot refrain from quoting the beginning:

*τούτω us two: . . . τούτω* is the direct accusative to *σπάσονται*, and *σάρκας* the so-called 'accusative of the part affected.'—The later MSS. destroy this line by substituting *τούτου*. If a possessive were required at all we should read *τούτῳ*. But the whole point lies in the use of the dual.

Then, later:

*αὐτῷ . . . τῷδε with only this, just with this, i.e.* with her woman's dress, . . .—*αὐτή* (for *αὐτῷ*) Pierson, Hermann, Dindorf and others, taking *τῷδε* as *for him*, in which case *αὐτῷ* would be superfluous. Others, as Paley, join *τῷδε* rightly with *κόλπῳ* but take *αὐτῷ* to mean *Πολυνείκει*; but even so *αὐτῷ* is unnecessary and not used after the manner of Aeschylus.

*Ag.* 1587. *καὶ προστρόπαιος ἑστίας μολὼν πάλιν*
*τλήμων Θυέστης μοῖραν ηὗρετ' ἀσφαλῆ*
*τὸ μὴ θανὼν πατρῷον αἱμάξαι πέδον*
*αὐτοῦ· ξένια δὲ τοῦδε δύσθεος πατὴρ . . .*

so f. (*αὐτός·* Blomfield: *ἀστοξένια* Hermann).

Dr. Verrall reads . . . *πέδον. αὐτοῦ ξένια δὲ τοῦδε. . .*

*αὐτοῦ ξένια δὲ κ.τ.λ.*: *but taking the very occasion of his arrival Atreus* . . . *αὐτοῦ ξένια* literally 'as an arrival-feast to (Thyestes) himself,' . . . The peculiar treachery and cruelty of Atreus showed itself first in making the home-coming of his reconciled brother the pretended occasion for the abominable feast . . .

*αὐτοῦ ξένια τοῦδε*, of course, could only mean '. . to this very man': it could not mean 'on the very occasion of his arrival,' for that would be *αὐτὰ ξένια τοῦδε*.

*Ag.* 635. *πότερα γὰρ αὐτοῦ ζῶντος ἢ τεθνηκότος*
*φάτις πρὸς ἄλλων ναυτίλων ἐκλῄζετο ;*

*αὐτοῦ* Menelaus himself, as opposed to the *ἄλλοι* . . .

*Ag.* 681. εἰ δ' οὖν τις ἀκτὶς ἡλίου νιν ἱστορεῖ
καὶ ζῶντα καὶ βλέποντα, μηχαναῖς Διός,
οὔπω θέλοντος ἐξαναλῶσαι γένος
ἐλπίς τις αὐτὸν πρὸς δόμους ἥξειν πάλιν.

αὐτὸν emphatic; 'for him, if for any, there is a hope.'

*Ag.* 868. ἐκ τῶνδέ τοι παῖς ἐνθάδ' οὐ παραστατεῖ, . . .
870. μηδὲ θαυμάσῃς τόδε.
τρέφει γὰρ αὐτὸν εὐμενὴς δορύξενος
Στρόφιος ὁ Φωκεύς,

τρέφει γὰρ αὐτὸν *he is under the separate care of Strophius*, literally 'Str. is taking care of him *by himself*': αὐτός is as usual emphatic.

*Ag.* 266. τορὸν γὰρ αὐτὸν ἥξει σύνορθον αὐταῖς.

so M. σύνορθρον Wellauer: αὐγαῖς Hermann.

*For it will come clear and right, when the science itself comes clear and right;* literally 'clear it will come, made right together with the divination itself' . . . αὐταῖς emphatic, as the position shows. In Aeschylus this pronoun almost always is so. There is no difficulty in supplying ταῖς τέχναις from *v.* 260, . . . Nor is the emphatic pronoun unsuited for its place; it marks the point and could not be placed otherwise. The objection made here arises from neglect of the emphasis. . . Prof. Goodwin, retaining the text, retains also the old interpretation, 'the future will come clear in accord with them (the prophecies).' But αὐταῖς cannot be unemphatic.

*Ag.* 1594. τὰ μὲν ποδήρη καὶ χερῶν ἄκρους κτένας
ἔθρυπτ' ἄνωθεν ἀνδρακὰς καθημένος.
ἄσημα δ' αὐτῶν αὐτίκ' ἀγνοίᾳ λαβὼν
ἔσθει βόραν ἄσωτον . .

1596. so MSS. ἄσημ'· ὁ δ' Dindorf.
αὐτὸν αὐτίκ' ἀγνοίᾳ, *not knowing the meat at the moment for what it was:* αὐτά, as usual, has an emphasis, literally 'the meat itself.' The adverb αὐτίκα belongs in sense to the substantive.

With a similar rendering we have an explicit statement of the doctrine at

*Theb.* 651. ἀλλ' οὔτε νιν φυγόντα μητρόθεν σκότον,
οὔτ' ἐν τροφαῖσιν οὔτ' ἐφηβήσαντά πω,
οὔτ' ἐν γενείου ξυλλογῇ τριχώματος,
Δίκη προσεῖδε καὶ κατηξιώσατο·
οὐδ' ἐν πατρῴας μὴν χθονὸς κακουχίᾳ
656. οἶμαί νιν αὐτῷ νῦν παραστατεῖν πέλας.

αὐτῷ νῦν. The pronoun is emphatic, and with νῦν would be approximately rendered in English by *his present self* or *him as he now is*. . . As has been observed before the use of αὐτός, unless for emphasis, is very rare in Aeschylus. As unemphatic pronouns can be supplied from the context, the insertion of them is a sacrifice of force to simplicity and clearness, and alien to the weighty and sententious Aeschylean style. With the light enclitic pronouns νιν, σφε etc., this is not felt, but αὐτός, if needless, has an incongruous effect, and where it occurs an emphasis is to be looked for.

Now, all this is due either to unverified assumption or to deliberate disregard of the evidence. The truth is stated by Dindorf (*Lex. Aesch. s.v.* αὐτός p. 52): *αὐτός is*, sed in casibus tantum obliquis, neque in initio sententiae, sed post unum vel plura vocabula, et plerumque in diverbiis, rarius in melicis, . .

According to his list there are in Aeschylus certainly not more than thirty-one instances of αὐτός emphatic in the oblique cases, and certainly not less than 44 unemphatic. Reference to that list will save me from disproving the assertion that 'except with emphasis αὐτός is excedingly rare in Aeschylus,' as it might have saved Dr. Verrall from making that assertion. Though indeed a lexicon would be of little use to the judgment that could propound such interpretations.

We are no better off in hearing about the article in Aeschylus:

*Ag.* 1607. τραφέντα δ' αὖθις ἡ δίκη κατήγαγεν . . . .
1610. οὕτω καλὸν δὴ καὶ τὸ κατθανεῖν ἐμοί,
ἰδόντα τοῦτον τῆς δίκης ἐν ἕρκεσιν.

The passage and the comment shall be treated another time; they are both too long to quote here. *v.* 1607 is translated 'that justice hath brought back again . .' *v.* 1611 'having seen him in the toils of this just revenge.' ἡ δίκη, we are told, is '*the* justice of the cause':

The use of the article with a mere general term or personification (*Justice*) is not according to Aeschylus' habit (so we have δίκη, not ἡ δίκη, in *vv.* 767, 1537, *Theb.* 633, 654, 658 etc. *passim*).

We have; and we have ἡ δίκη and not δίκη at:

*Supp.* 345. ἀλλ' ἡ δίκη γε ξυμμάχων ὑπερστατεῖ.
*Eum.* 217. εὐνὴ...τῇ Δίκῃ φρουρουμένη.
*fr.* 266. τοῦ θανόντος ἡ Δίκη πράσσει κότον.

*Ag.* 1669. πράσσε, πιαίνου, μιαίνων τὴν δίκην.

τὴν δίκην *doing outrage to the rightful cause*, that of Orestes : not *justice*; see on *v.* 1607.

As μιαίνειν τὰ τῶν θεῶν Eur. *H.F.* 1219, νόμους βροτῶν *Supp.* 379, νόμον *Trag. fr. adesp.* 486, μιαίνων εὐσέβειαν Ἄρης Aesch. *Theb.* 331 and Δίκης ἱερὰ κρήδεμνα μιήνας Metrodor. *A.P.* xiv. 122, so here τὴν δίκην, *Right.*

*Ag.* 1621. δεσμῶν δὲ καὶ τὸ γῆρας αἵ τε νήστιδες
δύαι διδάσκειν ἐξοχώταται φρενῶν
ἰατρομάντεις.

[δεσμὸν fg. δεσμὸς h. δεσμοὶ Karsten. δεσμῶν Dr. Verrall.]

δεσμῶν . . αἵ τε νηστίδες δύαι *the pains of imprisonment and the pains of hunger.* The genitive δεσμῶν (depending on δύαι) is required by the article αἱ, justifiable according to the use of Aeschylus only if αἱ νηστίδες δύαι are contrasted with some other δύαι . . καὶ το γῆρας . . . διδάσκειν *to teach even your age* . . τὸ γῆρας has the article (*the*, or rather *that, such*) as referring to γέρων preceding. In the archaistic language of Aeschylus the 'article' is still felt as a demonstrative, and very rarely employed except where it is indispensable.

which explains the remark on :

*Ag.* 588. νικώμενος λόγοισιν οὐκ ἀναίνομαι.
ἀεὶ γὰρ ἥβᾳ τοῖς γέρουσιν εὖ μαθεῖν.

Note that the article is indispensable ; with γέρουσιν alone we should be bound to supply ἡμῖν.

So we are told on

*Theb.* 1002. τέθνηκεν οὗπερ τοῖς νέοις θνῄσκειν καλὸν,

(Dr. Verrall's emendation of which may be seen on p. 92) that

Aeschylus would have written νέοις not τοῖς νέοις.

*Theb.* 335. βλαχᾳ̂ δ' αἱματόεσσαι
τῶν ἐπιμαστιδίων
ἀρτιτρεφεῖς βρέμονται.

The trivial misaccentuation βλαχαὶ in M, an ingeniously simple error by which every word down to the very article becomes meaningless, converts the sentence into this, 'and the bloody bleatings of those babes being new-suckled, roar.'

The passage is treated on p. 126. It is interesting to find Dr. Verrall elsewhere implying the exact opposite of his own view as here stated. Thus:

*Theb.* 560. μέγιστον Ἄργει τῶν κακῶν διδάσκαλον
Ἐρινύος κλητῆρα, πρόσπολον φόνου,
κακῶν τ' Ἀδράστῳ τῶνδε βουλευτήριον.

Between Ἄργει τῶν κακων in *v.* 560 and κακῶν Ἀδράστῳ τῶνδε in *v.* 562 there is obviously an antithesis, that of the general to the particular——*strongest to persuade Argos to evil and adviser of Adrastus in this evil now.*

*Theb.* 580. βαθεῖαν ἄλοκα διὰ φρενὸς καρπούμενος
ἀφ' ἧς τὰ κεδνὰ βλαστάνει βουλεύματα.

. . . note τὰ in *v.* 581, which indicates that κεδνὰ βουλεύματα, and therefore βαθεῖαν ἄλοκα, is to be understood generally.

It is enough to have shown by these contradictions of what value Dr. Verrall's views are to himself. How full of error they are here I have not stayed to prove, because the instances of the article in Aeschylus are given and classified in Dindorf's *Lex. Aesch.* pp. 233—236, and the truth may be learnt therefrom.

One note on the article I could not place with the preceding:

*Theb.* 596. οὕτως δ' ὁ μάντις, υἱὸν Οἰκλέους λέγω,

υἱὸν Οἰκλέους λέγω. The purpose of this parenthesis is to mark at once that ὁ μάντις is not to be taken in the general sense of 'the prophet,' *i.e.* a prophet as such, which the previous context would rather suggest.

It will be as well to give some further facts in face of which Dr. Verrall makes this extraordinary statement. The title ὁ μάντις is used in Tragedy with noticeable frequency: Aesch. *Theb.* 24, 366, 577, *Ag.* 1274, *Eum.* 598, *fr.* 394; Soph. *Aj.* 760, 780, *O.T.* 526, 747, *Ant.* 992, 1053, *Phil.* 614; Eur. *Phoen.* 172, 1118, *I. A.* 84, 995. It is used here to emphasise the *holiness* of Amphiaraus, which for the point of the speech it is necessary to emphasise. Cf. Soph. *O.T.* 298 τὸν θεῖον μάντιν, and *Theb.* 369 θείνει δ' ὀνείδει μάντιν Οἰκλείδην σοφόν, to which we shall come presently. The intention of the phrase is 'the holy prophet Amphiaraus will be involved in the destruction of his impious associates.' For the use of λέγω = *namely* see Aesch. *Theb.* 476, 645, *Cho.* 251, *fr.* 169, 175; Soph. *Aj.* 569, *Ant.* 198, *Trach.* 9; Eur. *Phoen.* 990, *Heracl.* 640. A good illustration of its use where emphasis is to be thrown on the attribute is

> Clem. Alex. *Cohort.* 10 ἡ μὲν οὖν ἀφρογενής τε καὶ κυπρογενής, ἡ Κούρᾳ φίλη, τὴν Ἀφροδίτην λέγω, τὴν φιλομηδέα, . .

To Dindorf's *Lexicon Aeschyleum* I am content to refer for disproof of another statement, that the word ἐστὶ without emphasis is very rarely admitted by Aeschylus, especially in lyrics, but almost always left to be supplied. (Note on *Ag.* 436.)

No better example of Dr. Verrall's method could be given than the following:

*Theb.* 241. ΧΟ. ὦ παγκρατὲς Ζεῦ, τρέψον εἰς ἐχθροὺς βέλος.
ET. ὦ Ζεῦ, γυναικῶν οἷον ὤπασας γένος.
ΧΟ. μοχθηρόν, ὥσπερ ἄνδρας ὧν ἁλῷ πόλις.
ET. παλινστομεῖς αὖ θιγγάνουσ' ἀγαλμάτων ;
ΧΟ. ἀψυχίᾳ γὰρ γλῶσσαν ἁρπάζει φόβος.

*Theb.* 369. θείνει δ' ὀνείδει μάντιν Οἰκλείδην σοφὸν
σαίνειν μόρον τε καὶ μάχην ἀψυχίᾳ.

370. ἀψυχία. This very rare word (literally *lifelessness* or *spiritlessness*) occurs in this play twice (see *v.* 245) both times in connexion with a 'mantic' subject (δυσφημία, μάντις), and in the *Alcestis* four times. In medical language ἀψυχεῖν, ἀψυχία signified to *swoon, swooning*. See *Lex. s. vv.* From this peculiar distribution it is clear that in Aeschylus and Euripides it is not a casual synonym for δειλία, but is chosen for some particular reason. In the present passage it is also clear that the taunt of ἀψυχία is pointed at Amphiaraus as a μαντίς, and for using religious arts to defer the fight; for the words μάντιν σοφὸν, to have any point, must be part of the taunt or at least explain its effect. Nor is it difficult to fix the point. One of the methods of divination was the *swoon* or *trance* in which the ψυχή of the seer was supposed to depart from his body and return with reports of its visions in distant places (see Smith, *Dict. Biog. Hermotimus*, Tylor, *Anthropology* p 345). The mockery of Tydeus turns upon this 'absence of spirit,' and upon the form of the word, which makes it a sort of contrary to εὐψυχία *courage.* Note also the formal antithesis between ἀψυχία and σαίνειν μόρον 'avoiding death by absence of soul.' . . . Equally in *v.* 245 ἀψυχία should receive its full meaning; it is when 'the spirit is gone,' as it

were, that fear surprises the masterless tongue, and speaks by it words which are not more controlled by the terrified person than those of one in a trance—or at least so the maidens would imply by their apology.—The four passages in the *Alcestis* (642, 696, 717, 954) all describe the conduct of Pheres, Admetus' father, in refusing to die for his son. The context, which in every case refers to Admetus' denial of his sonship *e.g.* καί μ' οὐ νομίζω παῖδα σὸν πεφυκέναι. ἦ τἄρα πάντων διαπρέπεις ἀψυχίᾳ, 642, leaves no doubt in what sense (a very natural one) *lifeless* or *spiritless* is there used. Cf. Eur. *Tro.* 619, where the women of Troy have been allotted each to the λέκτρα of some Greek, Cassandra to Agamemnon, Andromache to Neoptolemus, but Polyxena to the dead Achilles, δῶρον ἀψύχῳ νεκρῷ, an expression very interesting in this connexion, as showing that Euripides knew or felt the primitive theory of female sacrifice at the tomb. And see also the use of ψυχή in Eur. *Med.* 247, where, in contrast with the license of husbands, it is said of wives, ἡμῖν δ' ἀνάγκη πρὸς μίαν ψυχὴν βλέπειν.

It is true that the word ἀψυχία is rare,[1] and that it occurs in Tragedy only in the two passages of this play and the four of the *Alcestis* to which Dr. Verrall refers. Concerning these last four passages we have three statements:

(1) they all describe the conduct of Pheres in refusing to die for his son Admetus:

(2) the context in every case refers to Admetus' denial of his sonship:

(3) in every case the context leaves no doubt that ἀψυχία is used in a very natural sense [which sense, it will be clear from the argument, is 'physical impotence'].

It will be profitable to examine the passages:

Eur. *Alc.* 645. ΑΔ. σὺ δ' ἐκποδὼν στὰς καὶ παρεὶς ἄλλῳ θανεῖν

[1] In the *Lex. Seguer.* ('Αντιαττικίστης. Anecd. Bekker, p. 78) is the following entry: ἀψυχίαν: ἀντὶ τοῦ δειλίαν. Πλάτων Γοργίᾳ. The word is not found in Plato anywhere according to Ast; certainly not in the *Gorgias*. In that dialogue δειλία occurs 477B, but there expressly as a quality of ψυχή: ΣΩ. οὐκοῦν καὶ ἐν ψυχῇ πονηρίαν ἡγεῖ τινα εἶναι; ΠΩΛ. πῶς γὰρ οὔ; ΣΩ. ταύτην οὖν οὐκ ἀδικίαν καλεῖς καὶ ἀμαθίαν καὶ δειλίαν καὶ τὰ τοιαῦτα; for which reason it seems improbable that ἀψυχίαν should be restored there. For the same reason it could hardly be substituted for the corrupt ἀδικίαν in 478E κάκιστα ἄρα ζῇ ὁ ἔχων ἀδικίαν καὶ μὴ ἀπαλλαττόμενος, where Thompson considers Dobree's κακίαν certain.

The word is used in the same lexicon (Λέξεις ῥητορικαί, p. 210) ἀθυμια: ἀψυχία καὶ τὸ ἀπαγορεῦσαι. And again (Συναγωγὴ λέξεων χρησίμων, p. 352) ἀθυμία: Ἡρόδοτος ἐν τῷ πρώτῳ αὐτοῦ λόγῳ (i. 37) τὴν ἀτυχίαν λέγει. Read τὴν ἀψυχίαν.

In Philemon *fr.* 136 Kock proposes to read it for εὐψυχία, but without sufficient reason.

νέῳ γέρων ὢν τόνδ' ἀποιμώξῃ νεκρόν;
οὐκ ἦσθ' ἄρ' ὀρθῶς τοῦδε σώματος πατήρ,
οὐδ' ἡ τεκεῖν φάσκουσα καὶ κεκλημένη
μήτηρ μ' ἔτικτε· δουλίου δ' ἀφ' αἵματος
μαστῷ γυναικὸς σῆς ὑπεβλήθην λάθρᾳ.
ἔδειξας εἰς ἔλεγχον ἐξελθὼν ὃς εἶ
652. καί μ' οὐ νομίζω παῖδα σὸν πεφυκέναι.
653. ἦ τἄρα πάντων διαπρέπεις ἀψυχίᾳ
ὃς τηλικόσδ' ὢν κἀπὶ τέρμ' ἥκων βίου
οὐκ ἠθέλησας οὐδ' ἐτόλμησας θανεῖν
τοῦ σοῦ πρὸ παιδός, ἀλλὰ τήνδ' εἰάσατε . .

'After standing out of the way and being ready in your age to let a young man die, shall you now bewail this corpse? You are not really my father, nor did my so-called mother give me birth, but I am a supposititious child. Put to the test you have shown what you are, and I don't consider myself to be your son. Or surely you are a most conspicuous example of *ἀψυχία*, when at your age, at the end of your life, you have neither the will nor the courage to die for your son, but allow her . .'

What is not seen from the two consecutive lines quoted by Dr. Verrall is seen from the whole passage, that *ἀψυχίᾳ* refers, not, as his quotation implies, to what precedes, but to what follows; that it signifies not inability in Pheres to have become the father of Admetus, but the conduct of the aged Pheres in refusing to die for Admetus his son.

The second passage is the retort of the father to that taunt:

*Alc.* 702. ΦΕ. χαίρεις ὁρῶν φῶς, πατέρα δ' οὐ χαίρειν δοκεῖς;
ἦ μὴν πολύν γε τὸν κάτω λογίζομαι
χρόνον, τὸ δὲ ζῆν σμικρόν, ἀλλ' ὅμως γλυκύ.
σὺ γοῦν ἀναιδῶς διεμάχου τὸ μὴ θανεῖν
καὶ ζῇς παρελθὼν τὴν πεπρωμένην τύχην
ταύτην κατακτάς· εἶτ' ἐμὴν ἀψυχίαν

λέγεις γυναικός, ὦ κάκισθ', ἡσσημένος,
ἣ τοῦ καλοῦ σοῦ προύθανεν νεανίου;

'You enjoy living, and do you think your father doesn't? The time below I reckon to be long, and life is short, but still sweet. You, at any rate, struggled shamelessly to avoid dying, and remain alive above your due time by putting her to death: and then do you talk of my ἀψυχία, after being outdone by a woman, that has died for that fine youth, yourself?'

Here is the third:

*Alc.* 726. ΑΔ. μακροῦ βίου γὰρ ᾐσθόμην ἐρῶντά σε.
ΦΕ. ἀλλ' οὐ σὺ νεκρόν γ' ἀντὶ σοῦ τόνδ' ἐκφέρεις;
ΑΔ. σημεῖα τῆς σῆς, ὦ κάκιστ', ἀψυχίας.

Ad. 'Because I see you are in love with long life.
Ph. Well, aren't you burying this corpse instead of yourself?
Ad. That shows your ἀψυχία.'
Your physical impotence!

The fourth passage is this:

*Alc.* 960. ΑΔ. ἐρεῖ δέ μ' ὅστις ἐχθρὸς ὢν κυρεῖ τάδε·
ἰδοῦ τὸν αἰσχρῶς ζῶνθ' ὃς οὐκ ἔτλη θανεῖν
ἀλλ' ἣν ἔγημεν ἀντιδοὺς ἀψυχίᾳ
πέφευγεν Ἅιδην· εἶτ' ἀνὴρ εἶναι δοκεῖ;
στυγεῖ δὲ τοὺς τεκόντας αὐτὸς οὐ θέλων θανεῖν.

Ad. 'And my enemies will say: See the man that is to his shame alive, that didn't dare to die, but through ἀψυχία has escaped death by giving his wife instead. Is he a man? And he hates his parent, refusing to die himself.'

Mere inspection of the passages has been enough to prove every one of the statements made about them to be false:

(1) it is not true that they all describe the conduct of Pheres, for the last passage describes the conduct not of Pheres but of Admetus.

(2) it is not true that the context 'in every case refers to Admetus' denial of his sonship,' for only once does Admetus use that rhetorical taunt; and there charges him with ἀψυχία as the alternative.

(3) it is not true that in every case the context 'leaves no doubt' that ἀψυχία is used with the 'very natural' meaning 'physical impotence'; for not only would that meaning in every case make nonsense, but the word is in every case predicated of the man that has not the pluck to die.

From ψυχὴ *life, consciousness, wit*, we have ἄψυχος )( ἔμψυχος: Simonid. 106, Soph. *El.* 1221, *O.C.* 1486, Eur. *Ion* 890, *fr.* 655, 472, *Hipp.* 949, Hdt. ii. 39, and throughout Greek.

Sopater (Ath. iv. 77). ᾧ λωτὸς ἐν πλευροῖσιν ἄψυχος παγεὶς
ἔμπνουν ἀνίει μοῦσαν.

A picture or statue etc. being properly ἄψυχον, as ἀ. εἰκὼ Eur. *Med.* 1151, *A.P.* xvi. 30, εἰδώλοισι Ap. Rhod. iv. 1280, γραφή *Com. fr. adesp.* 410, etc., so by an *oxymoron* we have ἔμψυχος (like ἔμπνους) applied to a *living* image, picture, etc., as ἐ. ἄγαλμα *A.P.* xii. 56, πλάσμα xvi. 97. And so we have

Soph. *Ant.* 1166. οὐ τίθημ' ἐγὼ
ζῆν τοῦτον ἀλλ' ἔμψυχον ἡγοῦμαι νεκρόν,

because a corpse is properly ἄψυχος:

Ar. *Ran.* 1332. ὄνειρον ψυχὰν ἄψυχον ἔχοντα.
Eur. *Tro.* 624. τέθνηκέ σοι παῖς πρὸς τάφῳ Πολυξένη
σφαγεῖσ' Ἀχιλλέως δῶρον ἀψύχῳ νεκρῷ.

'The women of Troy,' we were told, 'have been allotted each to the λέκτρα of some Greek, Cassandra to Agamemnon, Andromache to Neoptolemus, but Polyxena to the dead Achilles, δῶρον ἀ. ν., an expression very interesting in this connexion as showing that Euripides knew or felt the primitive theory of female sacrifice at the tomb.'

Now, nowhere in this play or in the *Hecuba*, in both of which we have the sacrifice of Polyxena, is there any suggestion that she is allotted to the λέκτρα of Achilles. Early in the *Troades* Talthybius brings news to Hecuba: 'you have been allotted——' 'To what city?' '*κατ' ἄνδρ' ἕκαστον κοὐχ ὁμοῦ λελόγχατε.*' 'Who has got Casandra?' '*ἐξαίρετόν νιν ἔλαβεν Ἀγαμέμνων ἄναξ.*' 'As a slave for his wife?' '*οὔκ, ἀλλὰ λέκτρων σκότια νυμφευτήρια.*' 'Polyxena, *ταύταν τῷ πάλος ἔζευξεν;*' '*τύμβῳ τέτακται προσπολεῖν Ἀχιλλέως.*' 'What Greek custom or law is this? . . . But what of Andromache?' '*καὶ τήνδ' Ἀχιλλέως ἔλαβε παῖς ἐξαίρετον.*' 'And I?' 'Odysseus has got you for a slave.' (240—277.) Later, Hecuba hears from Andromache that Polyxena is sacrificed, in the sentence we are considering. 'Ah me,' she says, '*τοῦτ' ἐκεῖν' ὅ μοι πάλαι Ταλθύβιος αἴνιγμ' οὐ σαφῶς εἶπεν σαφές*' (*i.e.* 'now I see what he meant by saying she was to be a *πρόσπολος* at the tomb').

In the *Hecuba* we get more definite information. The ghost of Achilles had appeared above his tomb and demanded *Πολυξένην τύμβῳ φίλον πρόσφαγμα καὶ γέρας λαβεῖν* (*Prologue* 37—41). So Hecuba says: 'the phantom of Achilles appeared above his tomb, *ᾔτει δὲ γέρας τῶν πολυμόχθων τινα Τρωιάδων*' (94, 5). The Chorus entering tell her it has been decided to sacrifice her daughter. Achilles had appeared and stayed the fleet, crying, *Ποῖ δή, Δαναοί, τὸν ἐμὸν τύμβον στέλλεσθ' ἀγέραστον ἀφέντες;* whereupon the Greeks were divided in opinion, some for sacrificing, some not. But the two sons of Theseus agreed *τὸν Ἀχίλλειον τύμβον στεφανοῦν αἵματι χλωρῷ* (107—27). That is the object of the offering—the blood (*αἱμακούριαι*). Odysseus, arguing with Hecuba, says: *ἡμῖν δ' Ἀχιλλεὺς ἄξιος τιμῆς... τύμβον δὲ βουλοίμην ἂν ἀξιούμενον τὸν ἐμὸν ὁρᾶσθαι* (307) 'I should like to see my own tomb honoured' (with a blood-offering). It is made for the ghost to drink; as Hecuba understands: 'If a favour must be done (*χάριν γενέσθαι*) to Achilles,' she pleads, 'kill me instead.' 'Nay,' says Odysseus, 'the ghost demanded not you but her.' 'Then,' says Hecuba, 'kill me with her, *καὶ δὶς τόσον πῶμ' αἵματος γενήσεται γαίᾳ νεκρῷ τε τῷ τάδ' ἐξαιτουμένῳ.*' '*ἅλις κόρης εἷς θάνατος,*' says Odysseus, '*οὐ προσοιστέος ἄλλος πρὸς ἄλλῳ*' (381—93). The same, finally, is the language of

Talthybius at the actual sacrifice: *ὦ παῖ Πηλέως, πατὴρ δ' ἐμός, δέξαι χοάς μου τάσδε κηλητηρίους, νεκρῶν ἀγωγούς· ἐλθὲ δ', ὡς πίῃς μέλαν κόρης ἀκραιφνὲς αἷμ', ὅ σοι δωρούμεθα* . . (Every one will remember how thirsty for blood are the ghosts in the eleventh book of the *Odyssey*). Such is the evidence that by *ἀψύχῳ νεκρῷ* Andromache means 'an impotent corpse.'

Eur. *Med.* 245. *ἀνὴρ δ' ὅταν τοῖς ἔνδον ἄχθηται ξυνών,*
*ἔξω μολὼν ἔπαυσε καρδίαν ἄσης*
*ἢ πρὸς φίλον τίν' ἢ πρὸς ἥλικα[ς] τραπείς·*[1]
*ἡμεῖς δ' ἀνάγκη πρὸς μίαν ψυχὴν βλέπειν.*

'A man when he is bored with his wife goes out and relieves his boredom with his friends: we have to look always to one soul.'

The 'licence of husbands' in the sense intended by Dr. Verrall is entirely his assumption: even if suggested, it is certainly not expressed. Antipater (*ἐκ τοῦ Περὶ Γάμου*: Stob. *fl.* 67, 25) saw no physical sense in *v.* 284: *οὐ γὰρ μόνον τῆς οὐσίας καὶ τῶν φιλτάτων πᾶσιν ἀνθρώποις τέκνων καὶ τῆς ψυχῆς, ἀλλὰ καὶ τῶν σωμάτων οὗτοι μόνοι κοινωνοῦσι. καὶ κατ' ἄλλον δὲ τρόπον εἰκότως μεγίστη ἐστίν. αἱ μὲν γὰρ ἄλλαι κοινωνίαι καὶ ἑτέρας τινὰς ἀποστροφὰς ἔχουσι· ταύτας δ'*

*ἀναγκὴ πρὸς μίαν ψυχὴν βλέπειν,*

*τὴν τοῦ ἀνδρός*. Had Euripides wished to express what Dr. Verrall would have the meaning to be, he would, I conceive, have used the word *κύπριν* instead of *ψυχήν*, as

*Andr.* 179. *εἰς μίαν βλέποντες εὐναίαν κύπριν.*

As it is, *μίαν ψυχὴν* means 'a single soul, life, person,' an indefinite word which suits the place. Cf.

Eur. *fr.* 402 *χρὴν γὰρ τὸν εὐτυχοῦνθ' ὅπως πλείστας ἔχειν*[2] *(γυναῖκας)* . .
*νῦν δ' εἰς μίαν βλέπουσι, κίνδυνον μέγαν*
*ῥίπτοντες· οὐ γὰρ τῶν τρόπων πειρώμενοι* . .

[1] Read *φίλων* and *ἡλίκων*?

[2] Read *τρέφειν*.

The whole passage may be compared with a similar complaint in an epigram of Agathias (*A.P.* v. 297):

> Ἠιθέοις οὐκ ἔστι τόσος πόνος ὁππόσος ἡμῖν
> ταῖς ἀταλοψύχοις ἔχραε θηλυτέραις·
> τοῖς μὲν γὰρ παρέασιν ὁμήλικες, οἷς τὰ μερίμνης
> ἄλγεα μυθοῦνται φθέγματι θαρσαλέῳ,
> παίγνιά τ' ἀμφιέπουσι παρήγορα, καὶ κατ' ἀγυιὰς
> πλάζονται γραφίδων χρώμασι ῥεμβόμενοι·
> ἡμῖν δ' οὐδὲ φάος λεύσσειν θέμις, ἀλλὰ μελάθροις
> κρυπτόμεθα ζοφεραῖς φροντίσι τηκόμεναι.

From ψυχὴ *spirit, courage, pluck* (Aesch. *Pers.* 442, *Ag.* 1643, Eur. *Hec.* 575), we have ἄψυχος )( εὔψυχος:

εὔψ. (= ψυχῆς εὖ ἔχων) Eur. *Andr.* 754, *Hel.* 851, *Rhes.* 499, Plat. *Legg.* viii. 830 E. Xen. *Cyneg.* iv. 6 (of hounds) εὔψ. μὲν οὖν ἔσονται ἐὰν μὴ λίπωσι τὰ κυνηγέσια ὅταν ᾖ πνίγη, *ib.* iii. 3. αἱ ἄψ. δὲ λείπουσι τὰ ἔργα καὶ ἀφίστανται τὸν ἥλιον . . , Aesch. *Theb.* 192. ἄψ. κάκην, *Trag. fr. adesp.* 337. ἄψ. ἄνδρα λαμβάνειν συνέμπορον.

So the substantives:

Aesch. *Pers.* 326 πρῶτος εἰς εὐψ., Eur. *Supp.* 843 διαπρεπεῖς εὐψυχίᾳ, *id.* 163, *Med.* 406, *El.* 391, *Cycl.* 645, *fr.* 329, *H.F.* 156, 162, *Heracl.* 569, 746, 812, Thuc. i. 121, Plat. *Tim.* 25 B, Eur. *Heracl.* 597

> ἀλλ' ὦ μέγιστον ἐκπρέπουσ' εὐψυχίᾳ
> πασῶν γυναικῶν

to Macaria who offers herself to death; so of Iphigeneia in the spurious passage *I.A.* 1559.

The contrary quality is ἀψυχία (κακοψ.), as in the four places of the *Alcestis* has been already shown. Yet there we were asked to suppose a peculiar physical sense, while in *Theb.* 244, 370 we are required to see another peculiar sense entirely different. For among other things it is 'also clear' that the taunt of ἀψυχία is pointed at Amphiaraus as a μάντις, because μάντιν σοφόν to have any point must be part of the taunt or at least explain its effect. To me there appears point enough in the words considered as the respectful phrase of the narrator shocked at abuse of the wise prophet. As for the maidens, all they mean is that they are frightened out of their wits and don't know what they are saying.

The note, I think, could hardly be surpassed in its kind. But the following is a similar piece of lexicographical method :

*Theb.* 497. ξυνοίσετον δὲ πολεμίους ἐπ' ἀσπίδων
θεούς· ὁ μὲν γὰρ πύρπνοον Τυφῶν' ἔχει,
Ὑπερβίῳ δὲ Ζεὺς πατὴρ ἐπ' ἀσπίδι
σταδαῖος ἧσται διὰ χερὸς βέλος φλέγων·
κοὔπω τις εἶδεν Ζῆνά που νικώμενον.
502. τοιάδε μέντοι προσφίλεια δαιμόνων.
πρὸς τῶν κρατούντων δ' ἐσμέν, οἱ δ' ἡσσωμένων,
504. εἰ Ζεύς γε Τυφῶ καρτερώτερος μάχῃ,
505. Ὑπερβίῳ τε—πρὸς λόγον τοῦ σήματος
506. εἰκός γε πράξειν ἄνδρας ὧδ' ἀντιστάτας—
507. σωτὴρ γένοιτ' ἂν Ζεὺς ἐπ' ἀσπίδος τυχών.

δὲ ειν
['504—507. β γ α δ praescripsit m'. 506. εἰκόσγε πρᾶξιν (δὲ et ειν scr. m') M. Versum eicit Francken.' W.]

I give Dr. Verrall's text and punctuation.

and on their shields they will bring to battle hostile gods; the one hath Typhon . . , and on Hyperbius' shield is Father Zeus, . . . and never anywhere was seen a Zeus defeated. We see, 'tis true, how frail is the gratitude of heaven ! Still we are with the victors, and they with the vanquished, if Zeus is anyway a mightier combatant than Typhon, and if Hyperbius—there is at least a likelihood that these human adversaries will prosper according to their blazons—may find protection from the fortunate Zeus upon his shield. (Transl. p. 157.)

502. *Such, it is true, is the gratitude of heaven. But etc.*, or *So much, however, for obliging a god ! Still etc.* The sense of the unique word προσφίλεια is to be determined by that of προσφιλής, which, applied to persons, signifies 'one who obliges' or 'is obliged.' See *Lex. s.v.* Soph. *Phil.* 532, 558, 587. The difference between φίλος and προσφιλής is well shown by Eur. *Hec.* 982 φίλος μὲν εἶ σύ προσφιλὲς δέ μοι τόδε στράτευμ' Ἀχαιῶν, 'thou art my friend (of old), and I have (now) obliged the Greeks.' . . . Note carefully μέντοι, which shows that this is a qualification, not a confirmation, of what precedes. The explanation is not far to seek. The story of the Titans and their war with Zeus is variously told, but it is agreed that the victor abused his strength and treated ungratefully and perfidiously even his allies, among them Γαῖα, the Earth (Aesch. *PV.* 226 *foll.*), and that his later conflicts (the subjugation of Typhoeus being the very last) were due to their anger. The story of Typhoeus had thus its sinister as well as its encouraging aspect for the worshipper of Zeus. . .

The meanings given for προσφιλὴς in the *Thesaurus* are Amatus, Carus, Gratus, Dilectus (qua etiam signif. dicitur interdum Amicus), Iucundus, Suavis, Acceptus.

of things, *acceptable, welcome, dear :*

Aesch.[1] *Theb.* 567. ἔργον καὶ θεοῖσι π.

Plat. *Euthyphr.* 6 E. ἔστι τοίνυν τὸ μὲν τοῖς θεοῖς π. ὅσιον,. .

„ „ 8 B. τῷ μὲν Διὶ προσφιλὲς ποιεῖς τῷ δὲ Κρόνῳ . . ἐχθρόν, καὶ τῷ μὲν Ἡφαίστῳ φίλον, τῇ δὲ Ἥρᾳ ἐχθρόν.

Eur. *Rhes.* 332. φράσω γὰρ δὴ ὅσον μοι ψυχᾷ π. ἐστιν εἰπεῖν.

Soph. *Phil.* 469. πρός τ' εἴ τί σοι κατ' οἶκόν ἐστι π.

„ „ 224. σχῆμα μὲν γὰρ Ἑλλάδος
στολῆς ὑπάρχει προσφιλεστάτης ἐμοί.

Plat. *Leg.* i. 642 C. καί μοι ἥ τε φωνὴ προσφιλὴς ὑμῶν.

„ *Tim.* 66 C. ἡδὺ καὶ π. πάντι πᾶν τὸ τοιοῦτον ἴαμα.

„ *Phil.* 64 C. πᾶσι γεγονέναι π. τὴν τοιαύτην διάθεσιν.

Xen. *Oec.* 5. 10. τίς δὲ [τέχνη] οἰκέταις προσφιλεστέρα ἢ γυναικὶ ἡδίων ἢ τέκνοις ποθεινοτέρα ἢ φίλοις εὐχαριστοτέρα ;

Xen. *Oec.* 15. 4. [τέχνην] προσφιλεστάτην θεοῖς τε καὶ ἀνθρώποις.

Eur. *Supp.* 489. εἰρήνη . . ἣ πρῶτα μὲν Μούσαισι προσφιλεστάτη,
γόοισι δ' ἐχθρά, τέρπεται δ' εὐπαιδίᾳ,
χαίρει δὲ πλούτῳ.

Soph. *El.* 672. παρὰ φίλου γὰρ ὢν
ἀνδρὸς, σαφ' οἶδα, π. λέξεις λόγους.

of persons, *in favour with, endeared, favourable to, attached, friendly :*

Hdt. i. 123. ἐόντι τῶν ἡλίκων ἀνδρηιοτάτῳ καὶ προσφιλεστάτῳ.

Hdt. i. 163. ἀπικόμενοι δὲ ἐς τὸν Τάρτησσον προσφιλέες ἐγένοντο τῷ βασιλέϊ . . . τούτῳ δὴ τῷ ἀνδρὶ π. οἱ Φωκαιέες οὕτω δή τι ἐγένοντο, ὡς . . .

[1] The word occurs first in Aeschylus ; never in lyric verse ; and only once in Comedy, Diphilus *fr.* 10.

Thuc. v. 40. [οἱ Ἀργεῖοι] ἔπεμπον . . ἐς τὴν Λακεδαίμονα πρέσβεις . . οἳ ἐδόκουν προσφιλέστατοι αὐτοῖς εἶναι.

Plat. *Gorg.* 507 E. οὔτε γὰρ ἂν ἄλλῳ ἀνθρώπῳ π. ἂν εἴη ὁ τοιοῦτος οὔτε θεῷ· κοινωνεῖν γὰρ ἀδύνατος· ὅτῳ δὲ μὴ ἔνι κοινωνία, φιλία οὐκ ἂν εἴη.

Plat. *Gorg.* 513 A. εἰ μέλλεις τούτῳ π. εἶναι.

„ *Lys.* 206 C. τί πράττων π. παιδικοῖς γένοιτο.

„ *Leg.* iv. 716 C. τὸν οὖν τῷ τοιούτῳ π. γενησόμενον.

„ *Menex.* 249 C. τοῖς ζῶσιν οὕτῳ ἂν προσφιλέστατοι εἴητε.

So with the adverb, προσφιλῶς διακεῖσθαι etc. Compare with this the following:

The verse is commonly interpreted by those who do not emend or eject it, 'Such is the friendship of gods to the respective combatants.' But this (as Hermann and others saw) takes no account of μέντοι: neither does it satisfy προσφίλεια.

Which of course implies not only that προσφιλὴς means *grateful*, but that anything short of this, as *friendly*, it cannot mean.

No such sense as *grateful* is acknowledged in the *Thesaurus* or in Ellendt's *Lex. Soph.* L. and S. however give:

. . . II. act. of persons, *kindly affectioned*, *grateful*, *well-disposed*, ὥς μ' ἔθεσθε προσφιλῆ Soph. *Ph.* 532, cf. Thuc. i. 92, vii. 86.

Dr. Verrall has added Soph. *Phil.* 558, 587 which we will take first:

Soph. *Phil.* 587. δεῖ δή σ', ἔμοιγ' ἐλθόντα προσφιλῆ, λόγων
κρύψαι πρὸς ἡμᾶς μηδέν' ὧν ἀκήκοας.

[λόγον L, etc. λόγων Burges (Nauck, Wecklein, Mekler, Jebb.]

'since thou hast come with a kindly purpose towards me' as Prof. Jebb translates. No notion of *gratitude* is possible in this place.

Soph. *Phil.* 557. ἀλλ' ἡ χάρις μὲν τῆς προμηθίας, ξένε,
εἰ μὴ κακὸς πέφυκα, προσφιλὴς μενεῖ.

Prof. Jebb translates 'the grace shown me by thy forethought . . shall live in my grateful thoughts.' But his note explains:

προσφιλής, *grata*, well-pleasing,—gratefully remembered. Aesch. *Theb.* 580. . .

(so rightly in Ellendt and L. S.). ἡ χάρις τῆς π. προσφιλὴς μενεῖ could not mean 'my gratitude for .. shall remain grateful.' The notion of *gratitude* is due to the context; it does not belong to the word here or at

Soph. *Phil.* 530. ὦ φίλτατον μὲν ἦμαρ ἥδιστός τ' ἀνήρ,
φίλοι δὲ ναῦται, πῶς ἂν ὑμὶν ἐμφανὴς
ἔργῳ γενοίμην ὥς μ' ἔθεσθε προσφιλῆ;

where Prof. Jebb rightly renders 'would that I could prove to you in deeds what love ye have won from me.'

Thuc. i. 92. ἅμα δὲ καὶ προσφιλεῖς ὄντες [οἱ Λακεδαιμόνιοι] ἐν τῷ τότε διὰ τὴν ἐς τὸν Μῆδον προθυμίαν τὰ μάλιστ' αὐτοῖς ἐτύγχανον.

'the patriotism which the Athenians had displayed in the Persian War had created a warm feeling of friendliness between the two cities.' Jowett.

Thuc. vii. 87. ἀνθ' ὧν οἱ Λακεδαιμόνιοι ἦσαν αὐτῷ προσφιλεῖς.

'Nicias surrendered to Gylippus . . . Nicias and Demosthenes they [the Syracusans and their allies] put to the sword . . . One of them, Demosthenes, happened to be the greatest foe, and the other the greatest friend of the Lacedaemonians, both in the same matter of Pylos and Sphacteria. For Nicias had taken up their cause, and had persuaded the Athenians to make the peace which set at liberty the prisoners taken in the island. The Lacedaemonians were grateful to him for the service, and this was the main reason why he trusted Gylippus and surrendered himself to him.' Jowett.

Add Soph. *O.T.* 322. οὔτ' ἔννομ' εἶπας οὔτε προσφιλὲς πόλει
τῇδ' ἥ σ' ἔθρεψε.

" *El.* 442. σκέψαι γὰρ εἴ σοι προσφιλῶς αὐτῇ δοκεῖ
γέρα τάδ' οὑν τάφοισι δέξασθαι νέκυς
ὑφ' ἧς . . . ἐμασχαλίσθη.

In all these last five passages we might in translation use the word *grateful* etc., but it is the context and that alone which would justify us in doing so; the notion of *gratitude* does not belong to the word.

Let us now take the passsage in the *Hecuba*, which according to Dr. Verrall well shows the difference between φίλος and προσφιλής. The case is this: the Greek army, after the fall of Troy, are detained by the ghost of Achilles on the coast of the Chersonese. Priam had placed his youngest son Polydorus with a large treasure in the keeping of Polymestor, king of that country. Troy fallen, Polymestor murders Polydorus for the sake of the treasure (*Prologue*, *v.* 25) and casts the body into the sea. It is discovered on the shore by a servant (*v.* 687), who informs her mistress Hecuba. Agamemnon immediately appears, enquires who is the dead man, and learns from Hecuba the story. He compassionates her, and she urges him to avenge her on the murderer Polymestor. Agamemnon replies he would willingly do so but fears the censure of the army, who regard Polymestor as a friend:

841. τὸν ἄνδρα τοῦτον φίλιον[1] ἡγεῖται στρατός
τὸν κατθανόντα δ' ἐχθρόν.

It is clear therefore that this regard exists already[2], independently of the murder. Hecuba thereupon devises her revenge and sends for Polymestor with his children on a false pretence. On his arrival in the next scene she says, 'I want to speak to you and your children on a private matter; bid your retinue leave the house.' Polymestor complies with these words:

962. χωρεῖτ'· ἐν ἀσφαλεῖ γὰρ ἥδ' ἐρημία.
φίλη[3] μὲν εἶ σύ, προσφιλὲς δέ μοι τόδε
στράτευμ' Ἀχαιῶν.

According to Dr. Verrall this means 'the Greek army is (now) obliged, grateful to me.' For what? Either for nothing, or for the murder of Polydorus. We have to suppose then that since the last scene he has informed the army

[1] Sch. προσφιλῆ.

[2] Sch. on 982: προσφιλες δὲ εἶναι αὐτῷ ὁ Πολυμήστωρ ἔφη τὸ Ἑλληνικὸν στρατευμα διὰ τὸ μὴ συμμαχῆσαι αὐτὸν τοῖς Τρωσί.

[3] Sch. προσφιλὴς μὲν εἶ σὺ, προσφιλὲς δὲ ἐμοὶ καὶ τόδε τὸ στοάτευμα . .

of the murder. Now, we might disbelieve his excuse made just before to Hecuba for his previous absence:

> τυγχάνω γὰρ ἐν μέσοις Θρῄκης ὅροις
> ἀπών, ὅτ' ἦλθες δεῦρ',

'and on my return I was just leaving the house when your messenger arrived'; but there is nothing in the play to suggest that the murder is yet even known to the army. And since presently in answer to Hecuba's questions he declares, not suspecting her knowledge, that Polydorus is alive and well, he must intend the last phrase, 'the Greek army is obliged to me,' to be quite unintelligible to Hecuba! But in any case the passage does not 'show' that προσφιλὲς in 963 means more than φίλιον in 841. The word is used regularly in scholiastic paraphrases as a mere synonym of φίλος and φίλιος, and it may clearly be seen so used in examples quoted above from classical Greek. It is habitual in Greek verse and ornamented prose to substitute synonyms for verbs or adjectives where these might be (as often they are) repeated: *e.g.*

Eur. *Bacch.* 1312. νῦν δ' ἄθλιος μέν εἰμ' ἐγώ, τλήμων δὲ σύ,
οἰκτρὰ δὲ μήτηρ, τλήμονες δὲ σύγγονοι.

Other instances may be seen in quotations given above (Xen. *Oec.* 5. 10, Eur. *Supp.* 489, Soph. *Phil.* 530). Another is immediately to our purpose:

Soph. *Ant.* 897. ἐλθοῦσα μέντοι κάρτ' ἐν ἐλπίσιν τρέφω
φίλη μὲν ἥξειν πατρί, προσφιλὴς δε σοί,
μῆτερ, φίλη δὲ σοί, κασίγνητον κάρα.

Does this passage too show the difference between φίλος and προσφιλής?

We have now seen that Dr. Verrall's method of ascertaining the meaning of a word is first to assume the meaning he desires; to ignore all instances of the word that will not admit that meaning, and to refer to such few as he can force to admit it; and upon such evidence to assert that no other meaning is admitted by the word.

If[1] προσφίλεια did mean 'gratitude,' the line would be meaningless, even if we suppose, as we are required to suppose, that, though both Typhoeus and Zeus are mentioned, yet δαιμόνων refers to Zeus alone. It is very easy to render 'such is the gratitude of heaven,'; but the Greek must mean 'such as I have described,' and there has been no description or mention of any one's gratitude. μέντοι does not 'show that this is a qualification of what precedes.' A full examination of this word would be worth the making. Whoever wrote this line intended it to mean 'So much for,' 'such then is the friendship of deities.' The following passages are sufficient illustration of the sentiment:

Eur. *Heracl.* 347. θεοῖσι δ' οὐ κακίοσι
χρώμεσθα συμμάχοισιν Ἀργείων, ἄναξ·
τῶν μὲν γὰρ Ἥρα προστατεῖ, Διὸς δάμαρ,
ἡμῶν δ' Ἀθάνα. φημὶ δ' εἰς εὐπραξίαν
καὶ τοῦθ' ὑπάρχειν, θεῶν ἀμεινόνων τυχεῖν·
νικωμένη γὰρ Πάλλας οὐκ ἀνέξεται.

" *Supp.* 595. ἓν δεῖ μόνον μοι, τοὺς θεοὺς ἔχειν ὅσοι
δίκην σέβονται· ταῦτα γὰρ συνόνθ' ὁμοῦ
νίκην δίδωσιν . . . .

" *Rhes.* 307. πολλούς, ἐπειδὴ τοὐμὸν εὐτυχεῖ δόρυ
καὶ Ζεὺς πρὸς ἡμῶν ἐστιν, εὑρήσω φίλους.

*Theb.* 556. καλεῖ· λέγει δὲ τοῦτ' ἔπος διὰ στόμα.

The force of one objection to this line has been already tested (p. 5 *seqq.*): five others are accumulated, some of which will be worth examining.

The addition of διὰ στόμα to λέγει is as pointless as 'speaks with his lips' would be in English.

---

[1] The word is not 'unique.' Dindorf (*Lex. Aesch.*) says: Vocabulum alibi non lectum, nisi quod Hasius ex Actis SS. Maii vol. 2 p. 775 attulit, τῆς τοῦ αὐτοκράτορος προσφιλείας ubi προσφιλίας scriptum. The Thesaurus and L.S. refer also to Aquila Psalm. lxiv. 1 ᾆσμα προσφιλίας (see Field *Origenis Hexapl.* ii. 161). Erroneous forms of this kind (due probably to itacism) are extremely common. In our line G. has προσφίλια.

Arguments from one language to another are likely to be more specious than sound. Consider the following:

Theognis 265. ἔνθα μέσην περὶ παῖδα βαλὼν ἀγκῶν' ἐφίλησα
δειρήν, ἡ δὲ τέρεν φθέγγετ' ἀπὸ στόματος.

*A.P.* ix. 571. λαρὰ δ' ἀπὸ στομάτων φθέγξατο Βακχυλίδης.

Antip. Sid. *A.P.* vi. 46. μέλπουσαν κλαγγὰν βάρβαρον ἐκ στομάτων.

Pamphilus, *A.P.* ix. 57. μυρομένη κελαδεῖς τραυλὰ διὰ στομάτων.

Lyc. *Al.* 263. κλάζων τ' ἄμικτον στόματι ῥιγίστην βοήν.

(Theocritus *A.P.* ix. 437, 11 may be compared but is not certain enough to be quoted.)

In all these cases an adjective is present, and the phrase may perhaps be thought an instance of *hypallage*. But the argument from English holds equally against these. For the following expressions see Ebeling *Lex. Hom.*:

Hom. *h. Cer.* 20. ἰάχησε δ' ἄρ' ὄρθια φωνῇ.
„ ω 530. ἤυσεν φ.
„ Γ. 161. Πρίαμος δ' Ἑλένην ἐκαλέσσατο φ.

Add Hegemon *ap.* Ath. xv. 698. εἶπέ τε φωνῇ. (parody.)
In Eur. *Or.* 103. Ἄργει τ' ἀναβοᾷ διὰ στόμα
the phrase is like διὰ σ. ἔχειν etc. Cf.

Ap. Rhod. iii. 792. τηλοῦ δε πόλις περὶ πᾶσα βοήσει
πότμον ἐμόν· καὶ κέν με διὰ στόματος φορέουσαι
Κολχίδες . . . μωμήσονται.

In *Batrachom.* 76. πολλὰ δ' ἐβώστρει,
καὶ τοῖον φάτο μῦθον ἀπὸ στόματος δ' ἀγόρευσεν.

ἀπὸ σ. cannot be used in the special sense 'off-hand,' 'from memory'; it is to be considered as a parody of Epic amplification. Unless indeed it should be suggested that it expresses the delivery of a consecutive *speech* as opposed to the *call* (ἐβώστρει). The same might then be urged for our passage.

Such is the evidence I have been able to find; which, if it does not establish our phrase, will yet show that it is not sufficient to argue from the use of English. Dr. Verrall omits to consider that the line may be corrupted in part. Keck proposed φλέγει (cf. *Theb.* 500). It is possible that λέγει is a gloss, and that the true reading is φέρει. Cf.

Aesch. *Supp.* 704. ἁγνῶν τ' ἐκ στομάτων φερέσθω
φῆμα φιλοφόρμιγξ.

Hom. Ξ. 90. μῦθον ὃν οὔ τις ἀνήρ γε διὰ στόμα πάμπαν
ἄγοιτο.

Sch. A εἴποι.

The third objection is:

τοῦτ' ἔπος λέγειν is not good Aeschylean Greek for 'to speak as follows'; ἔπος when used in this way, is not a speech but a *phrase* or formula of some kind, an exclamation or a 'proverb' such as . . *Pers.* 126, . . *Eum.* 513, . . *v.* 250, . . *P. V.* 1012, . . *v.* 704, . . *Cho.* 92.

But in *P.V.* 1097. οὐ γὰρ δή που
τοῦτό γε τλητὸν παρέσυρας ἔπος

τοῦτο ἔπος refers to neither phrase, formula, exclamation nor proverb, but to the piece of advice that Prometheus has just given. Just like that is Eur. *Hipp.* 232 τί τόδ' αὖ παράφρων ἔρριψας ἔπος; τόδ' ἔπος is used in Pindar of a long speech to follow, *N.* x. 80, τοιοῦτον ἔ. *O.* vi. 16, *I.* vi. 42. In Sophocles ἔπος refers but once to a following speech of any length: *Ant.* 1210. οἰμώξας δ' ἔπος ἵησι δυσθρήνητον· ($7\frac{1}{2}$ lines). This it remains for Dr. Verrall to eject. Otherwise one may argue that this epic use can hardly be permitted to Sophocles and upon the same evidence denied to Aeschylus.

Objections 4 and 5 I need not discuss. Here is objection 6:

on *v.* 567 the Scholl. give the note καθ' ὑπόκρισιν 'acted' or 'spoken in character' (see the *Lex. s. vv.* ὑπόκρισις, ὑποκριτής), indicating that here the ἄγγελος begins to speak as Amphiaraus; this note is useless as the text stands, and must have been written before the spurious verse was inserted.

There is here no admission of doubt, no hint of misgiving.

ὑπόκρισις is used in schol. L Soph. *Aj.* 864 of 'acting,'

'impersonation': δεῖ καρτερόν τινα εἶναι τὸν ὑποκριτὴν ὡς ἄξει τοὺς θεατὰς . . . ὁποῖα περὶ . . Τιμοθέου φασὶν ὅτι ἦγε τοὺς θεατὰς καὶ ἐψυχαγώγει τῇ ὑποκρίσει. Cf. sch. Eur. *Med.* 497. But καθ' ὑπ. is never so used. It is a phrase regularly used in scholia, not always easy to render accurately in English, but meaning *in pretence, hypocritically*, or *ironically, sarcastically* : cf. Athen. xiii. 585 f., Zenob. v. 85, Hesych. *s.v.* ἀφοσιούμενοι, Fab. Aesop. 69.

καθ' ὑπόκρισιν, ἐν ὑποκρίσει, ὑποκριτικῶς, all equivalent, are synonymous with κατ' εἰρωνείαν, ἐν εἰρωνείᾳ, εἰρωνικῶς : thus on our passage schol. rec. has εἰρωνευόμενος. Cf. sch. on Eur. *Med.* 880 ὑποκρίνεται δὲ νῦν καὶ μετ' εἰρωνείας ταῦτα λέγει.

Anecd. Bekker, p. 40. Ἐγὼ σιωπῶ τῷδε; Ἀριστοφάνης ταύτην ἐσχημάτισε τὴν σύνταξιν, καθ' ὑπ. δέ. λέγει γάρ·...εἶτ' ἀποκρίνεται Αἰσχύλος· ἐγὼ σιωπῶ τῷδε; βούλεται γὰρ λέγειν καθ' ὑπ. εἶτα ἐγὼ τούτῳ σιωπήσομαι; οἷον ἄξιόν ἐστιν ἐμὲ τῷδε ὑποστέλλεσθαι καὶ ὑπείκειν λόγοις;

Sch. Plat. *Protag.* 341 D. πολλοῦ γε δεῖ] τοῦτο καθ' ὑπ. λέγεται ἀποφατικῶς ἀπὸ [l. ἀντὶ] τοῦ πολὺ ἐνδεῖ.

Sch. Eur. *Or.* 482. ταῦτα δὲ ἐν ὑπ. λέγει καὶ οὐ σπουδῇ.

See scholl. on Eur. *Tro.* 971, *Hec.* 651, 661, 1086, *Ph.* 521, *Andr.* 194.

Sch Soph. *El.* 164. ἀκάματα: ἀκαμάτως καὶ ἀδιαλείπτως. λέγοι δ' ἂν ταῦτα ἐν ὑποκρίσει . .

Sch. Soph. *O.C.* 1232. τίς οὐ καμάτων ἔνι; φόνοι: ταῦτα ὑποκριτικῶς [ὑπεροπτικῶς L : corr. Papag.] εἴρηται κατὰ τοιαύτην ὑπόκρισιν καθ' ἣν . . .

This use is not recorded in 'the *Lex.*', nor indeed in the *Thesaurus* or by Sophocles *Lex. Byzant.* But one might expect a competent editor to know the meaning of so common a scholiastic phrase. If he did not, he might have found most of the instances in Euripides in the index to Dindorf's edition of the scholia. And in the index to Dindorf's edition he might have found the only other instance in the Aeschylean scholia :

*Theb.* 165. ὑμᾶς ἐρωτῶ θρέμματ' οὐκ ἀνασχετά,
ἦ ταῦτ' ἄριστα καὶ πόλει σωτήρια, . .

Sch. M. 166. καθ' ὑπόκρισιν ἀναγνωστέον. ἢ ὡς ἐν ἐρωτήσει μετ' ἐπιτιμήσεως.

*i.e.* we may take the line either as an ironical exclamation, *Verily this is best . . !* or interrogatively, *Is this best . . ?* Had Dr. Verrall not read this schol. upon his own play? Exactly the same is the meaning on our passage:

ἦ τοῖον ἔργον καὶ θεοῖσι προσφιλές,
καλόν τ' ἀκοῦσαι . .

*Verily the deed is grateful to heaven and brave for . . !* It is the ironical force of which we are here warned by καθ' ὑπ. as, for instance, at

*Pers.* 761. τοιγάρ σφιν ἔργον ἐστὶν ἐξειργασμένον
μέγιστον, ἀείμνηστον, . .

by a synonymous phrase in sch. rec., ἔστι δὲ ὁ λόγος ἐν εἰρωνείᾳ.

*Theb.* 459. ET. πέμποιμ' ἂν ἤδη τόνδε, σὺν τύχῃ δέ τῳ
καὶ δὴ πέπεμπτ' οὐ κόμπον ἐν χεροῖν ἔχων
Μεγαρεὺς Κρέοντος σπέρμα τοῦ σπαρτοῦ γένους.

Scribendum erat, remota negatione, καὶ δὴ πέπεμπται, graviore multo sententia, idque vidit etiam Erfurdtius ad Soph. *Aj.* 514. . . HERMANN

The MSS. add οὐ before κόμπον, and some give πεμπτ' or πέμπετ'. Hermann has ejected the οὐ (as had formerly been done by the present editor), and so Erfurdt on Ajax p. 514. He also removes the stop usually placed at the end of the preceding verse; 'and indeed there is already sent one who bears his vaunting (not on his tongue but) in action.' Inf. 549 ἀνὴρ—δράσιμον. There is a similar instance of the intrusion of οὐ arising from a misconception of the sense, inf. 1041. Dindorf condemns 467—8 as spurious. PALEY.

οὐ and μὴ are often so inserted wrongly from misapprehension of the meaning or the construction. κόμπον ἐν χεροῖν ἔχων, a form of expression characteristically Greek, is well illustrated by

Eur. *Supp.* 904. οὐκ ἐν λόγοις ἦν λαμπρός, ἀλλ' ἐν ἀσπίδι
[1][δεινὸς σοφιστὴς πολλά τ' ἐξευρεῖν σοφά.]
γνώμῃ δ' ἀδελφοῦ Μελεάγρου λελειμμένος
ἴσον παρέσχεν ὄνομα διὰ τέχνης δορὸς
εὑρὼν ἀκριβῆ μουσικὴν ἐν ἀσπίδι·
φιλότιμον ἦθος πλούσιον, φρόνημα δὲ
ἐν τοῖσιν ἔργοις οὐχὶ τοῖς λόγοις ἔχων.

The critic not perceiving the antithetical force of *κόμπον ἐν χεροῖν*, inserts *οὐ*, meaning of course *πέπεμπται οὐ*. Dr. Verrall, retaining this, supposes it to be *ἐπέπεμπτο οὐ*:

From all the expressions here, from ἤδη τόνδε, which marks that the choice is ready and obvious, and from σὺν τύχῃ τῳ *with a certain happiness* or *good fortune* in the choice, it is plain that the selection is suggested by some patent fact. The same thing is conveyed still more strongly by the pluperfect ἐπέπεμπτο, *and indeed he was already sent*, which implies according to the use of the tense, that the choice may be said to have made itself, the fitness of the person being patent *a priori*. And further, as the position of the words οὐ κόμπον ἐν χεροῖν ἔχων, bearing in his hands no idle brag, shows that here lies the explanation of ἐπέπεμπτο, we can scarcely be wrong in supposing that the reference is to the blazon upon his shield, which by an 'undesigned coincidence' represents *Ares*, the very god insulted by his opponent's impious emblem (*v.* 456). That Megareus might well bear this device 'not as an idle brag' is shown by his pedigree, the stock of the Σπαρτοί having sprung from the seed ὧν Ἄρης ἐφείσατο (*v.* 399) and being therefore entitled to claim his patronage. . . The later copies, misled by the omission of the mark of elision before 'πέπεμπτ', change πέπεμπτ' οὐ into πέπεμπται, and are followed by all modern editions. As however the text so produced is scarcely intelligible, it is further supposed by most commentators that the passage is defective, and it is argued, in support of this, that the speech wants 6 lines of the 15 assumed to be normal. . .

It will be noticed that *κόμπων* is translated 'an idle brag'; not for nothing, as we shall see:

[1] δεινὸς παλαιστὴς πολλά τ' ἐξευρεῖν σοφός Valckenaer on *Hippol.* 921. 'legendum πολλά τ' ἐξευρὼν σοφά' Kirchhoff, 1855. (Or πόλλ' ἀνεξευρὼν σοφά?) Cf. Eur. *fr.* 267 δεινὴ πόλις νοσοῦσ' ἀνευρίσκειν κακά, *Trag. fr. adesp.* 488 δαίμων βροτοῖσι πόλλ' ἀνευρίσκει κακὰ, 509 χρόνος . . πόλλ' ἀνευρίσκει σοφὰ μαιομένοις and Meleag. *A.P.* vii. 79

ὤνθρωφ', Ἡράκλειτος ἐγὼ σοφὰ μοῦνος ἀνευρεῖν
φημί· τὰ δ' εἰς πάτραν κρείσσονα καὶ σοφίης.

(So read for MSS. ἀνευρών.) See also *Trag. fr. adesp.* 323 N.

*Theb.* 540. ἔστιν δὲ καὶ τῷδ', ὃν λέγεις τὸν Ἀρκάδα,
ἀνὴρ ἄκομπος, χεὶρ δ' ὁρᾷ τὸ δράσιμον, . .
ὃς οὐκ ἐάσει γλῶσσαν ἐργμάτων ἄτερ
ἔσω πυλῶν ῥέουσαν ἀλδαίνειν κακά.

What could be simpler? The language here is just like that in 460, the same antithesis being sustained. This is what we get:

χεὶρ δ' ὁρᾷ. . . The explanation of this curious phrase . . . is perhaps to be found in its antithesis to ἄκομπος. From the language of the scene throughout, and immediately before (*v.* 537), it is natural to suppose that κόμπος refers to blazonry, and the comparison of οὐ κόμπον in *v.* 460 shows that ἄκομπος may well signify not 'without a blazon,' but 'having a blazon not false or over-boastful.' . .

This is not the only place where Dr. Verrall has contrived to see in a single word more than it can possibly contain. Thus

*Theb.* 646. τάχ' εἰσόμεσθα τοὐπίσημ' ὅποι τέλεῖ,
εἴ νιν κατάξει χρυσότευκτα γράμματα
ἐπ' ἀσπίδος φλύοντα, συμφοίτω φρενῶν.

648. συμφοίτω φρενῶν: *his mad pair of wanderers, viz.* the figures of Right and the warrior represented upon his shield. For the form σύμφοιτος . . cf. περίφοιτος, and for the construction with it of the genitive . . φρενῶν cf. παράκοπος φρενῶν and the like. The description 'wanderers' is of course literally as well as metaphorically appropriate to the exiles. . .

Appropriate or not, συμφοίτω φρενῶν could not possibly mean 'a mad pair of wanderers,' unless φρενῶν by itself can mean 'out of their minds'; but only 'a mad pair,' 'fellow-wanderers from their minds.'

The corrector m' has gone far to spoil this verse by the marginal note σὺν φοίτω, from which and his gloss μανίᾳ comes the current reading σὺν φοιτῷ: apart from the injury to the sense, σὺν is misused, and φοῖτος (*distraction*) is a word not known to exist and not regularly formed. The verb is φοιτάω (not φοιτέω) and the substantive, if it was used, would naturally be φοίτη.

The evidence for the existence of φοῖτος is as follows:

Hesych. φοῖτος: μανία, λύσσα

" φοιτῶντα ἄνδρα μανιάσι: λυσσήμασι. τὴν . . ἑδραίαν μανίαν φοιτὸν ἔλεγον, τουτέστι τὸν μεθ' ὁρμῆς μεμηνότα. [μανιάσι νόσοις: M. Schmidt, φοῖτον Musur.]

Suid. φοῖτος: ἡ μανία

„ φοιτῶντα: μεθ' ὁρμῆς μεμηνότα, μαινόμενον. φοῖτος γὰρ ἡ μανία . . .

Sch. G. Soph. *Aj.* 59. ἤτοι μαινόμενον· φοῖτος γὰρ ἡ μανία.

Sch. L. „ „ 332. διαπεφοιβάσθαι: ἐκμεμηνέναι, παρὰ τὸν φοῖτον (legit διαπεφοιτάσθαι Papag. Similar confusion appears to have happened elsewhere).

Sch. M. Ap. Rhod. iv. 55. φοιταλέην: ἐμμανῆ, μανιωδῶς πορευομένην. φοῖτος γὰρ ἡ μανία.

Sch. Eur. *Or.* 327 (319 K) φοιταλέου] λύσσα καὶ μανία καὶ φοῖτος ἔνεστι.

Sch. Opp. *Hal.* i. 45. φοιταλέων] ἀπὸ τοῦ φοῖτος, ἡ μανία.

Eustath. 732, 61. ὡς δὲ καὶ τὸ ἐνθουσιωδῶς ὁρμᾶν καὶ μαίνεσθαι φοιτᾶν ἐλέχθη, ὅθεν καὶ φοῖτος ἡ μανία, δηλοῦσιν οἱ παλαιοί.

„ 585, 15. εἰ δὲ, κατὰ τοὺς παλαιοὺς, φοῖτος ἡ μανία, . .

It is quite likely that the authority of one of these places is the authority of all; but they are not to be ignored as though m′ had invented the word himself.

As to the formation of the word; in the first place, how does Dr. Verrall know that there was never a verb φοιτέω? Cf. the form φοίτεσκον Asius *fr.* ap. Ath. xii. 525. Suidas records the form φοιτεία [Küst. for φοιτία MS.]: ἡ πορεία. Is this also to be rejected because 'the verb is φοιτάω'? There is also a verb φοιτίζω Hom. *h.* 26, 8, Callim. *fr.* 148, Ap. Rhod. iii. 54. Are we also to reject κοῖτος because there is no verb κοιτέω? and οἶτος because οἰτέω does not exist? To οἶμος, at any rate, we may object as 'not regularly formed' because the verb is not οἰμέω but οἰμάω. This is indeed schoolboy philology. On φοῖτος and its root see Lobeck *Paralip.* p. 349, and authorities quoted by Ebeling *Lex. Hom.* s.v. φοιτάω.

For the plot of the *Seven against Thebes* Dr. Verrall had not at the time of editing conceived a new interpretation. In the Introduction to the *Agamemnon* however he holds out hope of innovation in the order in which the *dramatis personae* of the *Theb.* come on the stage:

I give the list in the order, which I now think may be correct, of the Medicean MS. On another occasion I hope to make some remarks upon it, which would here be out of place. (*Agam.* Introd. p. xlix. note.)

I shall have some remarks, perhaps more instructive, to make upon this note when I come to speak about the *Agamemnon.*

But we are already presented with a new reading of the character of Eteocles. We thought him before to be high-spirited, impatient, headstrong. We are now to consider him a sarcastic scoffer at religion. It is not needful here to enquire how far it is probable that such a character was considered by Aeschylus necessary to the fulfilment of the father's curse, or indeed how far the character is consistently drawn. But it will be worth while to see how the new reading of the character is obtained:

*Theb.* 21. ET. *καὶ νῦν μὲν ἐς τόδ' ἦμαρ εὖ ῥέπει θεός·*
*χρόνον γὰρ ἤδη τόνδε πυργηρουμένοις*
*καλῶς τὰ πλείω πόλεμος ἐκ θεῶν κυρεῖ.*

21. *θεός*, equivalent to *τύχη*, *fortune.* The personal sense of the word is wholly lost, as the phrase *εὖ ῥέπει* shows.
23. *ἐκ θεῶν*—apparently a false accentuation for *ἐκθέων*; *our war in sallies has been for the most part successful.* *ἐκθεῖν* is the proper term for sallies of the beleaguered. *ἐκ θεῶν* does not suit the character of the speaker. Contrast *v.* 4 and see the Introduction.

This phrase *πόλεμος ἐκθέων* (to read which no letter need of course be changed) Dr. Verrall places in his text. At v. 4, which we are to contrast, Eteocles makes the shrewd remark that while success would be ascribed to heaven, all the blame for misfortune would fall on himself:

*Theb.* 4. *εἰ μὲν γὰρ εὖ πράξαιμεν, αἰτία θεοῦ·*
*εἰ δ' αὖθ', ὃ μὴ γένοιτο, συμφορὰ τύχοι, . .*

Every one knows how common a sentiment is this; to the numerous parallels quoted by the commentators add the words of Pericles in Thuc. ii. 64. According to Dr. Verrall the man who could utter this is not of a character to say also *καλῶς τὰ πλείω πόλεμος ἐκ θεῶν κυρεῖ.* His character permits him to say *εὖ ῥέπει θεός*, but then *θεὸς* there is merely *fortune*, with no personal sense whatever. One might ask why this should not be also true of *αἰτία θεοῦ* in v. 4. That, however, though in the translation rendered 'fortune hath the praise,' is presently given as equivalent to *πρὸς θεῶν*, at 202—4, where

Eteocles speaks with the same sceptical irony as elsewhere. If the town is to be saved, it must be by means of the wall and the human defence, and this, he adds maliciously, will be *πρὸς θεῶν* (*αἰτία θεοῦ* *v.* 4) after all; as for the gods, religion herself explains that when a town is taken the gods (of the citadel) leave their posts.

I do not quote the passage because the way it should be taken is very doubtful: as to the phrase which in Dr. Verrall's view Eteocles 'maliciously adds,' it is quite uncertain whether it should be taken positively or negatively, and whether it should be assigned to Eteocles or to the Chorus. Here and in the rest of his remonstrance with the maidens Eteocles urges that Heaven helps those who help themselves; one of the general doctrines of Greek religion. 'Trust in Providence, certainly,' he says, in effect, 'but do not therefore expose our powder to the rain.' If *ἐκ θεῶν* in v. 23 'does not suit the character' of Eteocles, one may wonder why the following passages are found in harmony with the character; 168,

244. ET. *παλινστομεῖς αὖ θιγγάνουσ' ἀγαλμάτων ;*

'And now thou blasphemest, with thy hand on the holy gods?'

252. ET. *εὔχου τὰ κρείσσω ξυμμάχους εἶναι θεούς*
*κἀμῶν ἀκούσασ' εὐγμάτων, ἔπειτα σὺ*
*ὀλολυγμὸν . . . παιάνισον, . .*

257—266. 'And for my part, unto the deities of this place, . . . unto these I vow that, if we prosper. . .'

612. ET. *θεοῦ δὲ δῶρόν ἐστιν εὐτυχεῖν βροτούς.*

649—658. the language about *ἡ Διὸς παῖς, παρθένος Δίκη*. Compare also the speech of the Theban herald, 936 *sqq.*, and Dr. Verrall's note on 1008, in which, arguing for another purpose, he speaks of Eteocles as (in the eyes of the Theban government) 'instrument of heaven' and 'champion of gods.'

For a 'touch of irrepressible scepticism and sarcasm . . . characteristic of the speaker' see Dr. Verrall's note on 502, concerning which I have had something to say at p. 68.

At 555 *seqq.* we have 'the recital of the final warnings addressed by Amphiaraus . . to Tydeus and Polynices, the chief authors of the war . . Eteocles replies with an edifying lamentation on the *recklessness of fortune, which confounds the judgments of heaven.*' (Introd. p. xiv.) Here is the 'edifying' lamentation (in Dr. Verrall's arrangement):

*Theb.* 584. φεῦ τοῦ ξυναλλάσσοντος ὄρνιθος βροτούς,
δίκαιον ἄνδρα τοῖσι δυσσεβεστέροις
ἐν πάντι πράγει δ' ἔσθ' ὁμιλίας κακῆς
κάκιον οὐδέν, καρπὸς οὐ κομιστέος·
ἄτης ἄρουρα θάνατον ἐκκαρπίζεται
ἢ γὰρ ξυνεισβὰς πλοῖον εὐσεβὴς ἀνὴρ
ναύτῃσι θερμοῖς καὶ πανουργίᾳ τινὶ
ὄλωλεν ἀνδρῶν σὺν θεοπτύστῳ γένει
ἢ ξὺν πολίταις ἀνδράσιν δίκαιος ὢν
ἐχθροξένοις τε καὶ θεῶν ἀμνήμοσιν
ταὐτοῦ κυρήσας ἐκδίκως ἀγρεύματος
πληγεὶς θεοῦ μάστιγι παγκοίνῳ 'δάμη.
οὕτως δ' ὁ μάντις, υἱὸν Οἰκλέους λέγω,
σώφρων δίκαιος ἀγαθὸς εὐσεβὴς ἀνήρ,
μέγας προφήτης ἀνοσίοισι συμμιγείς,
θρασυστόμοισιν ἀνδράσιν βίᾳ φρενῶν.
τείνουσι πομπὴν τὴν μακρὰν πάλιν μολεῖν,
Διός θ' ἑλόντος συγκαθελκυσθήσεται.

601. θελοντος M.

601. The letters here (θέλοντος) are ambiguous, but the tenor of the passage shows that the division and accentuation adopted in the MS. is wrong. According to the orthodox Greek theology, as here set forth, God does *not* either 'will,' or properly speaking 'permit,' that the righteous should perish with the wicked: but by the perverse entanglements of chance the one is sometimes involved in the punishment of the other. It must be remembered that neither the popular nor the critical philosophy of the Greeks supposed the divine power to be omnipotent or omniscient.

Let us first pause to wonder that Eteocles, the irreligious scoffer whose sarcasm has elsewhere been irrepressible, should here be accepted without remark as setting forth quite accurately 'the orthodox Greek theology.' Now what was orthodox theology at the time this play was written? Upon that point there cannot be two opinions: it was that defined by Homer and Hesiod. As Herodotus says (ii. 53): Ἡσίοδον γὰρ καὶ Ὅμηρον . . . οὗτοι δέ εἰσι οἱ ποιήσαντες θεογονίην Ἕλλησι καὶ τοῖσι θεοῖσι τὰς ἐπωνυμίας δόντες καὶ τιμάς τε καὶ τέχνας διελόντες καὶ εἴδεα αὐτῶν σημήναντες. It is these authors then that we must consult. Now what do we find in them to be the common language about Zeus?

First, as to *omniscience*: Athene speaking of Δία τερπικέραυνον says:

Hom. υ. 75. ὁ γάρ τ' εὖ οἶδεν ἅπαντα
μοῖράν τ' ἀμμορίην τε καταθνητῶν ἀνθρώπων.
Hes. *Op*. 267. πάντα ἰδὼν Διὸς ὀφθαλμὸς καὶ πάντα νοήσας
καί νυ τάδ', αἴ κ' ἐθέλῃσ', ἐπιδέρκεται.

Secondly, Zeus is constantly called *omnipotent*, as I shall show in passages where he is at the same time said to send good fortune or ill to men *according to his own caprice*, without regard to merit:

Hom. α. 348. (Telemachus) ἀλλά ποθι Ζεὺς αἴτιος, ὅστε δίδωσιν
ἀνδράσιν ἀλφηστῇσιν ὅπως ἐθέλῃσιν ἑκάστῳ.
„ ζ. 187. (Nausicaa) ξεῖν', ἐπεὶ οὔτε κακῷ οὔτ' ἄφρονι φωτὶ ἔοικας·
Ζεὺς δ' αὐτὸς νέμει ὄλβον Ὀλύμπιος ἀνθρώποισιν
ἐσθλοῖς ἠδὲ κακοῖσιν ὅπως ἐθέλῃσιν ἑκάστῳ.
καί πού σοι τά γ' ἔδωκε, σὲ δὲ χρὴ τέτλαμεν ἔμπης . .
„ δ. 235. (Helen) Ἀτρείδη Μενέλαε διοτρεφὲς ἠδὲ καὶ οἵδε
ἀνδρῶν ἐσθλῶν παῖδες· ἀτὰρ θεὸς ἄλλοτε ἄλλῳ
Ζεὺς ἀγαθόν τε κακόν τε διδοῖ· δύναται γὰρ ἅπαντα.

Hom. ξ. 443. (Eumaeus) ἔσθιε, δαιμόνιε ξείνων, καὶ τέρπεο τοῖσδε
οἷα πάρεστι· θεὸς δὲ τὸ μὲν δώσει, τὸ δ' ἐάσει,
ὅττι κεν ᾧ θυμῷ ἐθέλῃ· δύναται γὰρ ἅπαντα.

So Pind. *I.* v. 52. Ζεὺς τά τε καὶ τὰ νέμει
Ζεὺς ὁ πάντων κύριος.

He will even destroy, at his own pleasure:

Hes. *Op.* 665. (on a certain day) οὔτε κε νῆα
καυάξαις οὔτ' ἄνδρας ἀποφθίσειε θάλασσα,
εἰ μὴ δὴ πρόφρων γε Ποσειδάων ἐνοσίχθων
ἢ Ζεὺς ἀθανάτων βασιλεὺς ἐθέλῃσιν ὀλέσσαι,
ἐν τοῖς γὰρ τέλος ἐστὶν ὁμῶς ἀγαθῶν τε κακῶν τε.

Hence the reproach of Theognis:

373. Ζεῦ φίλε, θαυμάζω σε· σὺ γὰρ πάντεσσιν ἀνάσσεις
τιμὴν αὐτὸς ἔχων καὶ μεγάλην δύναμιν·
ἀνθρώπων δ' εὖ οἶσθα νόον καὶ θυμὸν ἑκάστου·
σὸν δὲ κράτος πάντων ἔσθ' ὕπατον, βασιλεῦ.
πῶς δή σευ, Κρονίδη, τολμᾷ νόος ἄνδρας ἀλιτροὺς
ἐν ταὐτῇ μοίρῃ τόν τε δίκαιον ἔχειν,
ἤν τ' ἐπὶ σωφροσύνην τρεφθῇ νόος, ἤν τε πρὸς ὕβριν
ἀνθρώπων ἀδίκοις ἔργμασι πειθομένων;

I leave Dr. Verrall's statements to be judged in the light of this evidence. Let us see what further warrant he can find for changing the division and accentuation of M:

*vv.* 596—601 are commonly taken, with the reading θέλοντος, as one sentence, τείνουσι being then the dative participle. But the long suspension of the syntax has an awkward effect.

It is hard to conceive how this could be said with conviction by any one accustomed to read Greek. For it is characteristic as well of the Greek sentence as of the Latin to make the *circumstances* or *conditions* subordinate to the *event* or *result*, it matters not how numerous the conditions or circumstances may be. 601 is the result affirmed of certain conditions; it is for the sake of the statement in 601 that the rest, from 595, exists. 600 is part of the conditions postulated. To make of this a sentence coordinate with the result would be natural in English (where such coordination is often carried to excess); in the Greek of Aeschylus I believe that as punctuated by Dr. Verrall the sentences 596—601 are impossible. But in any case the argument that 'the long suspension of the syntax has an awkward effect' declares unfamiliarity with one of the most characteristic features of Greek style.

It may be observed that Dr. Verrall's punctuation requires in 596 'the verb (δαμήσεται or the like)' to be 'supplied from the previous sentences'; that βίᾳ φρενῶν is taken together with θρασυστόμοισιν, '*bold with their lips in despite of sense*'; and that on 591 we read

ἀνδρῶν, antithetic to ἀνὴρ in *v.* 582; so also ἀνδράσιν in *v.* 592.

Why not also ἄνδρα in 585 and ἀνδράσιν in 599?

Let us return to Eteocles:

*Theb.* 705. ΧΟ. *ἀλλ' αὐτάδελφον αἷμα δρέψασθαι θέλεις;*
ΕΤ. *θεῶν διδόντων οὐκ ἂν ἐκφύγοις κακά.*

I could not wish to state the situation better than Dr. Verrall himself: 'it has now become apparent that the king has destined the seventh gate for himself, and is publicly committed to the enterprise. But the spy knows nothing of this, and announces point-blank that the assailant, still unnamed, whom chance has placed among the seven and the order of the lot has assigned to the seventh gate,—is Polynices . . . Eteocles for the moment is utterly appalled: but ashamed and afraid to go back from his promise, stung to fury by the challenge of Polynices, and above all, convinced by the course of these incidents that the destiny of his race is not to be averted, he puts on a desperate assurance, dashes aside the expostulations of the women, and rushes to meet his fate.' (Introd. p. xv.) The note on 706 tells us that

In διδόντων there is a last touch of Eteocles' irony.

Since Dr. Verrall himself speaks of Eteocles as 'convinced by the course of these incidents that the destiny of his race is not to be averted,' he clearly does not mean that the whole statement in 706 is made ironically, but that, as the note says, there is irony in διδόντων. From the form of the line any one might suspect in 706 a proverb, even if he had not met with it elsewhere. But whether an editor should have met with it I will leave my readers presently to judge.

The gifts of the gods are good or evil:

Hom. Ω. 528. *δοιοὶ γάρ τε πίθοι κατακείαται ἐν Διὸς οὔδει*
*δώρων οἷα δίδωσι κακῶν ἕτερος δὲ ἑάων.*
„ δ. 237. *ἄταρ θεοὶ ἄλλοτε ἄλλῳ*
*Ζεὺς ἀγαθόν τε κακόν τε διδοῖ.*
Hes. *Theog.* 219. *Κλωθώ τε Λάχεσίν τε καὶ Ἄτροπον αἵτε βροτοῖσι*
*γεινομένοισι διδοῦσιν ἔχειν ἀγαθόν τε κακόν τε.*
„ *fr.* 68, *Scut.* 400. *οἷα Διώνυσος δῶκ' ἀνδράσι χάρμα καὶ ἄλγος.*
Theognis 133. *οὐδείς, Κύρν', ἄτης καὶ κέρδεος αἴτιος αὐτός,*
*ἀλλὰ θεοὶ τούτων δώτορες ἀμφοτέρων.*

so 271, Bacchyl. *fr.* 36, Menander *fr.* 425.

Mention is frequent of their evil gifts:

Hom. η. 241, ι. 15. *κήδε' ἐπεί μοι πολλὰ δόσαν θεοὶ οὐρανίωνες.*
„ β. 135. *ἐκ γὰρ τοῦ πατρὸς κακά πείσομαι, ἄλλα δὲ δαίμων | δώσει.*
„ δ. 262. *ἄτην δὲ μετέστενον ἣν Ἀφροδίτη | δῶκ'.*
„ T. 270. *Ζεῦ πάτερ, ἦ μεγάλας ἄτας ἄνδρεσσι διδοῖσθα.*
Hes. *Op.* 638. *κακὴν πενίην τὴν Ζεὺς ἄνδρεσσι δίδωσι.*

Mimnermus 2, 15. οὐδέ τις ἔστιν | ἀνθρώπων ᾧ Ζεὺς μὴ κακὰ πολλὰ διδοῖ.

Archil. *fr.* 10. κρύπτομεν ἀνιηρὰ Ποσειδῶνα ἄνακτα δῶρα (so quoted by Schol. M Aesch. *P.V.* 643; κρύπτωμεν Rob. δ' ἀ. Ποσειδάωνος Schneidewin ἄνακτος Rob.).

Hes. *Op.* 741. τῷ δὲ θεοὶ νεμέσωσι καὶ ἄλγεα δῶκαν ὀπίσσω.

Hom. A. 96. τούνεκ' ἄρ' ἄλγε' ἔδωκε ἑκηβόλος ἠδ' ἔτι δώσει: so B. 375, Σ. 431, Ω. 241, δ. 722, ξ. 39, Hes. *Op.* 57, 86, 176, Archil. *fr.* 125, Pind. *fr.* 42, Soph. *fr.* 588, Eur. *fr.* 140, *Trag. fr. adesp.* 489, Lycophr. *Al.* 909, Orph. *fr.* i. 11, etc.

Whether good or evil, as they are not to be escaped, so they must not be shunned but patiently endured:

Hom. σ. 142. τῷ μή τίς ποτε πάμπαν ἀνὴρ ἀθεμίστιος εἴη,
ἀλλ' ὅ γε σιγῇ δῶρα θεῶν ἔχοι ὅττι διδοῖεν.

Solon 13, 63. Μοῖρα δέ τοι θνητοῖσι καλὸν φέρει ἠδὲ καὶ ἐσθλόν·
δῶρα δ' ἄφυκτα θεῶν γίγνεται ἀθανάτων.

Theognis 444. ἀθανάτων δὲ δόσεις
παντοῖαι θνητοῖσιν ἐπέρχοντ', ἀλλ' ἐπιτολμᾶν
χρὴ δῶρ' ἀθανάτων οἷα διδοῦσιν ἔχειν.

„ 591. τολμᾶν χρὴ τὰ διδοῦσι θεοὶ θνητοῖσι βροτοῖσι,
ῥηϊδίως δὲ φέρειν ἀμφοτέρων τὸ λάχος.

„ 1033. θεῶν δ' εἱμαρμένα δῶρα
οὐκ ἂν ῥηϊδίως θνητὸς ἀνὴρ προφύγοι.

Hom. Γ. 64. μή μοι δῶρ' ἐρατὰ πρόφερε χρυσέης Ἀφροδίτης (cf. Theogn. 1383)
οὔτοι ἀπόβλητ' ἐστι θεῶν ἐρικυδέα δῶρα
ὅσσα κεν αὐτοὶ δῶσιν, ἑκὼν δ' οὐκ ἄν τις ἕλοιτο.

Soph. *fr.* 879. θεῶν τὸ δῶρον τοῦτο· χρὴ δ' ὅσ' ἂν θεοὶ
διδῶσι φεύγειν μηδέν,' ὦ τέκνον, ποτέ.

*h. Cer.* 147, 216. θεῶν μὲν δῶρα καὶ ἀχνύμενοί περ ἀνάγκῃ
τέτλαμεν ἄνθρωποι.

Aesch. *Pers.* 249. ὅμως δ' ἀνάγκη πημονὰς βροτοῖς φέρειν
θεῶν διδόντων.

Aesch. *Theb.* 706. θεῶν διδόντων οὐκ ἂν ἐκφύγοις κακά.
Eur. *Hipp.* 1433. ἄκων γὰρ ὤλεσάς νιν· ἀνθρώποισι δὲ
θεῶν διδόντων εἰκὸς ἐξαμαρτάνειν.
Soph. *Phil.* 1317. ἀνθρώποισι τὰς μὲν ἐκ θεῶν
τύχας δοθείσας ἔστ' ἀναγκαῖον φέρειν·
ὅσοι δ' ἑκουσίοισιν ἔγκεινται βλάβαις...

so Hom. ζ. 190, Hes. *Op.* 717, Eur. *Alc.* 1070, *Hel.* 662, *fr.* 491, Nymphodorus *ap.* Ath. vi. 265.

I give so long a history to show how familiar were the thought and phrase of which the note betrays no recognition. Knowledge appreciating the proverbial expression is a better thing in my view than the false literary opinion that sees in διδόντων 'a last touch of Eteocles' irony.'

Later in the play the notion is again expressed by the poet and again missed by his Editor. The central idea of the play is the accomplishment of the curse uttered by Oedipus upon Eteocles and Polynices, that they should one day divide their possessions σιδαρονόμῳ χερί (l. 770 *sqq.*). That has now been brought to pass in the death of the two at each other's hand; and the Chorus, perceiving the fulfilment of the curse, dwells upon the irony of their fate in many a phrase of bitter ambiguity. See ll. 890—932. 'They have so divided their possessions as to get an equal share (*in the grave*) . . . *one in blood* are they indeed.'

929. ἔχουσι μοῖραν λαχόντες ὦ μελέοι
διοσδότων ἀχέων [= 918 διατομαῖς οὐ φίλαις]
ὑπὸ δὲ σώματι γᾶς
πλοῦτος ἄβυσσος ἔσται.

'They have got their portion—*of god-given woe*, . .' Or διοσδότων ἀχέων may be dependent on ὦ μελέοι, as Paley prefers; in which case μοῖραν alone bears the irony, in the double sense of 'share' and 'fate': 'they have obtained their *portion*, their *lot*.' Either way διοσδότων ἀχέων is 'god-sent woe' as

Pind. *fr.* 42. εἰ δέ τις ἀνθρώποισι θεόσδοτος ἄτα
προστύχῃ, ταύταν σκότει κρύπτειν ἔοικεν.

(v. Bergk and cf. Archil. *fr.* 10.)

ἀχέων. Unless—a possibility not to be overlooked—this ἆχος is an unknown (perhaps local) word, it must be an error; ἄχος *woe* suits neither the metre nor the sense. The sense refuses both ἀχθέων (Hermann) and ἀλγέων (Blomfield). The word must be descriptive of the royal property or inheritance—διόσδοτος, because the right of kings (διοτρεφεῖς βασιλῆες) are especially the gift of Zeus. Perhaps ἀρχέων, genitive of ἀρχαί *sovereignty, realm*: there is nothing improbable in the use of such an 'epic' form in the composite and irregular language of tragic lyrics.

Since ἄχος, ἄλγος, ἄχθος are constantly confused in MSS. ἀχθέων or ἀλγέων (which is preferable according to the epic use: ἄλγεα are bestowed by other gods and, Hom. B. 375, Σ. 431, Ω. 241, δ. 722, by Zeus) might easily be substituted for ἀχέων, if οὐ φίλαις is right in 918. But ἄχος *woe* does not suit the sense, and the sense refuses both ἀχθέων and ἀλγέων!

For δοῦναι, δωρεῖσθαι ἐπιτίμια see Porson on Eur. *Hec.* 1070. Upon these phrases there is no need to enlarge, but I may take this occasion of remarking upon a note of Dr. Verrall's on

Eur. *Med.* 127. τὰ δ' ὑπερβάλλοντ'
οὐδένα καιρὸν [δύναται θνητοῖς]
μείζους δ' ἄτας, ὅταν ὀργίσθῃ
δαίμων οἴκοις, ἀπέδωκεν.

I punctuate thus (and not δαίμων, οἴκοις ἀπέδωκεν) because I cannot find a clear example of ἀποδοῦναί τινι, *to inflict retributively on a person*. . .

So Mr. A. E. Housman (*Classical Review* iv. 1 and 2, Feb. 1890):

Before Mr. Verrall editors used to punctuate ὅταν ὀργίσθῃ δαίμων, οἴκοις ἀπ.; but as ἀποδιδόναι means to pay and not to inflict a penalty this cannot be.

It seems then to be worth quoting

Hes. *Theog.* 221. οὐδέ ποτε λήγουσι θεαὶ δεινοῖο χόλοιο,
πρίν γ' ἀπὸ τῷ δώωσι κακὴν ὄπιν, ὅστις
ἁμάρτῃ.

Plut. *Mor.* 551 E ἐὰν δ' ἐπιμένωσι, καὶ τούτοις ἀπέδωκε
τὴν δικην (ὁ θεός).

*Theb.* 1000. στυγῶν γὰρ ἐχθροὺς θάνατον εἵλετ' ἐν πόλει
ἱερῶν πατρῴων ὅσιος ὢν μομφῆς ἄτερ
τέθνηκεν οὗπερ τοῖς νέοις θνῄσκειν καλόν.

οἷσπερ ὀρνέοις θνῄσκειν καλόν *with such augury as makes death fair.* With ὀρνέοις here contrast the grim irony of πετηνῶν ὑπ' οἰωνῶν in *v.* 1011. παρὰ τὸ εἷς οἰωνὸς ἄριστος ἀμύνεσθαι Schol. . .—I have ventured to place this correction in the text, as the note cited appears to make it absolutely certain. In the MS. reading there is nothing even remotely suggesting the highly peculiar expression which the scholium cites as the model of it. The cause of error was probably the resemblance of letters in οἷσπΕΡΟΡνέοις, which became οἷσπερ νέοις, and was then patched up as we find it. . . The form ὄρνεον for ὄρνις, though rare in poetry, is ancient and Homeric (*Il.* 13. 64), which would be sufficient recommendation to Aeschylus. Apart from the schol. the MS. reading might be suspected if not condemned on its own demerits: patriotism is not honourable in *the young* only; and Aeschylus would have written νέοις, not τοῖς νέοις.

τέθνηκεν οἰωνοῖσιν οἷς θνῄσκειν καλὸν might have borne argument; but I will not dwell upon the judgment that does not hesitate to give to ὀρνέοις, a word which occurs nowhere in tragedy, a special sense which the word bears nowhere in Greek. But 'patriotism,' it is urged, 'is not honourable in the young alone.' It is not; nor is it merely patriotism that is here spoken of; nor is *honourable* the only meaning of καλον

By the Greeks counsel was regarded as proper to the old, action to the young: μόχθος γὰρ οὐδεὶς τοῖς νέοις σκῆψιν φέρει (Eur. *I. T.* 122).

Harpocrat. Ἔργα νέων. τοῦτο καὶ Ὑπερείδης ἐν τῷ κατ' Αὐτοκλέους Ἡσιόδου φησὶν εἶναι. παροιμία τίς ἐστιν ἣν ἀνέγραψε καὶ Ἀριστοφάνης ὁ γραμματικὸς οὕτως ἔχουσαν
Ἔργα νέων, βουλαὶ δὲ μέσων, εὐχαὶ δὲ γερόντων.

Eur. *fr.* 508. παλαιὸς αἶνος· ἔργα μὲν νεωτέρων
βουλαὶ δ' ἔχουσι τῶν γεραιτέρων κράτος.

as Nestor says:

Hom. Δ. 321. εἰ τότε κοῦρος ἔα, νῦν αὖτέ με γῆρας ὀπάζει·
ἀλλὰ καὶ ὣς ἱππεῦσι μετέσσομαι ἠδὲ κελεύσω

βουλῇ καὶ μυθοῖσι, τὸ γὰρ γέρας ἐστι γερόντων.
αἰχμὰς δ' αἰχμάσσουσι νεώτεροι, . .

and of actions war in chief:

Eur. *fr.* 1052. νεανίας γὰρ ὅστις ὢν Ἄρη στυγεῖ
κόμη μόνον καὶ σάρκες, ἔργα δ' οὐδαμοῦ.

The exhortations to battle of Tyrtaeus, as that attributed by Stobaeus to Callinus (*fr.* 1), are addressed expressly to the young. This thought alone might sufficiently explain the use in reference to Eteocles of the words τοῖς νέοις. But we need not rest with this. It will not be necessary for me to show how keenly the Greeks felt the bitterness of an early death. But to die young in battle for one's country that they held to be καλόν.

Tyrtaeus 10, 1. τεθνάμεναι γὰρ καλὸν ἐπὶ προμάχοισι πεσόντα
ἄνδρ' ἀγαθὸν περὶ ᾗ πατρίδι μαρνάμενον . . .
15. ὦ νέοι, ἀλλὰ μάχεσθε παρ' ἀλλήλοισι μένοντες, . . .
19. τοὺς δὲ παλαιοτέρους ὧν οὐκέτι γούνατ' ἐλαφρά,
μὴ καταλείποντες φεύγετε, τοὺς γεραιούς·
αἰσχρὸν γὰρ δὴ τοῦτο, μετὰ προμάχοισι πεσόντα
κεῖσθαι πρόσθε νέων ἄνδρα παλαιότερον, . . .
27. νέοισι δὲ πάντ' ἐπέοικεν
ὄφρ' ἐρατῆς ἥβης ἀγλαὸν ἄνθος ἔχῃ.
ἀνδράσι μὲν θηητὸς ἰδεῖν ἐρατὸς δὲ γυναιξίν,
ζωὸς ἐών, καλὸς δ' ἐν προμάχοισι πεσών.

the last part of which is after

Hom. X. 71. νέῳ δέ τε πάντ' ἐπέοικεν
Ἀρηικταμένῳ, δεδαιγμένῳ ὀξέι χαλκῷ,

κεῖσθαι· πάντα δὲ καλὰ θανόντι περ ὅττι φανήῃ·
ἀλλ' ὅτε δὴ πολιόν τε κάρη πολιόν τε γένειον
αἰδῶ τ' αἰσχύνωσι κύνες κταμένοιο γέροντος,
τοῦτο δὴ οἴκτιστον πέλεται δειλοῖσι βροτοῖσιν.

Tyrtaeus 12, 1. οὔτ' ἂν μνησαίμην οὔτ' ἐν λόγῳ ἄνδρα τιθείμην . .

9. οὐδ' εἰ πᾶσαν ἔχοι δύναμιν πλὴν θουρίδος ἀλκῆς.
οὐ γὰρ ἀνὴρ ἀγαθὸς γίγνεται ἐν πολέμῳ,
εἰ μὴ τετλαίη μὲν ὁρῶν φόνον αἱματόεντα
καὶ δηΐων ὀρέγοιτ' ἐγγύθεν ἱστάμενος.
ἥδ' ἀρετή, τόδ' ἄεθλον ἐν ἀνθρώποισιν ἄριστον
κάλλιστον τε φέρειν γίγνεται ἀνδρὶ νέῳ.

23. ὃς δ' αὖτ' ἐν προμάχοισι πεσὼν φίλον ὤλεσε θυμόν . .

27. τὸν δ' ὀλοφύρονται μὲν ὁμῶς νέοι ἠδὲ γέροντες,
ἀργαλέῳ τε πόθῳ πᾶσα κέκηδε πόλις·
καὶ τύμβος καὶ παῖδες ἐν ἀνθρώποις ἀρίσημοι
καὶ παίδων παῖδες καὶ γένος ἐξοπίσω·
οὐδέ ποτε κλέος ἐσθλὸν ἀπόλλυται οὐδ' ὄνομ' αὐτοῦ,
ἀλλ' ὑπὸ γῆς περ ἐὼν γίγνεται ἀθάνατος,
ὅντιν' ἀριστεύοντα μένοντά τε μαρνάμενόν τε
γῆς πέρι καὶ παίδων θοῦρος Ἄρης ὀλέσῃ.

It is by these passages, I think, that the expression in our line is to be understood : 'he has died where for the young to die is fair.' It is not only *honourable* for a young man so to die, though honourable of course it is; but a young man's death, *ἀεκὲς* generally, is *beautiful* and *seemly* when in battle for his native land. This sentiment I cannot but feel to be natural and in place as applied to the death of young Eteocles. The schol. refers to the line of Homer only as the most famous praise of fight in defence of one's country. The quotation is so familiar that there is no need for him to finish it. The argument that for 'the young' generally Aeschylus would have νέοις without the article is sufficiently criticised at p. 57.

A few remarks may be added upon

*Theb.* 1000. στυγῶν γὰρ ἐχθροὺς θάνατον εἵλετ' ἐν πόλει.

In the first place, over στυγῶν in M is written εἴργων δηλονότι, whence Wakefield, Dobree, Hartung etc. read στέγων. στέγειν is elsewhere explained by εἴργειν or ἀπείργειν, as at *Theb.* 202, *Supp.* 141. I hesitate only because of the presence of δηλονότι, which usually signifies *subaudi* as *e.g.* at *Cho.* 108 . . τοῖσιν εὔφροσιν] sch. M . . . τοῖς εὖ φρονοῦσι τῷ 'Αγαμέμνονι δηλονότι. It could not indeed have that signification here, but it is rarely used with a mere explanatory synonym. The nearest approach to such use that I have found in the Medicean scholia to Aeschylus is *Cho.* 110 πρῶτον μὲν αὑτὴν (factum ex αὐτὴν) χὤστις Αἴγισθον στυγεῖ] σεαυτὴν δηλονότι κἀκεῖνον ὅστις Αἴγισθον στυγεῖ. Dr. Verrall's arguments against στέγων are that the sense of 'holding off the foe' is very doubtful, and that 'στυγῶν is thoroughly characteristic of ancient sentiment and should on no account be changed.' I cannot feel any objection to the use of στέγειν in this sense, though it does not elsewhere occur in the best authors. The following references I owe to the *Thesaurus*: Polyb. 3, 53, 2 οὗτοι ἔστεξαν τὴν ἐπιφορὰν τῶν βαρβάρων: *id.* 18, 8, 4 οὐ δυναμένους στέγειν τὴν τῆς φάλαγγος ἔφοδον: cf. Diod. xi. 32. The best support I have yet found is in an epigram of Parmenio (*A.P.* ix. 304):

τὸν γαίης καὶ πόντου ἀμειφθείσασι κελεύθοις
ναύτην ἠπείρου, πεζοπόρον πελάγους,
ἐν τρίσσαις δοράτων ἑκατοντάσιν ἔστεγεν ἄρης
Σπάρτης.

It is hard to see any point in ἐν πόλει, but θάνατον εἵλετο, *chose death*, might be defended by Aristotle's explanation of ἀνδρεία: ἀνδρείας δέ ἐστι . . . τὸ μᾶλλον αἱρεῖσθαι τεθνάναι *ἢ αἰσχρῶς διασωθῆναι*, (as Isocr. *πρὸς Νικοκλ.* 22 *b ἐὰν δ' ἀναγκασθῇς κινδυνεύειν, αἱροῦ καλῶς τεθνάναι μᾶλλον ἢ ζῆν αἰσχρῶς*), and by an epigram of Damagetus (*A.P.* vii. 231), which is applicable to the whole passage:

*ὧδ' ὑπὲρ 'Αμβρακίας ὁ βοαδρόμος ἀσπίδ' ἀείρας*
*τεθνάμεν ἢ φεύγειν εἵλετ' 'Αρισταγόρας,*
*υἱὸς ὁ Θευπόμπου· μὴ θαῦμ' ἔχε· Δωρικὸς ἀνὴρ*
*πατρίδος, οὐχ ἥβας ὀλλυμένας ἀλέγει.*

I have said that Dr. Verrall appears to be bent on retaining at any cost exactly the text of M. He is quite justified in acting upon the general opinion that this is the sole independent authority for the text of Aeschylus. But when he retains and defends the readings of M in all smallest details, he is acting upon an opinion which could not be held by any one with a scholar's knowledge of Greek and of MS. errors. No one with that knowledge could deny that the text of M is very faulty. The extremities to which Dr. Verrall carries his superstitious belief in the integrity of M may be seen throughout this criticism. I will add a couple of illustrations:

*Theb.* 721. *ἐπεὶ δ' ἂν αὐτοκτόνως* *στρ.*
*αὐτοδάικτοι θάνωσι, . .*
725. *τίς ἂν καθαρμοὺς πόροι,*
*τίς ἄν σφε λούσειεν; ὦ πόνοι δόμων*
*νέοι παλαιοῖσι συμμιγεῖς κακοῖς.*

*παλαιγενῆ γὰρ λέγω* *αντ.*
*παρβασίαν ὠκύποινον*

721. so Triclinius. M *αὐτοκτόνωσιν*, the letters of which Dr. Verrall retains, retaining

*ἐπεὶ δ' ἂν αὐτοκτονῶσιν*
*αὐτοδάικτοι θάνωσι,*

*But when by kindred murderers kinsmen are murderously slain.* The reference as the sequel shows, is to the parricide of Laius, which entailed on the house the curse now being fulfilled. The subject is general, *men.* For a similar 'riming' effect in parallel clauses see *vv.* 895, 896.—*αὐτοκτόνως* Triclinius, for metre. but the adverb is not satisfactory, and see the *Appendix.*

We have seen enough of the Appendix on metre: but is it metre alone that supports Triclinius' emendation? Dr. Verrall gives no literal rendering of his text, but the remark about 'parallel clauses' shows that he translates, 'but when (men) do kindred murder, (and) die slain by kinsmen'; a pretty omission of connecting particle! I think I need not argue against the statement that 'the reference, as the sequel shows, is to' Oedipus' parricide of Laius, 'which entailed on the house the curse' of Oedipus. The reference is of course to Eteocles and Polynices who slay each other *αὐτοκτόνως*. 'The adverb,' says Dr. Verrall, 'is not satisfactory.' Why so, without a reason? Having it in

*Ag.* 1635. *δρᾶσαι τόδ' ἔργον οὐκ ἔτλης αὐτοκτόνως*

according to one meaning of *αὐτοκτόνος*, why may we not have it here according to another equally common meaning of the adjective? It is this final calamity of which the Chorus exclaim '*ὦ πόνοι δόμων νέοι*, entangled in the sins of ancient days! that ancient transgression of Laius . . .'

In the following passage all the copies agree in giving *προσάψαι*:

*Ag.* 1564. *τίς ἂν γονὰν ἀραῖον ἐκβάλοι δόμων;*
*κεκόλληται γένος προσάψαι.*

1565. *It is a sort that sticketh fast*, literally, 'the kind is glued for the fixing on,' where 'fixing on' is *transitive*. . . . . *προσάψαι* is an explanatory infinitive. . .—*πρὸς ἄτᾳ* Blomfield, 'the family is fastened (glued) to calamity,' a suggestion not deserving the vogue which it has obtained. . .

We shall see much more of the same sort in the *Agamemnon*.

'My own few corrections,' says Dr. Verrall, 'are chiefly in the division of the letters into words and in the accentuation. It is needless to say that these in any Greek MS., if the author dates from the time of uncial writing, are strictly part of the commentary, not of the text.' (*Theb.* Introd. p. xxxiv.) That is true, of course; only it would really seem as if Dr. Verrall had sought to change accentuation and division wherever he could, without regard to probability. Some examples of this we have already noticed (see p. 82 for *Theb.*

23, p. 84 for *Theb.* 601), and in the *Agamemnon* we shall notice more. I will only add one here:

*Theb.* 269. ET. *ἐγὼ δ' ἐπ' ἄνδρας ἓξ ἐμοὶ σὺν ἑβδόμῳ*
*ἀντηρέτας ἐχθροῖσι τὸν μέγαν τρόπον*
*εἰς ἑπτατειχεῖς ἐξόδους τάξω μολών.*

So M. Dr. Verrall reads '*ἐπανδρὰς* aor. part. from *ἐπαναδιδράσκω, I will haste back again.*' To the rest of the note I would refer the reader. Dr. Verrall records Canter's conjecture *ἐπάρχους*, but Paley's *φῶτας* and Blomfield's *ἐγὼ δέ γ'* (which I believe to be right) he does not mention.

But in the lacunae of M (*Ag.* 323—1050, 1159—1673) Dr. Verrall follows another superstition, treating f as a hardly fallible copy of M. 'Fortunately,' he says, 'it appears to represent M very closely. Cases such as *v.* 23, where the genuine *φάος* of M could not be recognised in the conjectural supplement (*νῦν φῶς*) of f, are rare.'

The faithfulness of f can be estimated only by comparing its readings with those of M. Having done this in the *Agamemnon* through the first 169 lines I find in these no fewer than 52 discrepancies. Such being the case, I cannot agree in the view that f represents M very closely. It is worth mentioning however that, while for a full apparatus we go of course to Hermann, Wecklein, giving only such readings of f as may tend to the immediate improvement of the text, records only 15 of these 52. Some of the variations within these limits (1—169) may be given to show whether the cases where the true reading of M could not be recognised are as rare as Dr. Verrall says:

| M | f |
|---|---|
| 23. *φάος* | *νῦν φῶς* |
| 26. *σημαίνω* | *σημανῶ* |
| 40. *πριάμω* | *πριάμου* |
| 48. *κλάζοντες* | *κλάγξαντες* |
| 87. *πειθοῖ* | *πυθοῖ* |
| 98. *αἰνεῖν* | *εἰπεῖν* |

| | M | f |
|---|---|---|
| 101. | *φαίνεις* | *φαίνουσ'* |
| 103. | *θυμοφθόρον* | *θυμοβόρον* |
| 122. | *ἐρικύματα* | *ἐρικύμονα* |
| | *φέρματι* | *φέρβοντο* |
| 129. | *ἀρχάς* | *ἀρχούς* |
| 130. | *δ'* | *δ' οὖν* |
| 145, 169. | *αἴλινον αἴλινον* | *αἴλινον* (*semel*) |
| 146. | *τόσσων* | *τόσον* |

In all these places the reading of M holds Dr. Verrall's text. One may venture to doubt whether, if M had been deficient here, Dr. Verrall would in most cases have been able to recognise its readings from those of f. Certainly nothing could be further from his practice than to do so; for in the parts where M fails he cleaves to f through thick and thin, as illustrations will show. Every one knows how liable to confusion are the letters *β*, *η*, *κ*, *υ*, in minuscules from the 9th century to the 12th. The confusion is especially easy in a hand so cursive as that of M:

*Ag.* 878. *ἔμοιγε μὲν δὴ κλαυμάτων ἐπίσσυτοι*
*πηγαὶ κατεσβήκασιν, οὐδ' ἔνι σταγών.*
*ἐν ὀψικοίτοις δ' ὄμμασιν βλάβας ἔχω,*
*τὰς ἀμφί σοι κλαίουσα λαμπτηρουχίας . . .*

f has *κλάβας*, which Dr. Verrall keeps, explaining it thus:

*κλάβας*, *eye-sores.* I do not see reason to reject this word. The representation of the ϝ by *β* is in the Doric and Aeolic dialects frequent and regular (*φάβος* = *φάϝος*, *ὤβεα* = *ὤϝεα* *ᾠά* etc.). From *κλαϝ* (cf. *κλαῦμα*) the regular formation in these dialects would be *κλάβ-α*. . .—The Farnesian editor substitutes *βλάβας*, but M, it is clear, had *κλάβας*, which is not in itself likely to be an error for *βλάβας* and, so far as I can judge, is not open to any suspicion.

The whole note will be found to be of a piece with this; but I need only call attention to the statement that because f has *κλάβας* it is 'clear' that M had it too.

*Ag.* 1007. *οὐδὲ τὸν ὀρθοδαῆ . . .*
*Ζεὺς αὔτ' ἔπαυσεν ἐπ' αὐλαβείᾳ*

is the reading of f (schol. . . ὥστε μὴ ἕτερον βλαβῆναι), though Hermann gave '. . ἐπ' εὐλαβείᾳ Flor.,' h has ἐπ' ἀβλαβείᾳ γε, cod. Vict. ἐπ' εὐλαβείᾳ γε. Dr. Verrall:

I retain under reserve the form αὐλαβείᾳ as given, perhaps rightly by the MS. The initial β of the stem βλαβ- is supposed by some to represent an original ϝ. From ἀϝλαβής the regular Aeolic formation would be αὐλαβής, as αὔρηκτοσ (α-ϝρηκτος) εὐράγη (ε-ϝράγη) in Alcaeus, and the preservation of that form might be due to some literary association.

*Ag.* 1465. μηδ' εἰς Ἑλένην κότον ἐκτρέψῃς.

ἐκτρέχῃς f and no doubt M also: ἐκτρέψῃς (g, h, probably from the margin of M) is a possible correction but not probable. It is more likely that ἐκτρέχῃς covers some unknown word or form, and I have therefore simply printed it as an error.

Nothing can be less doubtful than that ἐκτρέχῃς of f is simply an error. There is no ground whatever for assuming that it was in M also: but whether it was or not, ἐκτρέψῃς of g and h is as certain as any reading can be.

As ἐκτρέπειν ῥέεθρον ἐς Hdt. i. 186, 11, 11, ὕδωρ ἐς Thuc. v. 65, so

Antiphon A. 119, 3: τὴν αὑτοῦ μιαρίαν εἰς ὑμᾶς αὐτοὺς ἐκτρέψαι.

Antiphon A. 123, 26: τὰς συμφορὰς τῶν ἁμαρτόντων εἶναι καὶ μὴ εἰς τοὺς ἀναμαρτήτους ἐκτρέπεσθαι.

Eur. *Supp.* 484. τὸ δυστυχὲς δὲ τοῦτ' ἐς ἄλλον ἐκτρέπει.

So Aesch. *Theb.* 615, Soph. *Aj.* 53.

*Ag.* 1361. ἦ καὶ βίον κτείνοντες ὧδ' ὑπείξομεν.

'Libri κτείνοντες, quod in Farn. ita explicare studuit interpres, ηγουν τροπον τινὰ τῷ θανάτῳ παραδιδοντες τὴν ζωὴν ἡμῶν. Sed nemo non probavit Canteri emendationem τείνοντες.' Hermann.

Dr. Verrall:

βίον κτείνοντες *slaying our life*, i.e. accepting a condition no better than death. Compare the common phrase οὐ βιώσιμον for an intolerable state. This explanation is offered by the *Cod. Farn.* nor does it seem to me impossible.—In any case βίον τείνοντες (Canter) is no solution: any editor finding this would have left it. . .

How οὐ βιώσιμον could be comparable with such a phrase I fail to see.

The value of the last remark will be appreciated when I point out that at *v.* 1295, μακρὰν ἔτεινας, g has ἔκτεινας·

and that is recorded at its place in the margin of Wecklein's text.

*Ag.* 966. τίπτε μοι τόδ' ἐμπέδως
δεῖμα προστατήριον
καρδίας τερασκόπου ποτᾶται;

δεῖγμα f. δεῖμα h.

Dr. Verrall reads δεῖγμα on the ground that

δεῖγμα must have been in M and is presumably right.

the argument being that δεῖγμα, being in f, must therefore have been in M; having been in M, is presumably right. Now whether f is so close a copy that it cannot have erred has been shown. But perhaps it could not have made the mistake of δεῖγμα for δεῖμα? We shall see.

The mistake occurs elsewhere in many places:

[1] Arat. *Phaen.* 629. τὸ δέ οἱ μέγα δεῖμα
κήτεος ἠερόεις ἐπάγει νότος.

'δεῖγμα CI' Bekker.

[1] Dionys. Hal. *A.R.* ii. 20. οἱ δὲ ταραχὰς ἐξαιρούμενοι ψυχῆς καὶ δείματα καὶ δόξας καθαιροῦντες οὐχ ὑγιεῖς.

'δείγματα Euseb.' Sylb.

[1] Dionys. Hal. *A.R.* vii. 68. ταραχαὶ δέ τινες ἐνέπιπτον ἐκ δειμάτων δαιμονίων τῇ πόλει συχναί.

δειγμάτων codd.

[1] Lucian i. 512. ἐλπίδες . . καὶ δείματα καὶ ἄνοιαι καὶ ἡδοναὶ . . .

v. l. δείγματα.

Lyc. *Al.* 225. νυκτίφοιτα δείματα.

'δείγματα Par. E.' Bachmann.

Libanius *Declam.* xxxvii. p. 807. ὁ δὲ τὴν μάχην διηγεῖται, τὴν φάλαγγα, τὸ σύνθημα, τὸ μεταίχμιον, τοὺς φόνους, τὴν δίωξιν· μὴ σύ γε ταῦτα, ὦ παῖ, τὰ ἐκ τοῦ πολέμου δείγματα.

'Var. Lect. διδάγματα, sed legendum δείματα *terrores.* Sic recte *Origeni* contr. Cels. III. p. 457. c. restituit *Delarue* pro δείγματα, et

---

[1] Thesaurus *s. vv.*

*Iuliano* Ep. ad Themist. p. 259. C. Petavius; et plura dat Cl. *Schwebel* ad Onosandr. p. 92.' D. Wyttenbach *Epistola Critica* etc. p. 60, by whom Cobet (*Collect. Crit.* p. 298) found himself anticipated.

Cannot the same mistake have been made by f or by M or by an earlier MS.?

*Ag.* 779. πολλοὶ δὲ βροτῶν τὸ δοκεῖν εἶναι
προτίουσι δίκην παραβάντες.
τῷ δυσπραγοῦντι δ' ἐπιστενάχειν
πᾶς τις ἕτοιμος· δῆγμα δὲ λύπης
οὐδὲν ἐφ' ἧπαρ προσικνεῖται·

δεῖγμα f, δῆγμα Stob. *fl.* 112, 12 and h.

δεῖγμα δὲ κ.τ.λ. *when the display of grief reaches not at all to the heart*... δῆγμα Stobaeus and (presumably by conjecture) *Cod. Farn.*.. But δῆγμα is much too strong a word for the place and consequently spoils the sense. The point is not that the grief does not *wound*, but that there is no grief at all.

Now perhaps of no word is the metaphorical use more common than of δάκνω:

Of *desire*:

Soph. *fr.* 757. ὅτῳ δ' ἔρωτος δῆγμα παιδικοῦ προσῆν.
Aesch. *Ag.* 742. δηξίθυμον ἔρωτος ἄνθος.
Eur. *fr.* 316. πόθῳ δεδηγμένοις.
*Anth. Plan.* 208, Plat. *Pol.* v. 474 C; for more see Valckenaer on Eur. *Hipp.* 1303.

far more often of *pain*, *grief*, *annoyance* and the like. The following examples are grouped, not according to shade of meaning, but roughly according to expression:

Hom. E. 493. δάκε δὲ φρένας Ἕκτορι μῦθος. Eur. *Ph.* 384, *Heracl.* 484.
„ θ. 185. θυμοδακὴς μῦθος. *A.P.* ii. (ἰάμβους). δακέθυμος Simonid. 58 (ἱδρώς), Soph. *Phil.* 705 (ἄτα). Anacreont. 35.
Hes. *Th.* 567. δάκεν δ' ἄρα νειόθι θυμὸν Ζῆν'.
„ *Op.* 451. κραδίην δ' ἔδακ' ἀνδρὸς ἀβουτέω. *A.P.* vii. 115, Ar. *Ach.* 1.
Simonid. 167. ἀνδρῶν ἀχλαίνων ἔδακε φρένας (Βορέης). *Batrachom.* 181.
Aesch. *Ag.* 1471. κράτος καρδιόδηκτον. Eur. *Hec.* 233.

Theognis 910. δάκνομαι ψυχήν. Soph. *Ant.* 317, Eur. *Med.* 111.

Aesch. *Pers.* 848. ἥδε συμφορὰ δάκνει. Eur. *fr.* 572, Lycophr. *Al.* 954.

„ *Eum.* 641. ταύτην τοιαύτην εἶπον ὡς δηχθῇ λεώς. Soph. *Phil.* 378, *Tr.* 254, Eur. *Med.* 1333, Ar. *Ach.* 18.

Soph. *Tr.* 1117, *Aj.* 1119, *Phil.* 1358, Ar. *Eq.* 1372, *Vesp.* 253, *Com. fr. adesp.* 114, 666, Menander 282, 365, Leon. *A.P.* vii. 648, Eur. *Hipp.* 692, *I.A.* 380, 687, *Med.* 812, 1359, *Bacch.* 344, *H.F.* 94, *El.* 240.

Eur. *El.* 290. αἴσθησις γὰρ οὖν
κἀκ τῶν θυραίων πημάτων δάκνει βροτούς.

„ *Alc.* 1103. λύπῃ καρδίαν δηχθήσομαι. *Rhes.* 587.

Hdt. vii. 16. ἐμὲ . . οὐ τοσοῦτο ἔδακε ἡ λύπη . .

From these materials (which might be very largely increased from [1] prose) it may be satisfactorily judged whether 'δῆγμα is much too strong a word for the place.' δάκνω, δῆγμα are merely equivalent to λυπῶ, λύπη, the words regularly given as their synonyms in lexicons and scholia. δῆγμα λύπης is a periphasis for λύπη just as δῆγμα ἔρωτος in Soph. *fr.* 757 (quoted above) is a periphrasis for ἔρως. The same MS. error is found in Lucian i. 24 οὔτε κίνησις ὁμοία πρόσεστιν οὔτε ψυχῆς δεῖγμά τι, ἀλλὰ τέρψις ἄλλως καὶ παιδιὰ τὸ πρᾶγμα, where Cobet (*q.v.*) *Var. Lectt.* p. 142 shows that δῆγμα is to be read.

*Ag.* 1445. ὁ μὲν γὰρ οὕτως, ἡ δέ τοι . .
κεῖται φιλήτωρ τοῦδ',
[so g and h, f has φιλήτως]

ὁ μὲν γὰρ οὕτως, ἡ δὲ . . . κεῖται φιλήτως τοῦδε *for he lies as ye see, and she also like his beloved*, literally 'she lies loveably to him (as he to her).' The construction of τοῦδε is modelled on the genitive of *relation in place*, as in Thuc. I. 36. 2 τῆς Ἰταλίας καὶ Σικελίας καλῶς παράπλου κεῖται (ἡ Κέρκυρα), Herod. 2. 112 τοῦ Ἡφαιστηΐου πρὸς νότον ἄνεμον κείμενον . . .—Here again f has faithfully preserved the reading of M.

*O soul of Sir John Cheke!*—
For the word φιλήτωρ see Blomfield and Hermann.

[1] A considerable list is given by Gataker on Marc. Anton. xi. 18.

Of Cod. a Wecklein says (*Praef.* p. ix.): Codex Marcianus 468 (a) ad paucos quorum liber Mediceus iacturam fecit versus pertinet, sed libro Florentino praestat et in v. 348 meliorem lectionem ἀπαλλαχθέντες conservavit. Yet there Dr. Verrall reads ἀπαλλαγέντες with f, remarking

ἀπαλλαχθέντες a. Both forms are good.

And so they are; but of the two readings ἀπαλλαχθέντες is the better, because in late Greek the second aorist passive was generally preferred to the first, no doubt as being easier of pronunciation. This same variation is found at

Eur. *Phoen* 975. φεῦγ' ὡς τάχιστα τῆσδ' ἀπαλλαχθεὶς χθονός·

ἀπαλλαχθείς [A] et a pr. m. B, bc: ἀπαλλαγείς E *C*, -ῇς F.

where Valckenaer says: . . . Attici quidam recentiores emollitam sequentes Dialectum, in plerisque secundos istos aoristos praetulerunt, qui faciliores erant pronuntiatu, atque aures iucundius incidebant; sed Ionas et veteres Atticos contra primos aoristos passivos frequentasse qui quidem hos attente legerint nunquam dubitabunt. *Eustathius* in *Il. E* [40] p. 395, 25 [519. 41] Σημείωσαι, inquit, ὅτι φιλεῖ Ὅμηρος Στρεφθέντα λέγειν οὐ μὴν στραφέντα· ὡς καὶ Εὐριπίδης Θρεφθῆναι εἶπεν ἀντὶ τοῦ τραφῆναι. προτιμῶνται γὰρ οἱ σοφοὶ τὴν καίριον τραχυφωνίαν τῆς ἀκαίρου λειότητος· ὡς δηλοῖ καὶ τὸ Βρεχθῆναι τὴν γῆν παρὰ Δίωνι, ἀντὶ τοῦ βραχῆναι, καὶ τὸ Θαφθεῖσι παρ' Ἡροδότῳ, ἀντὶ τοῦ ταφεῖσι, καὶ χλανιδίων ἔσω κρυφθεὶς παρ' Εὐριπίδῃ, καὶ Βλαφθεὶς παρὰ τῷ ποιητῇ, ἀντὶ τοῦ βλαβείς. In Eclogis *Thomae Mag.* tres quatuorve sunt in universum huius generis observationes, ex Atticista veteri transcriptae: βλαφθέντες, δόκιμον· τὸ δὲ βλαβέντες κοινόν. καταλεχθεὶς κάλλιον ἢ καταλεγείς. Συλλεχθεὶς κάλλιον ἢ συλλεγείς. [1] Φανθεὶς καὶ Ἀποφανθεὶς Ἀττικοὶ οὐ φανεὶς οὐδὲ ἀποφανείς. . . .

[1] Wecklein *Studien zu Aeschylus* p. 17 note, on *Ag.* 101 τότε δ' ἐκ θυσίων ἀγανὰ φαίνεις . . says: Die Lesart des Med. φαίνεις, wofür die Lesart des Flor. φαίνουσ' nur metrische Correktur ist, weist auf φανθεῖσ' hin, welches schon [Pauw] Welcker und Panzerbieter vorgeschlagen

So sch. Eur. *Hipp.* 1181 (1170 K) ἀπαλλαχθεὶς γόων] ἀπαλλαγείς B. Rhes. 463 εἰ τοῦ παρόντος τοῦδ᾽ ἀπαλλαχθεὶς κακοῦ] sch. . . εἰ τοῦ παρόντος ἀπαλλαγεὶς κακοῦ. .
We should expect therefore in MSS. to find the heavier forms wrongly ousted by the weaker. As we do frequently find; *e.g.* at

Eur. *Bacch.* 948 κρύψῃ σὺ κρύψιν ἥν σε κρυφῆναι χρεὼν

is the MS. reading, while the Christus Patiens 1506 has [1]κρυβῆναι, the Aldine ed. rightly κρυφθῆναι. So Christ. Pat. 281 = Eur. *Med.* 1285.

'Duo MSS. Herodoti II. 81 ταφῆναι pro θαφθῆναι' [2]Porson, Eur. *Phoen.* 986 (l. c.). At *Theb.* 514, for προσταχθέντα, ed. Rob. has προσταγέντα.

That of all this Dr. Verrall knows nothing is explicitly shown by his note on

*Ag.* 736 ἐκ θεοῦ δ᾽ ἱερεύς τις ἄ-
τας δόμοις προσετράφη.

[προσετρέφθη Heath, προσεθρέφθη Porson; Dr. Verrrall προσετράφθη.]

προσετράφθη: *it was directed* by the unconscious agency of those who captured it. For the Homeric form see τρέπω προστρέπω and compare πολέα for πολλά in *v.* 724. . . The omission of θ, a kind of error always liable to happen in heavy combinations of consonants (cf. *v.* 1186 σύμφογγος for σύμφθογγος), was here facilitated by the exceptional form.—προσεθρέφθη Heath and many texts: but (1) the supposed corruption of this familiar form, protected by metre, to προσετράφη, is incredible; (2) προσεθρέφθη δόμοις is not grammatical Greek nor indeed a significant expression at all; and (3) the stolen whelp was not 'reared by' the god.—The verb προστρέφω, though possible, is not apparently extant, which is not surprising, as it would not, except in a very peculiar context, be required or admissible.

θρεφθῆναι, which is here called a familiar form, is found at

haben; φανθεῖσ᾽ ging in φανεῖσ᾽ über *nach der Gewohnheit der Abschreiber den ersten Aor. Passiv in den gebräuchlicheren zweiten Aorist zu verwandeln* (z. B. Ag. 736 προσεθρέφθη in προσετράφη, Eur. Hec. 335 ῥιφθέντες in ῥιφέντες). . .

[1] Sch. Eur. *Hec.* 897 οἱ Ἀττικοὶ ἐκρύφθην γράφουσιν, οἱ δὲ πεζογράφοι ἐκρύβην.

[2] Ellendt *Lex. Soph.* s.v. ἀπαλλάσσω refers to both Porson and Valckenaer.

Hes. *Theog.* 192, 198, [1]Empedocles 139, Eur. *Hec.* 349, 596, Nicand. *Alex.* 231, Epigr. *ap.* Strabon. x. 463 (τρεφθέντα MS., θρεφθέντα Brunck); 'in Attic prose, only Plat. *Politicus* 310' (Veitch); in Attic inscriptions once (Meisterhans p. 150) and that in verse (Kaibel 71, 5). There was no ground therefore for assuming it to have been familiar to a scribe.

Of the two places where the form is found in Tragedy, one is

Eur. *Hec.* 349. ἔπειτ' ἐθρέφθην ἐλπίδων καλῶν ὕπο.

'ἐτραφειν (η above ει) sic Cod. A' Beck.

Sch., ἔπειτα ἐτράφην ὑπὸ καλῶν ἐλπίδων . . ὁ δὲ νοῦς καὶ ἡ σύνταξις οὕτως, ἐτράφην. . .

the other is

Eur. *Hec.* 596. ἔχει γέ τοί τι καὶ τὸ θρεφθῆναι καλῶς.

[2] 'τραφῆναι c cf. Eustathium in *Il.* p. 519' K.

Sch. B. Gr. θρεφθῆναι] ἀνατραφῆναι. See the sch.

Therefore in each case 'this familiar form, protected by metre' has been [3]ousted by the 2nd aorist. With knowledge of the matter we should expect to find τραφῆναι (or ἀνατραφῆναι) in the schol.; we should be prepared for a variant τραφῆναι in the text. But if we have not that knowledge, we shall not call such a corruption 'incredible' without moving one step towards ascertaining its credibility.

I proceed with the rest of the note: "The stolen whelp was not 'reared by' the god." This implies that ἐκ θεοῦ προσεθρέφθη could only mean 'reared by.' Dr. Verrall is unaware, then, that ἐκ θεοῦ may be used like ἐκ θεῶν, θεόθεν

[1] At Emped. 65 θρεφθεῖσα is read by Stein, Panzerbieter, Schneidewin for θρυφθεῖσα.

[2] Wecklein *Studien zu Euripides* p. 311: 'Hierher gehört auch die Herstellung des geläufigen zweiten aor. pass. wie ἀπαλλαγεὶς Phoen. 902 für ἀπαλλαχθεὶς, Hec. 600 τραφῆναι (unmetrisch) für θρεφθῆναι . . .' with a note 'Auch Aesch. Ag. 336 ist aus dem cod. Ven. ἀπαλλαχθέντες herzustellen. Vergl. dazu meine *Studien zu Aesch.* S. 17 Note.'

[3] In a fragment (4) of Dicaeogenes in Stob. *fl.* 79, 6:

αὐτὸς τραφεὶς δὲ τῶν φυτευσάντων ὕπο

('δὲ τραφεὶς] τραφεὶς δὲ A. ut edidit Grotius. δὲ θρεφθεὶς Porsonus *Advers.* p. 304. et Wakefield.' Gaisford), Porson's reading is only of equal probability.

(which in scholia are often explained θεῶν βουλήσει) in the sense *under the influence of . . . , by the will of . . .*, etc. The following examples will show how all these phrases are similarly used:

Hom. P. 101. ἐκ θεόφιν πολεμίζει.
„ Ω. 617. θεῶν ἐκ κήδεα πέσσει.
Hes. *Scut.* 22. ἔργον ὅ οἱ Διόθεν θέμις ἦεν.
Pind. *P.* xi. 50. θεόθεν ἐραίμαν καλῶν.
Aesch. *Cho.* 1004. ὀλοίμην πρόσθεν ἐκ θεῶν ἄπαις.
„ *Theb.* 23. καλῶς τὰ πλείω πόλεμος ἐκ θεῶν κυρεῖ.
Eur. *Or.* 357. θεόθεν πράξας ἅπερ ηὔχου.
„ *Heracl.* 794. πράξας ἐκ θεῶν κάλλιστα δή.
„ *Andr.* 670. Ἑλένη δ' ἐμόχθησ' οὐχ ἑκοῦσ' ἀλλ' ἐκ θεῶν.
Amphis *fr.* 21. ἐκ θεῶν τε δυστυχής.
Eur. *Med.* 1273. Ἰνὼ μανεῖσαν ἐκ θεῶν.
Ap. Rh. iv. 413. θεόθεν δὲ κακὰς ἤνυσσα μενοινάς.
Philodem. *A.P.* v. 112. ἐμάνην· ἐκ τίνος; οὐχὶ θεοῦ;
(so Eur. *Hipp.* 140 ἔνθεος . . εἴτ' ἐκ Πανὸς εἴθ' Ἑκάτας).
Pind. *P.* x. 20. μὴ φθονεραῖς ἐκ θεῶν μεταροπίαις ἐπικύρσαιεν.
Hdt. i. 34. ἔλαβε ἐκ θεοῦ νέμεσις μεγάλη Κροῖσον.
Moschus iv. 68. τοιῆσδ' ἐκυρήσαμεν ἐκ θεοῦ αἴσης.
Pind. *O.* x. 10. ἐκ θεοῦ δ' ἀνὴρ σοφαῖς ἀνθεῖ πραπίδεσσιν ὁμοίως.

Thus at

*Theb.* 308. οἰκτρὸν γὰρ πόλιν . .
Ἀΐδᾳ προϊάψαι . . ,
ὑπ' ἀνδρὸς Ἀχαιοῦ θεόθεν
περθομέναν ἀτίμως.

the last phrase is in itself perfectly legitimate, heaven being the remoter influence, the Achaean the immediate instrument. The only objection to which it is open is that it is unsuitable in this place, and that might be maintained. For the Chorus have in the preceding passage 288—307 been *addressing* the gods, and if they be supposed to continue their address, θεόθεν is certainly very clumsy. But Dr. Verrall's reason for objecting to the phrase is very different:

It by no means follows that, because πέρθειν πόλιν θεόθεν is a possible phrase (if it is), a city could be said πέρθεσθαι θεόθεν.

Now, I conceive that a man might be said πέρθειν πόλιν θεόθεν, as ἐκ θεόφιν πολεμίζειν; but it is of course not necessary to assume the possibility of that phrase in order to hold πόλιν θεόθεν περθομένην possible; for which if enough support be not found in the quotations given above, let the following be compared

Soph. *Ant.* 586. οἷς γὰρ ἂν σεισθῇ θεόθεν δόμος.

As for the last remark by which Dr. Verrall tries to excite prejudice against προσεθρέφθη, that 'the verb προστρέφω, though possible, is not apparently extant,' not only is an example quoted by Hase in the *Thesaurus*, but the same example is quoted thence by Dindorf *Lexicon Aeschyleum s.v.* προστρέφω:

Teles (Stob. *fl.* 97, 13) κἂν ἄλλον προστρέφειν.

Hase gives this the sense *innutrio*, which Dindorf also assigns to the word in our passage. In my opinion προσ- means rather *in addition*, and I understand in the fragment of Teles *to keep another as well*, and in our passage *was reared as an additional inmate in the house*. That is all I wish to say upon the remaining objection, that 'προσεθρέφθη δόμοις is not grammatical Greek nor indeed a significant expression at all.'

Dr. Verrall's belief in the infallibility of f does not hinder him from heretically deserting it in favour of g (see *Ag.* 1594), or from paying a reverent regard to what g offers:

*Ag.* 1544. ἀλλ' Ἰφιγένειά νιν ἀσπασίως
θυγάτηρ, ὡς χρή,
πατέρ' ἀντιάσασα πρὸς ὠκύπορον
πόρθμευμ' ἀχέων
περὶ χεῖρα βαλοῦσα φιλήσει.

'ἀχέων fh. ἀχείῶν (factum ex ἀχαιῶν) g.' W.

ἀχείῶν (originally ἀχαιῶν) g. It is probable therefore that M had ἀχείων. ἀχέων (f) may be accepted provisionally.

Did Dr. Verrall but know, the error of ἀχαιῶν for ἀχέων (which is interesting for more reasons than one) is frequent; as

Aesch. *Supp.* 13. κύδιστ' ἀχαιων (ε above αι) ἐπέκρανε M.

" " 886. ἴυζε καὶ βόα πικρότερ' ἀχέων

Sch. M. καὶ αὐτῶν τῶν ἀχαιῶν (ἐ above αι) πικρότερ' ἴυζε.

(Therefore quite probably it was ἀχαιῶν (ἐ above αι) in M that caused ἀχείῶν in g.)

Soph. *El.* 852. δεινῶν στυγνῶν τ' αχαιων L pr. m.; ἀχέων per ras. L.[Σ]

Euseb. *praep. evang.* xiii. p. 684 quoting Empedocles 388 ἀνδρείων ἀχαιῶν ἀπόκληροι ἀτειρεῖς [ἀχέων Stephanus].

Apollon. Dysc. *de pron.* 381 C quoting Alcaeus *fr.* 105 ἀμμετέρων ἀχαιῶν [ἀχέων Bergk].

cf. Ath. iv. 184 f quoting Ion *fr.* 39 ἐπὶ δ' αὐλὸς ἀλέκτωρ Λύδιον ὕμνον ἀχαιῶν [ἀχέων Emper.].

Schuetz was the first to quote the following passage in illustration of the phrase πόρθμευμ' ἀχέων:

Stob. *ecl. phys.* I. 41, 50. τοῦ δὲ Ἀπολλοδώρου ἐν τῷ εἰκοστῷ περὶ τῶν θεῶν συγγράμματι ὅ ἐστι περὶ τοῦ ᾅδου, τάδε περὶ τῆς Στυγὸς λεγόμενα εὕρομεν (ἀρκτέον γὰρ ἀπὸ τούτων τῆς τε ἐκ τῶν ὀνομάτων παρεμφάσεως οὐ καταφρονητέον)· Ἐκ γὰρ τοιούτων ὁρμώμενοι πιθανῶς καὶ τοὺς ἐν ᾅδου νομιζομένους ποταμοὺς κατωνομάκασιν· Ἀχέροντα μὲν διὰ τὰ ἄχη, ὡς καὶ [1]Μελανιππίδης ἐν Περσεφόνῃ

καλεῖται δ' ἐν κόλποισι γαίας
ἀχαιοῖσι προχέων Ἀχέρων.

[1] Melanippides *fr.* 3 sic vulgo, ἀχεοῖσι VAE. ἄχεα Grotius. ἄχε' ἀνθρώποισι Schneidewin.

ἔτι καὶ [1]Λικύμνιός φησι

μυρίαις παγαῖς δακρύων ἀχέων τε βρύει·

καὶ [2]πάλιν

Ἀχέρων ἄχεα βροτοῖσι πορθμεύει.

In the light of this evidence it will be admitted that ἀχέων in our passage is as certainly right as any reading can ever be. The example will show that it is worth while to study the phenomena of MSS. Dr. Verrall is content to spin theories out of his own head rather than deduce them from the evidence:

*Ag.* 112. ξύμφρονα τὰν γᾶν.

'112—114, quos M omiserat spatio vacuo relicto, addidit m.' W.

ξύμφρονε ταγώ Dindorf. Dr. Verrall prefers τάγα (τάγης) which may be right. His account however is:

The source of error was probably an accidental (or intentional, see on *v.* 1164) doubling of the γ. Hence τάγγα, τάνγα, τὰν γᾶν.

*Ag.* 1164. δυσαγγεῖ τύχᾳ μινυρὰ θρεομένας
θραύματ' ἐμοὶ κλύειν.

δυσαλγεῖ Canter. Dr. Verrall reads δυσᾱγεῖ.

δυσαγεῖ . . . κλύειν *at the breaking misery of her piteous song which shatters me to hear it. . .* δυσαγεῖ from ἀγή *breaking* (ἄγνυμι): cf. δυστυχής, τύχη. The spelling δυσαγγής was probably adopted on purpose, to distinguish δυσᾱγής from δυσᾰγής impious; cf. Ἐριννύς for Ἐρῑνύς and see on *v.* 112.—δυσαλγεῖ (Canter) would not have been so mistaken, and besides the strong metaphor in θραύματα requires something to lead up to it.

Since all the copies have δυσαγγεῖ, that was most probably in M. But from a cursive hand such as M the mistake of δυσαγγεῖ for δυσαλγεῖ might be made with the greatest ease; and it might be made from many earlier hands. Dr. Verrall, however, says it would not have been made. As to this theory of a doubled γ, it is entirely invented. Some letters are constantly found doubled, as λ, σ, ρ, ν, and oftenest μ. These, as labials or sibilants, might be prolonged in pronunciation. Not so the explosive γ. The cause, therefore, being absent, so is the result. γ is not erroneously doubled in MSS.

[1] Licymnius *fr.* 1. [2] id. *fr.* 2.

Dr. Verrall suggests this groundless theory yet again:

*Ag.* 504. τὸν ἀντίον δὲ τοῖσδ' ἀποστέργω λόγον.

where reading ἀποστέγω he says:

The MS. reading may have arisen from a double γγ, but is more probably a deliberate change made by one who did not recognise the meaning of στέγω.

Would any one think it necessary to suppose a deliberate change, if he was aware that στέγω and στέργω are constantly [1]confused in MSS.?

*Ag.* 230. τόθεν τὸ παντότολμον φρονεῖν μετέγνω.
βρότοις θρασύνει γὰρ αἰσχρόμητις
τάλαινα παρακοπὰ πρωτοπήμων.
[M has μετέγνω βροτοῖς·].

So Dr. Verrall reads, without indeed changing one letter of the MS.

..literally, 'for by bloodshed takes (or 'gives') confidence an obstinate delusion,' etc.

which is supposed to mean

*For to put faith in the shedding of blood is an obstinate delusion....* βρότοις: (instrumental dative) the plural (cf. αἵματα) of the Homeric word βρότος *blood...*

Paley follows Klausen in defending βροτοῖς as a 'dative of relation,' with little probability. Spanheim's correction βροτοὺς is generally accepted:

βροτοὺς (Spanheim) is the common reading, but is for many reasons not to be accepted: for (1) it does not account for the MS., (2) the emphasis on βροτοὺς has no point, (3) there is then no excuse for the position of γάρ, and (4) the sense is incomplete, and there is nothing to show what particular delusion is intended.

Because no particular delusion is intended. I pass over this now, since I shall have occasion to speak of this famous thought in treating *Ag.* 396—7.

To account for the MS. is not difficult. It is due first of all to the position of γάρ, which was assumed to be as usual the second word in the clause. βροτοὺς accordingly

[1] See statements of lexicographers quoted by Bachmann on Lycophr. *Al.* 525.

was supposed to belong to the preceding sentence. This is shown by the explanation of schol. M, *ὅθεν ἔγνω πάντας τοὺς ἀνθρώπους τολμᾶν*, . . and by the punctuation of M itself, which has *μετέγνω βροτοῖς· θρασύνει γὰρ*. . Whether *βροτοῖς* was written merely through carelessness I could not say: *-οις* for *-ους* is not so frequently an error of inadvertence as might be expected; but in any case it was more likely to happen here when *βροτοὺς* was no longer connected with *θρασύνει*. That schol. M was written to *βροτοὺς* seems to me indubitable. Dr. Verrall ignores the schol.

Objections (2) and (3) imply that with the order *βροτοὺς θρασύνει γὰρ* . . *βροτοὺς* is emphasised, or else *γὰρ* holds an inexcusable position. With his own reading Dr. Verrall remarks:

> Note the position of *γάρ*. The principal emphasis is on *βρότοις*, but there is also a joint emphasis on *βρότοις θρασύνει*, which are closely connected together and distinguished, as subject from predicate, from the rest of the sentence. It is this which justifies the place of the conjunction.

('predicate from subject,' I suppose, is meant). So on

*Ag.* 610. *ἥκειν ὅπως τάχιστ' ἐράσμιον πόλει*
*γυναῖκα πιστὴν δ' ἐν δόμοις εὕροι μολών*, . .

> *ἐράσμιον πόλει . . . γυναῖκα πιστὴν δέ*: these are antithetical in meaning though not exactly in form. 'Let him come swiftly to find his people loving and his wife faithful' is the sense. It is this antithetic emphasis on *πιστὴν* which justifies the position of *δέ*.

*Ag.* 954. *πολλῶν πατησμὸν δ' εἱμάτων ἂν εὐξάμην.*

> *πολλῶν* is displaced for emphasis. The full sense is 'as for trampling of tapestries I would have devoted *many* to the trampling.'

*πολλῶν* is doubtless the emphatic word and is therefore placed first; but that does not account for the position of *δέ*; for *πολλῶν* would be equally emphatic if *δὲ* were in its usual place *πολλῶν δὲ πατησμὸν εἱμάτων*. Dr. Verrall's theory therefore requires that he should say '*πατησμὸν* is displaced for emphasis.'

*Ag.* 743. παρακλίνασ' ἐπέκρανεν δὲ γάμου πικροῦ τελευτάς.

The conjunction is so placed in order that ἐπέκρανεν, marking what happened *in the result*, may receive the antithetic emphasis as well as παρακλίνασα.

Elsewhere Dr. Verrall adopts the usual account:

*Theb.* 41. αὐτὸς κατόπτης δ' εἴμ' ἐγὼ τῶν πραγμάτων.

Note the position of the conjunction, justified by the fact that αὐτὸς κατόπτης form one idea.

*Ag.* 249. κρόκου βαφὰς δ' ἐς πέδον χέουσα.

δέ: the position is natural, κρόκου βαφὰς being inseparable and in fact one word.

But he objects to

*Theb.* 1015. ἄτιμον εἶναι δ' ἐκφορᾶς.

(where he thinks that εἶναι δ' ἄτιμον could not be read because εἶναι being unemphatic should not stand first in the clause), saying

but the displacement of εἶναι emphasises it as much as if it stood first.

*Ag.* 1316. θανούσῃ μαρτυρεῖτέ μοι τάδε
ὅταν γυνὴ γυναικὸς ἀντ' ἐμοῦ θάνῃ,
ἀνήρ τε δυσδάμαρτος ἀντ' ἀνδρὸς πέσῃ.
ἐπιξενοῦμαι ταῦτα δ' ὡς θανουμένη.

where he punctuates ἐπιξενοῦμαι· ταῦτα δ'..

literally 'I claim ξενία, but *that* as one about to die': cf. the common καὶ ταῦτα 'and that' and see *v.* 556.—If this verse be taken as one clause the sense is the same, but the position of δέ awkward and hardly justifiable.

The passage to be compared for support of this new use of ταῦτα δὲ is

*Ag.* 566. εὖ γὰρ πέπρακται. ταῦτα δ' ἐν πολλῷ χρόνῳ
τὰ μέν τις ἂν λέξειεν εὐπετῶς ἔχειν
τὰ δ' αὖτε κἀπίμομφα.

[ἂν Auratus: εὖ MSS. retained by Dr. V.]

which Dr. Verrall punctuates thus

εὖ γὰρ πέπρακται, ταῦτα δ' ἐν π. χρόνῳ.

*Aye, all is well, with allowance for the time*, literally 'but *that* in a long time,' ταῦτα standing for the verb εὖ πέπρακται: compare the common use of καὶ ταῦτα 'and that,' and see also *v.* 1319. . . . *A man must speak well of his fortune, though some of it be not so good.* . .

In the matter of the postponed conjunction I am unable to consider Dr. Verrall successful in these cases that he rejects; which however must doubtless be rejected if his theory is to stand. The reasonable view I must hold to be that, except in such cases as *P.V.* 1101 τοὺς προδότας γὰρ. ., the postponement is a licence for metrical convenience; a licence, however, seldom admitted except when the words preceding the conjunction are closely connected in grammatical construction. To treat the question satisfactorily it would be necessary to consider together with the instances in Tragedy not only the instances in Epic and Lyric poetry, which are few, but the instances in Comedy, which are multitudinous. But the following case is hardly to be explained by Dr. Verrall's theory:

Aesch. *Eum.* 622. τὸ μὲν δίκαιον τοῦθ' ὅσον σθένει μαθεῖν,
βουλῇ πιφαύσκω δ' ὔμμ' ἐπισπέσθαι πατρός.

The position of the conjunction is certainly not here justified by the fact that βουλῇ πιφαύσκω form one idea. The words are in no way connected by grammatical construction. Nor am I able to see that either is 'displaced for emphasis.'

But in MSS. δὲ and γὰρ are constantly transferred from the unusual position to the usual:

Aesch. *fr.* 161 (*Niobe*). μόνος θεῶν γὰρ θάνατος οὐ δώρων ἐρᾷ.

so Ar. *Ran.* 1392, Stob. *fl.* 118. 1, schol. Hom. I. 158; but μόνος γὰρ θεῶν schol. Soph. *El.* 139, schol. Eur. *Alc.* 55.

*Pers.* 721. πεζὸς ἢ ναύτης δὲ πεῖραν τήνδ' ἐμώρανεν
τάλας;

so M. But πέζὸς δ' ἢ ναύτης Cantabr. 2.

*Supp.* 924. ἀλλ' ἢ γυναικῶν ἐς πόλιν δοκεῖς μολεῖν;
κάρβανος δ' ὢν Ἕλλησιν ἐγχλίεις ἄγαν;

so. M. κάρβανος ὢν δ' Porson.

*Eum.* 617. λέξω πρὸς ὑμᾶς τόνδ' Ἀθηναίας μέγαν
θεσμὸν δικαίως, μάντις δ' ὢν οὐ ψεύσομαι.

so M. μάντις ὢν δ' Canter.

*Theb.* 1011. οὕτω πετηνῶν τόνδ' ὑπ' οἰωνῶν δοκεῖ
ταφέντ' ἀτίμως τοὐπιτίμιον λαβεῖν
καὶ μήθ' ὁμαρτεῖν τυμβοχόα χειρώματα
μήτ' ὀξυμόλποις προσσέβειν οἰμώγμασιν
ἄτιμον εἶναι δ' ἐκφορᾶς φίλων ὕπο.

ἄτιμον * εἶναι δ' M. 'ἄτιμον δ' εἶναι δ' Vit. Lips. ἄτιμον δ' εἶναι Ox. Ald. ἄτιμον δ' εἶν' ex Par. L. affertur. Ceteri ἄτιμον εἶναι δ'.' H.

Doubtless therefore M before erasure had ἄτιμον δ' according to the common tendency.

ἄτιμον εἶναι was the regular legal phrase:

Law in Dem. *c. Aristocr.* 640: ὃς ἂν . . αἴτιος ᾖ . . , ἄτιμον εἶναι καὶ παῖδας ἀτίμους καὶ τὰ ἐκείνου.

(ἄτιμος ἔστω in *oratio recta*: Dem. *Philip.* iii. 121 τί οὖν λέγει τὰ γράμματα; Ἄρθμιος, φησίν, ὁ Ζηλείτης ἄτιμος ἔστω καὶ πολέμιος τοῦ δήμου τῶν Ἀθηναίων καὶ τῶν συμμάχων αὐτὸς καὶ γένος. So *c. Aristocr.* 640, *in Neaer.* 1363, 1374.)

Aesch. *Supp.* 616. τόνδε κραινόντων λόγον, . .
τὸν μὴ βοηθήσαντα τῶνδε γαμόρων
ἄτιμον εἶναι ξὺν φυγῇ δημηλάτῳ.

Andoc. *de M.* 74, Dem. *Pro Megalop.* 200, Alexis 262.

But Dr. Verrall reads εἶναι δ' ἄτιμον and this is his account:

The MS. itself shows that εἶναι (without aspirate) is an error. As the unemphatic εἶναι should not stand first in the clause the order was changed to ἄτιμον δ' εἶναι, and this, to restore metre, into ἄτιμον εἶναι δ'.

But the displacement of *εἶναι* emphasizes it as much as if it stood first. The change of subject also, from the mourners to the corpse, is inappropriate and confuses the sense.

That *εἶναι* unemphatic should not stand first in the clause is quite a mistake. It is no doubt rarely found so placed in Tragedy:

Aesch. *P.V.* 766. *οὓς γὰρ νῦν ἀκήκοας λόγους,*
*εἶναι δόκει σοι μηδέπω 'ν προοιμίοις.*

Eur. *Ion* 601. *εἶναί φασι τὰς αὐτόχθονας*
*κλεινὰς 'Αθήνας οὐκ ἐπείσακτον γένος. . .*

In Comedy more frequently:

Ar. *Ran.* 886. ΑΙΣ. *Δήμητερ ἡ θρέψασα τὴν ἐμὴν φρένα,*
*εἶναί με τῶν σῶν ἄξιον μυστηρίων.*

„ *Plut.* 830. *εἶναι νομίζων χρήσιμον πρὸς τοῦ βίου.*

„ „ 1074. *εἶναί σ' ὑβριστήν φησι καὶ λέγειν ὅτι . .*

Menand. *fr.* 649. *τὸ γυναῖκ' ἔχειν εἶναί τε παίδων . .*
*πατέρα μερίμνας τῷ βίῳ πολλὰς φέρει.*

Philippides *fr.* 18. *εἶναι δ' ὑπόλαβε καὶ σὲ τῶν πολλῶν ἕνα.*

Anaxippus *fr.* 1. 9. *εἶναι δ' ὑπέλαβον*
*τὸν τοῖς τοιούτοις παντοπώλην χρώμενον.*

So *fr.* 18, Ar. *Vesp.* 1423, *Nub.* 1311. It is often so placed in prose, *e.g.* Hdt. ii. 147 *νόμοισι τοισίδε χρεώμενοι, μήτε καταιρέειν ἀλλήλους μήτε πλέον τι δίζησθαι ἔχειν τὸν ἕτερον τοῦ ἑτέρου, εἶναί τε φίλους ὡς μάλιστα.*
For which reason it is not probable that *εἶναι δ' ἄτιμον* (which Brunck and Porson read) would have been changed to *ἄτιμον δ' εἶναι.* For the notion that the 'displacement of *εἶναι*' emphasizes it see p. 113.

It remains to deal with the last statement. Change of subject with infinitives in sentences of this kind occurs again and again, but without confusing the sense any more than it does here; *e.g.*:—

Eur. *Ion* 1317. τοὺς μὲν γὰρ ἀδίκους βωμὸν οὐχ ἵζειν
ἐχρῆν,
ἀλλ' ἐξελαύνειν.

„ *Or.* 513. εἰς ὀμμάτων μὲν ὄψιν οὐκ εἴων περᾶν
οὐδ' εἰς ἀπάντημ', ὅστις αἷμ' ἔχων κυροῖ,
φυγαῖσι δ' ὁσιοῦν, ἀνταποκτείνειν δέ μή.

I would add many examples were not a change of subject equally confusing and inappropriate supplied by a closely parallel passage from Aeschylus himself:

Aesch. *Cho.* 290. καὶ τοῖς τοιούτοις οὔτε κρατῆρος μέρος
εἶναι μετασχεῖν, οὐ φιλοσπόνδου λιβός,
βωμῶν τ' ἀπείργειν οὐχ ὁρωμένην πατρὸς
μῆνιν, δέχεσθαι δ' οὔτε συλλύειν τινά,
πάντων δ' ἄτιμον κἄφιλον θνῄσκειν χρόνῳ
κακῶς ταριχευθέντα παμφθάρτῳ μόρῳ.

This last line, we are informed at *Theb.* 407, is a 'clear' example of *μόρος* in Tragedy with the meaning *corpse:*

literally '*ill-mummied* in a perishing corpse.' So in *Ag.* 1245 Ἀγαμέμνονός σέ φημ' ἐπόψεσθαι μόρον it is not the death of Agamemnon which the Chorus are to see or do see, but Agamemnon dead. In *Cho.* 443 λέγεις πατρῷον μόρον the context proves that μόρον means the *corpse* (or *funeral*), not the death, and this explains *ib.* 440 μόρον κτίσαι μωμένα ἄφερκτον (so the MS. rightly) αἰῶνι σῷ (*she mutilated thy murdered father*) *wishing to put a bar between the corpse and thy life. . .*

Let us pause here and look at the passage:

*Cho.* 438. ΧΟ. ἐμασχαλίσθη δέ γ', ὡς τόδ' εἰδῇς,
ἔπρασσε δ' ἅπερ νιν ὧδε θάπτει,
440. μόρον κτίσαι μωμένα
441. ἄφερτον αἰῶνι σῷ.
κλύεις πατρῴους δύας ἀτίμους.
443. ΗΛ. λέγεις πατρῷον μόρον· ἐγὼ δ' ἀπεστά-
τουν
ἄτιμος, οὐδὲν ἀξία,

445. μυχῷ δ' ἄφερκτος πολυσινοῦς κυνὸς δίκαν
ἑτοιμότερα γέλωτος ἀνέφερον λίβη.
χέουσα πολύδακρυν γόον κεκρυμμένα.
τοιαῦτ' ἀκούων ἔσω φρενῶν γράφου.

438 ἐμασχαλίσθης M, corr. Rob. 440 κτεῖναι M, corr. Stanley. 441 ἄφερκτον M, corr. Rob. 442 κλύεις M, corr. Turneb. 445 μυχοῦ M, corr. Stanley. 448 ἔσω φρενῶν Enger, ἐν φρεσσὶν M.

How in 443 the context proves that *μόρον* means not 'fate' but 'corpse' or 'funeral' I am willing to confess myself unable to understand. However, this is proved, and explains 440, the literal rendering of which Dr. Verrall must intend to be 'wishing to make the corpse barred from thy life.' One would expect *αἰῶνος σοῦ*, but let that pass. Four lines below, at 455, *ἄφερκτος* in the text[1] is certain. It could have no reference to *ἄφερκτον*, if that were read in 441. Which then is the more likely, that Aeschylus carelessly repeated the same unusual word, or that *ἄφερκτον* in 441 is a copyist's mistake caused by the near presence of *ἄφερκτος* in 445? The presence of the word in 445 is not mentioned by Dr. Verrall, neither is

*Ag.* 1600. μόρον δ' ἄφερτον Πελοπίδαις ἐπεύχεται.

We are to compare also (besides *Cho.* 8—9, *Ag.* 338, 341)

Soph. *Ai.* 1059 θανόντες ἂν προυκείμεθ' αἰσχίστῳ μόρῳ where *αἴσχιστος μόρος* is the exposure of the corpse.

Now, this belongs to a form of expression common in Greek, as for example,

Hom. ψ. 79. κτεῖναί μ' οἰκτίστῳ ὀλέθρῳ.
Simon. Amorg. i. 18. οἱ δ' ἀγχόνην ἅψαντο δυστήνῳ μόρῳ.
Aesch. *Pers.* 447. τεθνᾶσιν αἰσχρῶς δυσκλεεστάτῳ μόρῳ.

[1] *μυχοῦ* in M I take to be due to a notion that the word was governed by *ἄφερκτος*. For Stanley's *μυχῷ* cf. Hes. *Theog.* 1015, Ap. Rhod. iii. 656.

In 439 Portus' alteration ᾇπερ seems to be generally accepted, but I incline to think the text is better: '*he was mutilated . . ., and it was she who thus* (429—432) *buries him that did the deed, meaning to.*'

Hdt. i. 110. ὀλέθρῳ τῷ κακίστῳ σε διαχρήσεσθαι.
„ „ 167. οὗτοι μὲν τὸν Φ. τοιούτῳ μόρῳ διεχρήσαντο.
„ iii. 65. οὗτος μὲν ἀνοσίῳ μόρῳ τετελεύτηκε.
„ ix. 17. διαφθαρῆναι αἰσχίστῳ μόρῳ.

Neophron *fr.* 3. τέλος γὰρ αὐτὸς ἐχθίστῳ μόρῳ φέρεις
βροχωτὸν ἀγχόνης ἐπισπάσας δέρῃ.

(αἰσχίστῳ Elmsley; but cf. Pind. *Nem.* i. 66).

These phrases shall be allowed to speak for themselves.

Let us leave corpses and return to our particles. The earlier use of δὲ where later Greek would more logically have γὰρ is frequent in Aeschylus. In such cases we often find in scholia the phrase ὁ δὲ ἀντὶ τοῦ γάρ. Thus

*Cho.* 237. ὦ τερπνὸν ὄμμα τέσσαρας μοίρας ἔχον
ἐμοί· προσαυδᾶν δ' ἔστ' ἀναγκαίως ἔχον
πατέρα τε καὶ τὸ μητρὸς ἐς σέ μοι ῥέπει
στέργηθρον.

238 Schol. M ὁ δὲ ἀντὶ τοῦ γὰρ,

as at *Cho.* 517, 622, 633, *Eum.* 693, *P. V.* 556, *Supp.* 4, *Pers.* 146. Often γὰρ is written above δέ; as

*Theb.* 274. μέλει, φόβῳ δ' οὐχ ὑπνώσσει κέαρ·
γείτονες δὲ καρδίας
μέριμναι ζωπυροῦσι τάρβος.

275 'δὲ particulae in M recentior manus γὰρ suprascripsit.' H.

*Theb.* 452. ἐσχημάτισται δ' ἀσπὶς οὐ σμικρὸν τρόπον·
ἀνὴρ δ' ὁπλίτης κλίμακος προσαμβάσεις
στείχει.

453 'super δ' scripsit γὰρ compendio m'.' W.

Or γὰρ is substituted[1] in the text, as

*P. V* 160. τὰ πρὶν δὲ πελώρια νῦν ἀιστοῖ.

'γὰρ pro δὲ G.' H.

---

[1] In many places the refore δὲ has been rightly restored for γὰρ, as at *P. V.* 194
ἐμὰς δὲ φρένας ἐρέθισε διάτορος φόβος·
δέδια γὰρ ἀμφὶ σαῖς τύχαις [= 174 θέμενος ἄγναμπτον νόον]
δέδια δ' by Porson.

*Ag.* 425. *εὐμόρφων δὲ κολοσσῶν.*

'γὰρ Farn. Vict.' H.

A good example of the tendency occurs at

Soph. *Ant.* 668. *καὶ τοῦτον ἂν τὸν ἄνδρα θαρσοίην ἐγὼ*
*καλῶς μὲν ἄρχειν εὖ δ' ἂν ἄρχεσθαι θέλειν, . .*
*ἀναρχίας δὲ μεῖζον οὐκ ἔστιν κακόν.*

ἀναρχίας ·γὰρ· δὲ L. superscr. L^Σ (as in relation to Sophocles m is called). And many of the later MSS. have γὰρ instead of δέ.

A history precisely similar is seen at

*Theb.* 111. *ἀλλ' ὦ Ζεῦ πάτερ παντελές, πάντως*
*ἄρηξον δαΐων ἅλωσιν.*
*'Αργέϊοι δὲ πόλισμα Κάδμου* [= 127 *καὶ Κύπρις ἅτε γένους προμάτωρ*]
*κυκλοῦνται, . .*

113 'ἀργεῖοι ·γὰρ· δε M (superscr. m).' W.
'habet δὲ etiam Par. L. Ceteri libri ἀργεῖοι γὰρ.' H.

on which passage Dr. Verrall's note is

γὰρ offered in M as an alternative reading or conjecture, is plainly preferable in sense. Perhaps γὰρ ὅπλισμα: where ὅπλισμα *armament* is for ὁπλίτας. For ὅπλισμα in a similar sense see Eur. *Iph. A.* 253, τῶν Βοιωτῶν δ' ὅπλισμα . . . εἰδόμαν τοῖς δὲ Κάδμος ἦν ἀμφὶ ναῶν κόρυμβα, possibly a reminiscence of this passage.

'Plainly preferable in sense' is what m thought; what writers continually thought in adscribing, superscribing, or substituting γάρ. The Chorus use almost the same language at

*Theb.* 233. *στένει πόλισμα γῆθεν ὡς κυκλουμένων.*

'the fortress groans from the earth, as though they were surrounding it.' From this interpretation, therefore, Dr. Verrall has to devise an escape:

233. πόλισμα may be either (1) from πολίζω to build a city, a synonym of πόλις, or (2) from πολίζω to go round and round, revolve about (cf. ἀναπολίζω, πόλος, πολεύω etc.) *a revolution* or *roll.* Etymologically the two words are identical πόλισμα (= πόλις) being properly a *circle.* The second gives a far better sense here, *there comes a low*

*sound from the earth, as it were the roll of them going round*, . . . With πόλισμα fortress γῆθεν cannot be fairly translated. . .

Now for the notion of *circling* in this root, which is here asserted as if it were true, there is no ground whatever. Philologists are their own tribunal; and I seem to find them in agreement with themselves as with the ancients in holding that the notion of the root is *frequenting*. πόλις = ἀναστροφή, ἐπιστροφαί, a *frequented* place; ἐν ᾗ ἀναστρέφονται οἱ ἄνθρωποι (*E.M.*). I may notice here that at

*Ag.* 961. ὅταν δὲ τεύχῃ Ζεὺς ἀπ' ὄμφακος πικρᾶς
οἶνον, τότ' ἤδη ψῦχος ἐν δόμοις πέλει
ἀνδρὸς τελείου δῶμ' ἐπιστρωφωμένου.

Dr. Verrall translates 'it is to the home like a sudden coolness to be visited by the crowned lord thereof,' instead of 'when the lord is about the home'; saying in the note:

Nor is ἐπιστρωφωμένου without bearing on this suggestion; for the victim which came by accident to the place of sacrifice. .

Sometimes γὰρ is inserted:

*Theb.* 1022. δεινὸν τὸ κοινὸν σπλάγχνον, οὗ πεφύκαμεν.

'δεινὸν γὰρ τὸ Par. K.L. Ven. B. Rob.' H.

*Eum.* 199. αὐτὸς σὺ τούτων οὐ μεταίτιος πέλῃ.

'αὐτὸς γὰρ σὺ Flor.' H.

*Eum.* 380. τοῖον ἐπὶ κνέφας [= 370 τακόμεναι κατὰ].

so Heath. τοῖον γὰρ M.

This may well account for

*Ag.* 790. σὺ δέ μοι τότε μὲν στέλλων στρατιὰν
Ἑλένης ἕνεκ', οὐ γὰρ ἐπικεύσω,
κάρτ' ἀπομούσως ἦσθα γεγραμμένος,

where I have as little doubt as Hermann that Aeschylus wrote οὐκ ἐπικεύσω. Hermann, however, accounts for the text differently:

. . . Quod Pauwio auctore posuit Blomfieldius, οὐ γὰρ ἐπικρύψω, non scripsisset Aeschylus; . . . Hic quoque versus paroemiacus in acatalectum mutatus est. Aeschylum enim non dubito scripsisse οὐκ ἐπικεύσω.

He supposes, therefore, that γὰρ was inserted to change a paroemiac into an acatalectic verse, a treatment which all but final paroemiacs are liable[1] to suffer; *e.g.* at

Pers. 41. δεινοὶ πλῆθός τ' ἀνάριθμοι.

*Par.* B. adds γρ. πλῆθος καὶ τ' ἀνάριθμον.
Triclinius (cod. h) is a great offender in this way; *e.g.* at

*Ag.* 780. προτίουσι δίκην παραβάντες.

he writes παραβαίνοντες. I show other supplements of his:

*Ag.* 795. ἀνδράσι[ν εὖ] θνήσκουσι κομίζων.
,, 1541. δροίτας [νῦν] κατέχοντα χάμευναν.

Let us now hear Dr. Verrall:

οὐ γὰρ ἔπη κεύσω *for I will speak out* (*what I am thinking*), literally 'will not suppress speech,' cf. Eur. *Suppl.* 295—96 AI. ἀλλ' εἰς ὄκνον μοι μῦθος ὃν κεύθω φέρει. ΘΗ. αἰσχρόν γ' ἔλεξας, χρήστ' ἔπη κρύπτειν φίλους, where the phrase κεύθειν ἔπη has exactly the same sense. The singular (κεύθειν ἔπος) is common in Homer, see L. and Sc. *s. vv.* κεύθω, ἐπικεύθω. —This seems the simplest correction. οὐκ ἐπικεύσω (Hermann) does not account for the MS.

Dr. Verrall must understand how Hermann accounts for the MS., for Paley, adopting Hermann's reading, gives also his explanation. He means therefore that the insertion of γὰρ here does *not* make an acatalectic dimeter. Which is true; but it may nevertheless have been intended to do so. Even Triclinius writes

*Ag.* 1339. ποίνας θανάτων [ἄγαν] ἐπικρανεῖ.

and Dr. Verrall might tell us that desire to complete an acatalectic dimeter does not there account for the text. That γὰρ may have been inserted merely for sense, as I have shown to be probable, he does not seem to know.

Nor does he seem to know that in the parallel he adduces

[1] At *Ag.* 1526 ἀλλ' ἐμὸν ἐκ τοῦδ' ἔρνος ἀερθὲν
τὴν πολύκλαυτόν τ' Ἰφιγένειαν
ἀνάξια δράσας ἄξια πάσχων

I suspect that τὴν (which Meineke ejects) is due to this cause; and I would therefore read πολυκλαύτην (Porson) Ἰφιγένειαν,
ἄξια (Hermann) δράσας etc.

from Eur. *Suppl.* 297 he is quoting merely a conjecture. The MSS. have *χρήστ' ἐπικρύπτειν φίλοις. φίλους* is due to Barnes. *ἔπη κρύπτειν* is Hermann's reading, which can hardly be held to have such certainty that it should be quoted to support *ἔπη κεύσω*, without any mention being made that it has no MS. authority. Indeed, considering

Eur. *Hipp.* 330. *κἄπειτα κρύπτεις χρήσθ' ἱκνουμένης ἐμοῦ ;*

I am scarcely inclined to accept it.

*κεύθειν* and *ἐπικεύθειν* are doubtless often used in Homer with *ἔπος* and *μῦθον*, as Ebeling's *Lexicon* will show. But *ἐπικεύσω* is also used absolutely :

Hom. K. 115. *ἀλλὰ . . . Μενέλαον*
*νεικέσω, εἴπερ μοι νεμεσήσεαι, οὐδ' ἐπικεύσω.*

,, ε. 143. *αὖτάρ οἱ πρόφρων ὑποθήσομαι, οὐδ' ἐ. , . .*

There is no need, therefore, of an expressed object to the verb. Here *οὐκ ἐπικεύσω* will be parenthetical as *οὐκ ἀρνήσομαι* (*P.V.* 282, *Eum.* 466, *Hec.* 301, *Or.* 1082).

Dr. Verrall, like little boys beginning Greek, seems to think that δὲ is always adversative, to be translated *but :*

*Theb.* 233. ΧΟ. *στένει πόλισμα γῆθεν ὡς κυκλουμένων.*
ΕΤ. *οὐκοῦν ἔμ' ἀρκεῖ τῶνδε βουλεύειν πέρι.*
ΧΟ. *δέδοικ', ἀραγμὸς δ' ἐν πύλαις ὀφέλλεται.*

Dr. Verrall punctuates *δέδοικ'—ἀραγμὸς δ'. . .*

Note the adversative *δὲ but.* *δέδοικα* is the beginning of a reply to the previous verse, which is cut short by a fresh alarm.

*Ag.* 74. *μίμνομεν ἰσχὺν*
*ἰσόπαιδα νέμοντες ἐπὶ σκήπτροις.*
*ὅ τε γὰρ νεαρὸς μυελὸς στέρνων*
*ἐντὸς ἀνᾴσσων*
*ἰσόπρεσβυς, Ἄρης δ' οὐκ ἐνὶ χώρᾳ,*
*τί θ' ὑπεργήρως ; . .*

*Ἄρης δ' οὐκ ἐνὶ χώρᾳ* : this qualifies the parallel, to the disadvantage of the old ; note *δέ*. 'The spirit of war' not being 'in the fort,' children do not miss the strength they have not known. '. . the young breast . . . is no better than eld but in this, that the spirit of war is not there. .' (Transl. p. 232.)

'In the fort'! here is a new meaning for *χώρα*. On the phrase *ἐνὶ χώρᾳ* see Blomfield (*'is not in its proper place'*), Hermann (*'non inest, non censetur in loco aliquo et numero'*), and Liddell and Scott, who have a good article upon the word.

That *τοι* always indicates a proverbial sentiment is another notion of schoolboys: also of Dr. Verrall, as one may judge from what we are told to 'note':

*Theb.* 391. *τῷ τοι φέροντι σῆμ' ὑπέρκομπον τόδε* . .
(see the passage)

Note that *τοι* marks the words *τῷ φέροντι* as familiar. They are probably from some proverb answering to our 'Curses come home to roost.'

*Theb.* 702. *τεθηγμένον τοί μ' οὐκ ἀπαμβλυνεῖς λόγῳ.*

*τοι* marks that the phrase is a proverb applied to the present case.

*Ag.* 1039. *οὔτοι θυραίαν τήνδ' ἐμοὶ σχολὴ πάρα*
*τρίβειν.*

*I have no leisure, you may know, to be dallying abroad.*—Clytemnestra, throughout this scene haughtily affects popular expressions and images (*vv.* 1024, 1028, 1034).

*Ag.* 241. *φράσεν δ' ἀόζοις πατὴρ* . .
*προνωπῆ λαβεῖν*
245. *ἀέρδην, στόματός τε καλλιπρῴ-*
*ρου φυλακὰν κατασχεῖν*
*φθόγγον ἀραῖον οἴκοις*
*βίᾳ χαλινῶν τ' ἀναύδῳ μένει.*

The construction is now generally taken to be *φυλακὰν*—*κατασχεῖν φθόγγον*, a form of construction for which there is good support. Dr. Verrall prefers

literally 'and, by way of guard upon her fair lips, they should restrain,' etc. *φυλακὰν* is acc. in apposition to the action. . .—*φυλακᾷ*, Blomfield cuts the knot, but does not account for the text.

I have quoted this only to comment on the last remark. Were it necessary, it would be quite easy to read *φυλακᾷ* with Blomfield for this reason, that final ι and ν are very often confused. There is a case of this at

*Theb.* 714. ξένος δὲ κλήρους ἐπινωμᾷ.

So m. M had κλήροις ἐπινωμᾶν, and Dr. Verrall of course has it still:

ξένος κλήροις (ἐστὶν) ἐπινωμᾶν (αὐτούς): *he is but a stranger to the inheritance, that he should award it.* ἐπινωμᾶν depends as an explanatory infinitive on ξένος literally 'foreign to award it.' . .—This is a better reading, as well as technically more probable, than κλήρους ἐπινωμᾷ.

The translation has: 'He is no native, that he should divide the inheritance,—this Chalyb from distant Scythia, this cruel steel, . .' This implies that there has been some mention before of the Chalyb, steel; but there has been not a word. The sense required is 'there is a stranger to divide the inheritance, a Chalyb . .', which is expressed by m's text but could not be expressed with ἐπινωμᾶν, for ἐστὶ cannot be *understood* except when it is a copula.

Final ι being so frequently confused with ν, at

*Ag.* 1621. δεσμὸν δὲ καὶ τὸ γῆρας αἵ τε νήστιδες
δύαι

I prefer Karsten's δεσμοὶ to δεσμὸς of h. Dr. Verrall reads δεσμῶν:

The genitive δεσμῶν (depending on δύαι) is required by the article αἱ, justifiable according to the use of Aeschylus, only if αἱ νήστιδες δύαι are contrasted with some other δύαι.

The statement about the article—

Both the trustworthy copies (f, g) give the impossible reading δεσμόν, reproducing doubtless that of M, in which ο and ω are not seldom accidentally confused, the sounds having been probably indistinguishable.

The confusion of *ον* and *ων* occurs again and again in any MS., oftenest in the neighbourhood of a similar termination, but often without that influence. We see that, where it suits him, Dr. Verrall is quite aware (as how could he not be?) that this confusion often happens accidentally. Let us now compare his language in opposing an accepted reading:

*Ag.* 146. τόσσων περ εὔφρων καλὰ
δρόσοισιν ἀέλπτοις μαλερῶν ὄντων.

so M. τόσον fh.

On the passage generally I say nothing now; but arguing against λεόντων (restored by Stanley from the *E.M.*) he says

In the first place λεόντων is of course inconsistent with τόσσων and requires us to assume that some one, without any motive, wrote τόσσων for τόσσον.

This rhetorical method, used throughout the two volumes, makes plain criticism at once difficult, invidious, and necessary. It is found in every form:

*Theb.* 335. βλαχαὶ δ' αἱματόεσσαι
τῶν ἐπιμαστιδίων
ἀρτιτρεφεῖς βρέμονται.

where he reads βλαχᾷ, he translates '*and the young mothers blood-red cry aloud at the bleating of their babes*':

βρέμονται *roar*, the French *frémir* or *rugir*... Unfortunately our corresponding English words *roar*, *bellow* have been spoilt for poetical purposes.

Yet in the translation of the passage according to the reading rejected, this word *roar* is given, *ad invidiam*:

The trivial misaccentuation βλαχαί in M, an ingeniously simple error by which every word down to the very article becomes meaningless, converts the sentence into this, 'and the bloody bleatings of those babes, being new-suckled, roar.'

I am with Blomfield, who remarks: durior est enallage, sed eo fortasse magis Aeschylea. But Euripides has

*Phoen.* 1351. λευκοπήχεις κτύπους χεροῖν.
*Cycl.* 58. ποθοῦσί σ' ἁμερόκοιτοι
βλαχαὶ σμικρῶν τεκέων.

For the article see p. 58.

*Ag.* 692. ἐπεὶ πρεπόντως . . . ἔπλευσεν
πολύανδροί τε φεράσπιδες κυναγοὶ

κατ' ἴχνος πλατᾶν ἄφαντον
κελσάντων Σιμόεντος
ἀκτὰς ἐπ' ἀξιφύλλους
δι' ἔριν αἱματόεσσαν.

ἀεξιφύλλους is the conjecture of Triclinius (*Cod. Farn.*), who here as in many places, has by his arbitrary change merely diverted attention from the much better reading of the faithful copy. ἀεξιφύλλους δι' ἔριν αἱματόεσσαν 'whose forests will grow because of the bloody fray' is in the first place hardly sense in itself. Wecklein refers to Hor. *Od.* 2. 1. 29 'quis non Latino sanguine pinguior campus?,' but it will be seen that the phrases differ materially.

Now I do not know that the words have ever been so interpreted by any editor but Wecklein. Nor does Dr. Verrall explicitly assert that they have. But he proceeds as though rejection of that interpretation involved rejection of the reading ἀεξιφύλλους. Yet he must be aware that the words δι' ἔ. αἱ. have been generally connected with κυναγοὶ (ἔπλευσαν), for Paley has 'δι' ἔριν. "Iungendum cum κυναγοί." Klausen.'

*Theb.* 259. Δίρκης τε πηγαῖς, οὐδ' ἀπ' Ἰσμηνοῦ λέγω, . .

Wecklein, who in his edition of 1885 places 'certain emendations' in his text, 'very probable conjectures' in his margin, and the rest in his appendix, admits here into the text οὐδ' ἀπ' Ἰσμηνὸν λέγω (Schuetz, Abreschio auctore); *i.e.* οὐδ' ἀπολέγω Ἰσμηνὸν *per tmesim*, as *Theb.* 1019, κἀνὰ κίνδυνον βαλῶ, *Ag.* 1569, ἀπὸ σφαγὴν ἐρῶν (Auratus, accepted by Dr. Verrall, for σφαγῆς). Dr. Verrall reads

Δίρκης τε πηγαῖς—οὔδατ' Ἰσμηνοῦ λέγω—,

The local form in the local name is a picturesque touch; and that it was actually used by Aeschylus the MS. hardly leaves room to doubt; the error and the exact form of it might have been predicted. . . ὕδατά τ' Ἰσμηνοῦ (W. Dindorf) is little less close to the MS., but bad in rhythm and not consistent with the usage of λέγω.

The conjecture admitted as certain by Wecklein is entirely ignored: W. Dindorf's, in Wecklein's appendix, not mentioned by Paley, is selected, as though the best, for unfavourable criticism.

*Theb.* 751. τέλειαι γὰρ παλαιφάτων ἀραὶ στρ. δ.
βαρεῖαι καταλλαγαί· τὰ δ' ὀλοὰ
πελόμεν' οὐ παρέρχεται
πρόπρυμνα δ' ἐκβολῶν φέρει
ἀνδρῶν ἀλφηστᾶν
ὄλβος ἄγαν παχυνθείς.
τίν' ἀνδρῶν γὰρ τοσόνδ' ἐθαύμασαν αντ. δ'.
θεοὶ καὶ ξυνέστιοι πόλεως
πολύβατός τ' ἀγὼν βροτῶν
ὅσον τότ' Οἰδίπουν τίον, . .

It was not an easy task to keep the text of M unaltered here; but Dr. Verrall has achieved it:

*For an inherited self-fulfilling curse is a dangerous ware to traffic withal: neither doth the merchantman's wealth, heaped over-high, escape the coming of destruction, but bringeth total wreck.* παλαιφάτων masculine, *of the men of old.*

τὰ ὀλοὰ πελόμενα is taken as an accusative,

literally 'things destructive when they occur,'

governed (as πρόπρυμνα ἐκβολῶν, another accusative,

*utter loss* or *utterness of loss,*

by ὄλβος φέρει) by ὄλβος οὐ παρέρχεται.

τὰ δ' ὀλοὰ κ.τ.λ. For a large number of suggested changes see Wecklein's *Appendix.* All of them . . proceed on the supposition that τὰ ὀλοὰ is nominative.

Wecklein places in his text (besides Bothe's ἀρᾶν) Buecheler's brilliant conjecture πενομένους. It gives a just and simple sense. σ is very liable to be lost before π when the two letters are written, as they are very frequently, together. πένεσθαι is similarly corrupted in

*Eum.* 434. τῶν σοφῶν γὰρ οὐ πένῃ.

'πέλῃ Ven. Flor.' H.

Yet to this certain reading Dr. Verrall has not a word of reference, but directs us to the vain suggestions, for ever superseded, in Wecklein's *Appendix.*

*Theb.* 508. πέποιθα τὸν Διὸς ἀντίτυπον ἔχοντ'
ἄφιλον ἐν σάκει τοῦ χθονίου δέμας
δαίμονος, ἐχθρὸν εἴκασμα βροτοῖς τε καὶ
δαροβίοισι θεοῖσι
πρόσθε πυλᾶν κεφαλὰν ἰάψειν.

510. δαίμονος et βροτοῖς Brunck : δαίμοσιν et βροτοῖσί M.

because, as Paley puts it:

δαίμονος. So Brunck from the Schol. Med., πιστεύω ἀπολεῖσθαι τὸν ἔχοντα ἐν τῷ σάκει τὸν ἐχθρὸν τοῦ Διὸς δαίμονα. . . Some ancient corrector wished to adapt the construction to ἄφιλον or ἐχθρόν, misled by βροτοῖς τε καὶ θεοῖσιν.

(so in Blomf., Dind., Herm., Weil, etc.). Dr. Verrall retains the exact text of M, with this note:

ἄφιλον . . . δαίμοσιν, *who hath no deity for friend*: δαίμοσιν is 'ethic' dative,' 'in the regard of deities.'—The correction of Brunck, δαίμονος, obliterates the meaning of the phrase, which replies obliquely to the insinuation of Eteocles (502); Typhon had never a friend in heaven. Nor perhaps would the maidens have bestowed the name δαίμων upon the monster.

in which it will be seen that the paraphrase in M, though expressly mentioned by all the commentators as the basis of Brunck's certain emendation, is absolutely ignored.

*Theb.* 661. ET. ἄρχοντί τ' ἄρχων καὶ κασιγνήτῳ κάσις
ἐχθρὸς σὺν ἐχθρῷ στήσομαι· φέρ' ὡς τάχος
κνημῖδας, αἰχμῆς καὶ πετρῶν προβλήματα,

'πετρῶν (eraso accentu super ε) M.' W. πτερῶν *recc.* αἰχμήν *recc.*

As for 663 nothing short of re-writing would get rid of the obvious flaws both in the whole conception and in almost every word. . . However the MS. no doubt represents the stage tradition, founded, as Paley and others point out, on the somewhat similar situation in Euripides (*Phoenissae* 779. ET. ἐκφέρετε τεύχη πάνοπλά τ' ἀμφιβλήματα); and it has the practical advantage of explaining the delay.—πετρῶν: it is scarcely worth while to correct the accent, for the writer of this verse may well have confused πέτρα and πέτρος.

The words 'obvious,' 'evident,' 'clearly' and the like are frequent weapons in Dr. Verrall's vocabulary. I have long learnt the value of advice once given me, to regard such words with distrust, as likely to be substituted for arguments not easy to present. The 'flaws in the whole conception,' at any rate, are by no means 'obvious' to me. For the expression the following may be compared:

[1]Alcaeus *fr.* 15. λάμπραι κνάμιδες, ἄρκος ἰσχύρω βέλεος.

Hom. Δ. 137. μίτρης θ' ἣν ἐφόρει, ἔρυμα χροός, ἕρκος ἀκόντων.

so of ἀσπίς, O. 646, Paul. Sil. *A. P.* vi. 81.

„ φ. 340. ὀξὺν ἄκοντα, κυνῶν ἀλκτῆρα καὶ ἀνδρῶν.

Ap. Rhod. iv. 200. βοείας ἀσπίδας .. δήων θοὸν ἔχμα βολάων,

Hybrias (Scolion 28). τὸ καλὸν λαισήιον, πρόβλημα χρωτός·

Ar. *Vesp.* 615. τάδε κέκτημαι πρόβλημα κακῶν, σκευὴν βελέων ἀλεωρήν.

The only objection of force seems to me to be that stated by [2]C. M. Francken '.. etsi in armis principem fere locum tenent ocreae (Hom. Il. iii. 330, xi. 17, et passim), mirum tamen has solas postulari.' The final remark is singularly ill criticism. For not only is it uncertain how far πέτρα and πέτρος may be interchangeably used, but these words are very often confused in passages indubitably authentic: and either may be confused with πτερόν.[3] It would be fairer therefore to consider our passage after the accent has been changed.

*Theb.* 577. τοιαῦθ' ὁ μάντις ἀσπίδ' εὔκηλον ἔχων
πάγχαλκον ηὔδα· σῆμα δ' οὐκ ἐπῆν κύκλῳ.
οὐ γὰρ δοκεῖν ἄριστος ἀλλ' εἶναι θέλει,

[1] Valckenaer, Eur. *Ph. l. c.* discussing our passage.

[2] *Disputatio critica de antiquarum Aeschyli interpretationum ad genuinam lectionem restituendam usu et auctoritate.* Trajecti ad Rhenum 1845.

[3] Cf. Pind. *O.* x. 72 ἔδικε πέτρῳ. Gl. γ. διὰ τῆς στρογγυλοειδοῦς πέτρας. Eur. *Or.* 618 πέτροις. Sch. I. διὰ τῶν πετρῶν. Compare Eur. *Ph.* 1148 with *I. T.* 319, *Or.* 59, 1478. See Ellendt *Lex. Soph. s.v.* πέτρος. For πτερόν, Eur. *Hel.* 76, Lyc. *Al.* 401 and sch. M, 839 and sch. M.

βαθεῖαν ἄλοκα διὰ φρενὸς καρπούμενος
ἐξ ἧς τὰ κεδνὰ βλαστάνει βουλεύματα.

577. So M. γρ. εὔκυκλον νέμων m.

This reading given by m, and almost universally adopted, is according to Dr. Verrall

merely a bad conjecture suggested by *v.* 629 ; νέμων has no meaning.

At 629 we have ἔχει δὲ καινοπηγὲς εὔκυκλον σάκος, where schol. m has γρ. εὔθετον, ἵν' ᾖ εὐβάστακτον. Wecklein is right, I think, in preferring εὔθετον to εὔκυκλον, which may easily in an earlier MS. have been written through reminiscence of this Homeric epithet in our line: for one can hardly doubt that in v. 577 εὔκηλον is simply an error due to the similarity in minuscules of υ κ η. It would not be easy for such a hand as M to write εὔκυκλον correctly, just as many people to-day would find it hard to write the word *minimum*. νέμων is 'wielding.' We have νωμᾶν ἔγχος Hom. E. 594, βέλη *Cho.* 163, δόρυ *Pers.* 323, Ap. Rhod. iv. 1156, λόγχην Eur. *Ph.* 1394, ἐν σάκει Σφίγγ' ἐνώμα *Theb.* 529, νωμᾶν σάκος Ap. Rh. iii. 1229. οἴακα νωμῶν (as οἰήια Hom. μ. 218, πόδα νηὸς κ. 32) is said *Theb.* 3, οἴακα νέμων *Ag.* 793, and though the simple verb may be more justly used of a rudder than of a shield, yet I shall not venture to call ἀσπίδα νέμων a meaningless expression. It has frequently been remarked that νέμειν is used often as little more than equivalent to ἔχειν, and Hesychius gives νέμει: . . . ἔχει. So ἔχων of M is probably a gloss. Dr. Verrall, however, has only to change one letter of M:

τοιαῦθ' ὁ μάντις ἀσπίδ' εὐκήλων ἔχων
πάγχαλκον ηὔδα, σῆμα δ' οὐκ ἐπῆν, κύκλῳ.

The correction εὐκήλων . . restores the metre with an irreducible minimum of alteration, and is strongly supported by the sense.

The sense of the extraordinary sentence produced is, we are expected to believe:

*Thus spake the prophet, bearing a shield of plain bronze, without device upon it, to a ring of careless listeners*. . . The emphasis thrown upon κύκλῳ is intentional; *surrounded* by opponents, he would still speak his mind.—σῆμα δ' οὐκ ἐπῆν (αὐτῇ): a parenthesis.

and is indicated by Plutarch's reference to 579, 580: Αἰσχύλος δὲ καὶ τὸ πρὸς δόξαν ἔχειν ἀτύφως, καὶ μὴ διασοβεῖσθαι, μηδὲ ἐπαίρεσθαι τοῖς παρὰ τῶν πολλῶν ἐπαίνοις, ἐν τῷ φρονεῖν τίθεται, περὶ τοῦ Ἀμφιαράου γράφων 'οὐ γὰρ δοκεῖν . . . βουλεύματα' (*de audiend. poet.* p. 32 E).

The behaviour which calls forth this famous and splendid eulogy, is as Plutarch says, the honesty of Amphiaraus in urging unpopular truths, though his audience is unsympathetic and his courage exposes him to the reproach of cowardice (see *v.* 369).

But Plutarch does not say so; there is nothing in his words to suggest that they are more than an amplification of the sole verses that he quotes. It is objected that with the ordinary reading and punctuation

the words οὐ γὰρ δοκεῖν κ.τ.λ. must naturally be referred to the absence of a device on the shield, which, though a suitable circumstance, is of very slight importance to the main purpose, as it is rightly explained by Plutarch.

One may claim leave to think that after the vaunting emblems of the previous champions, described with so much stress, it is not of such very slight importance that Amphiaraus should bear his shield unblazoned; that not for nothing does Euripides record so carefully the same contrasted fact:

*Phoen.* 1118. ὁ μάντις Ἀμφιάραος, οὐ σημεῖ' ἔχων
ὑβρισμέν', ἀλλὰ σωφρόνως ἄσημ' ὅπλα.

But Dr. Verrall's correction has still further merits:

It also explains κύκλῳ which in the MS. and editions is joined to ἐπῆν in the supposed sense of *orb*, *i.e. shield*. But this . . . is bad Greek: κύκλος is not a synonym of ἀσπίς, nor is it the Greek habit, as in English and other modern languages, to use a synonym as a pronoun, nor with κύκλῳ should the preposition be ἐπί, but ἐν, as in Eur. *El.* 455 ἀσπίδος ἐν κύκλῳ τοιάδε σήματα τετύχθαι.

It will be convenient to take with this passage the arguments upon another shield:

*Theb.* 473. τεταρτος ἄλλος . . . παρίσταται
Ἱππομέδοντος σχῆμα καὶ μέγας τύπος·
ἅλω δὲ πολλήν—ἀσπίδος κύκλον λέγω—
ἔφριξα δινήσαντος·

*And I shuddered to see the long path—the circuit of the shield, that is—which it described.* δινήσαντος is intransitive, the subject being τύπου; the genitive depends upon ἅλω, literally 'of it turned about.' The description is strictly appropriate, in that the τύπος, the work in high relief, belonged as the sequel shows, to the circular border. . .—The *Lex.* and the commentators generally render πολλὴν ἅλω *vast orb* or *disc* and δινήσαντος *when he swung it round. . .*

Of the same shield:

*Theb.* 482. ὀφέων δὲ πλεκτάναισι περίδρομον κύτος
προσηδάφισται κοιλογάστορος κύκλου.

. . A central part of high curvature (κοιλογάστωρ κύκλος) was enclosed by a frame (περίδρομον κύτος) comparatively flat. (Hence the comparison to the ἅλως: see previous note). . .

It will now be seen that the ambiguous phrases 'path,' 'circuit of the shield' (made still more confusing by the words 'which it described') mean not 'circular course' but physically the 'circular border' of the shield. So that a more accurate rendering according to Dr. Verrall's view would have been 'I shuddered at the long path—namely the circular border of the shield—of the device as it turned about.' In this sense he identifies ἅλω πολλήν, ἀσπίδος κύκλον and περίδρομον κύτος. At this rate therefore κοιλογάστωρ κύκλος, the 'central part' of the shield, is opposed to ἀσπίδος κύκλος, the 'circular border.'

'κύκλος,' says Dr. Verrall, 'is not a synonym of ἀσπίς.' But he is wrong: for when sufficiently defined κύκλος may well be used as a synonym of ἀσπίς, and it is so used at

Eur. *El.* 1255. γοργῶφ' ὑπερτείνουσά σου κάρᾳ κύκλον.

*i.e.* Ar. *Ach.* 1124. γοργόνωτον[1] ἀσπίδος κύκλον.

Certainly it is sufficiently defined in our passage. ἐπῆν Dr. Verrall understands with ἀσπίδι: but with κύκλῳ, he says

[1] I find Blaydes has anticipated me in suggesting γοργονωπόν.

the preposition should not be ἐπὶ but ἐν. Now ἐπὶ and ἐν are used quite interchangeably of devices on a shield:

ἐπί:—Ar. *Ran.* 928. ἢ 'π' ἀσπίδων ἐπόντας γρυπαέτους.
Eur. *Phoen.* 1137. σιδηρονώτοις δ' ἀσπίδος τύποις ἐπῆν Γίγας.
so 1127, 1131, *fr.* 530. Pind. *P.* viii. 45. Aesch. *Theb.* 387, 497, 507, 546, 648. Hdt. ix. 74. Dioscor. *A.P.* vi. 126, vii. 430. Athenaeus xiii. 83.

ἐν:—Aesch. *Theb.* 376, 509, 526. Eur. *Phoen.* 1114, 1121, *El.* 465.

From these examples it may be found that in Tragedy while with ἀσπὶς we have always ἐπί, with σάκος we have ἐν. But no one, I imagine, would maintain that ἐν ἀσπίδι (Ap. Rh. i. 746, Nonnus xxv. 421, 445) or ἐπὶ σάκους would be wrong. Yet Dr. Verrall goes further even than that when, because at one place, Eur. *El.* 456, we find ἀσπίδος ἐν κύκλῳ, he argues that we might not have ἐπῆν κύκλῳ in the same sense at *Theb.* 578. Doubtless the change of preposition is merely for sake of metre: other things equal, ἐπὶ is preferred, for metrically it would be as easy in many places to write ἐν ἀσπίδι as ἐπ' ἀ.

That at Eur. *El.* 456 ἀ. κ. means the whole orb of the shield is beyond dispute, for both border and centre are expressly included in it:

> 453 ἔκλυον . . κλεινᾶς ἀσπίδος ἐν κύκλῳ
> τοιάδε σήματα . . . τετύχθαι·
> περιδρόμῳ μὲν ἴτυος ἕδρᾳ. . .
> 465 ἐν δὲ μέσῳ κατέλαμπε σάκει. . .

at Ar. *Ach.* 1124 φέρε δεῦρο γοργόνωτον ἀ. κ. the paratragic phrase means the same, and at Eur. *El.* 1255 γοργῶπα κ. alone means 'disc.' These are the only other places in the dramatists where κύκλος is used of a shield. It is natural to consider that here too ἀσπίδος κύκλον, the phrase by which the messenger explains his metaphor ἅλω, means the whole disc. But 'the ἅλως,' says Dr. Verrall, 'was not a disc but a circular path.' His only argument for this assertion is—

The Schol. import the later meteorological sense of 'halo,'... But this use (probably unknown to Aeschylus) is really a proof that the ἅλως proper was *not* conceived as a disc, but as a circle surrounding a disc.

I must decline to consider this to be a 'proof' that the ἅλως proper was not conceived by Aeschylus as a circular *area*, surrounded by a path; in the words of the *Classical Dictionary*, 'an open space ... of a circular form, slightly raised in the centre to allow moisture to run off.' Dr. Verrall himself has previously admitted the whole ἅλως:

The whole ἅλως is slightly domed to drain it, and the centre rises above the path.

His arguments fail therefore to weaken my belief that Aeschylus compared ἀσπίδος κύκλον, the shield with its border, to the ἅλως with its surrounding path.

For the phrase δινεῖν ἀσπίδα compare

Theocr. xix. 10. ὣς φαμένα δίνασε σάκος μέγα·

Hdt. ix. 74. ἐπ' ἀσπίδος αἰεὶ περιθεούσης καὶ οὐδαμὰ ἀτρεμιζούσης ἐφόρεε ἐπίσημον ἄγκυραν ..

Dr. Verrall urges against the sense *orb* for ἅλω that

πολύς is not a synonym of μέγας: πολλὴ χώρα (*Eum.* 837) cited by Paley proves nothing, as it does not describe a definite figure: hence the conjectures πολιάν Wakefield, λευκήν Heimsoeth, etc.

But does not the same objection hold equally against the sense *border?* Is not that a 'definite figure'? Though certainly the only phrase I have found closely resembling ours is

Arat. *Diosem.* 115 πολὺς δ' ὅτε οἱ περὶ κύκλος ..

Perhaps πολλὴν is a false explanation of ἄπειρον: cf.

Hesych. ἄπειρον: πολύ. ἄγευστον. περιφερές, στρογγύλον ..

ἀπείρῳ: πολλῇ.

For the use of ἄπειρος, ἀπείρων see Empedocles 61, Aesch. *fr.* 379, Soph. *fr.* 483, Eur. *Or.* 25, *Hel.* 1500, Ar. *fr.* 250.

*Theb.* 42. ἄνδρες γὰρ ἑπτά, θούριοι λοχαγέται,
ταυροσφαγοῦντες ἐς μελάνδετον σάκος
καὶ θιγγάνοντες χερσὶ ταυρείου φόνου
Ἄρη τ' Ἐνυὼ καὶ φιλαίματον Φόβον
ὡρκωμότησαν.

The difficulty in the construction of the passage is well known:

. . . Perhaps however we have the name of a masculine deity Ἄρης Ἐνυώς (the Homeric Ἄρης Ἐνυάλιος) making with Ἐνυώ a pair like Φοῖβος and Φοίβη, etc.

Ἐνυὼ (daughter of Phorcys and Ceto, Hes. *Theog.* 273) is constantly associated with Ares:

Hom. E. 592. ἦρχε δ' ἄρα σφιν Ἄρης καὶ πότνι' Ἐνυώ,
ἡ μὲν ἔχουσα κυδοιμὸν ἀναιδέα δηιοτῆτος, .

Callim. *h. Del.* 276. οὐδέ σ' Ἐνυώ,
οὐδ' Ἀίδης οὐδ' ἵπποι ἐπιστείβουσιν Ἄρηος
(where however Schneider and Meineke read Ἐλευθώ).

Lycophr. *Al.* 518. τοὺς Ἄρης ἐφίλατο
καὶ δῖ' Ἐνυώ. *A.P.* ix. 283, Nonnus xxxiii. 156.

Pausan. I. viii. 5 (of the temple of Ares at Athens). ἐνταῦθα καὶ Ἐνυοῦς ἄγαλμά ἐστιν, ἐποίησαν δὲ οἱ παῖδες οἱ Πραξιτέλους.

[1]Cornut. *de nat. deor.* p. 56. Ἐνυὼ οἱ μὲν τροφόν, οἱ δὲ μητέρα, οἱ δὲ θυγατέρα Ἄρεως παρέδωκαν.

Schol. Ar. *Pax* 457. τινὲς δὲ Ἄρεως καὶ Ἐνυοῦς τὸν Ἐνυάλιον. .

The presumption is that the two deities are so associated here. But according to Dr. Verrall's theory, Aeschylus introduced a title which can hardly have been known to his audience, for of a masculine Ἐνυὼς there is no trace anywhere. It is difficult to believe that in doing so he used that name in such a case as to be indistinguishable from that signifying a feminine deity familiar to the audience through Homer as the companion of Ares.

[1] Blomfield *ad loc.*

*Theb.* 43. For ταυροσφαγοῦντες Weil (ed. 1862) proposed and Herwerden (independently, as it seems, *Emendationes Aeschyleae* 1878) strongly urges the substitution of μηλοσφαγοῦντες, from the reference

Ar. *Lys.* 188. εἰς ἀσπίδ', ὥσπερ φασ' ἐν Αἰσχύλῳ ποτέ,
μηλοσφαγούσας.
(Sch. ἀντὶ τοῦ ταυροσφαγούσας μηλοσφαγούσας εἶπεν, εἰ μὴ ἄρα μῆλα πάντα τὰ τετράποδα.)
[1]Hesych. μῆλα: κοινῶς μὲν πάντα τὰ τετράποδα· . . κατ' ἐπικρατίαν δὲ τὰ πρόβατα καὶ αἶγες.
Eustath. 1648, 61. ἰστέον . . καὶ ὅτι μῆλα εἰ καὶ ὡς ἐπὶ πολὺ τὰ πρόβατα, ὅμως καὶ τὰ πλείω τῶν τετραπόδων ὡς καὶ ἀλλαχοῦ ἐγράφη μῆλά τε καλοῦνται καὶ πρόβατα. Σοφοκλῆς γοῦν (*fr.* 966) φασὶ τὸν 'Αχιλλέα τραφῆναι εἰπὼν ἐν τῷ Πηλίῳ πᾶν μῆλον θηρῶντα δόξαι ἂν τὰ θηρία πάντα μῆλα καλεῖν· καὶ ὁ εἰπὼν δὲ "μῆλα βόας κεραοὺς καὶ ὄϊς καὶ πίονας αἶγας" καὶ τοὺς βοῦς ἐν τοῖς μήλοις τίθησι. Σιμωνίδης δέ φασι τὸν ταῦρον ὁτὲ μὲν μῆλον ὁτὲ δὲ πρόβατον ὀνομάζει. .
('Haec sec. Aristoph. Byz., ut elucet ex p. 877. 51.' Ellendt *Lex. Soph.* *s.v.* μῆλον. See also 1814. 31, etc.)
[1]Aesch. *fr.* 151. Ἴδη δὲ μυκηθμοῖσι καὶ βρυχήμασι ἕρπουσι μήλων.

I quote these passages not because Dr. Verrall ignores the conjecture here, but with another note in view:

*Ag.* 718. ἔθρεψεν δὲ λέοντος
ἶνιν δόμοις ἀγάλακτον
οἴτας ἀνὴρ φιλόμαστον.
'720. οὗτος.' Dr. V.

---

[1] Herwerden *l.c.*

*οἶτας ἀνὴρ a shepherd*: *οἴτης* from *ὄϊς*, as *βούτης* from *βοῦς*. This correction if worth anything, should be credited to Heusde and Wecklein, who write respectively *βότας* and *βούτας*. Something like this, some description attached to *ἀνήρ*, is plainly to be sought in the MS. reading, *οὗτος*. (The *υ* in f has both accentuations, ῞ over ῀: but ῞ must be what M gave, the other merely the familiar accentuation written first by mistake.) But *οἶτας* is preferable, not only for obvious technical reasons, but because the sequel (*v.* 731 *μηλοφόνοισιν*) shows that a *shepherd* not an *oxherd* was in the poet's mind.—*οὕτως* h, an idle guess. If *οὕτως* had been the word, it would have been preserved nor does the place admit *οὕτως* or indeed, I feel, anything except an epithet to *ἀνήρ*.

From which it appears that the wider sense of *μῆλον* is unknown to Dr. Verrall, though it is duly given in Liddell and Scott.

As for the argument from the MS. accentuation, even the statement of f's reading is wrong. Wecklein gives quite clearly and correctly, '*ἀγάλακτον οὗτος* (*οὗτος* [῞ and ως written above] f, *οὕτως* h) libri.'; and Hermann expressly says '*οὗτος ἀνὴρ* Flor. Vict. sed in Flor. ad ultimam *οὗτος* vocabuli syllabam *ως* supra adscriptum est, habetque *οὕτως* Farn.' That is, f has merely written *οὕτως* above *οὗτος*. All the argument therefore becomes entirely vain. (The variation may have arisen through a compendium: '*οὕτως, οὗτος, οὗτοι* saepe indicantur hoc compendio, *οὗ* [with τ written above]: quae causa est confusionis harum vocum' etc. Bast *Greg. Cor.* p. 828; or M may at least have presented both readings; or *οὕτως* in f and h may be due to regard for metre or for sense.)

Appendix II. to the *Seven against Thebes* contains an argument (adapted with modification from the *Journal of Philology* vol. ix.) concerning the use of the word *ἔτυμος* and its congeners in Aeschylus. This argument is conducted upon the plan with which we have now become familiar: there is no attempt to weigh the evidence at large; none is placed before us but such as may appear to support the view maintained. Though it has been now some time before the world, the view has met with no argued opposition, but seems on the contrary in some quarters at any rate to have found acceptance.[1] Since the matter is of interest in itself and the discussion will strongly exhibit the worthlessness of argument without method, I have thought it worth while, for the conclusion of this criticism, to treat the question at the necessary length.

Dr. Verrall's position is that of the fourteen cases of ἔτυμος and ἐτήτυμος in Aeschylus no less than ten refer to an etymology. For the manner in which the argument is presented I must refer to the Appendix itself. Briefly, it is urged that in four of the examples, *P.V.* 309, 621, *Pers.* 739, *Ag.* 483, there is no trace of *etyma*; and in none of these accordingly is there the slightest ambiguity in the use of ἔτυμος or ἐτήτυμος, which applies, in the strictest sense of the word *true*, to a proposition, a thing said'; but that (*Theb.* 82, the theme of the Excursus, being excluded) in the remaining nine a satisfactory sense cannot be given by an ordinary rendering of the words:

> To appreciate fully the cumulative force of these difficulties, as proof that the use of the words in question is peculiar and must have some special explanation, it would be well to try a similar experiment upon fourteen examples *taken at random* of ἀληθής and ἀληθῶς.

Why Dr. Verrall lays so much stress upon random selection in the case of ἀληθὴς it is not for me to say. Random selection would be not more but less likely to ensure a true conclusion. It happens that there are but just fourteen examples of ἀληθὴς in Aeschylus. We may surely infer that in the case of ἀληθὴς Dr. Verrall will permit argument from the use of other authors. If so, it cannot be called fair to refuse it in the case of ἔτυμος.

[1] In *Hermathena* xv. (1889) Mr. J. B. Bury has the following note on *Ag.* 1298:

> εἰ δ' ἐτητύμως
> μόρον τὸν αὑτῆς οἶσθα, πῶς θεηλάτου
> βοὸς δίκην πρὸς βωμὸν εὐτόλμως πατεῖς;

'The poet clearly intends a play on βοός and βωμόν in l. 1228. This coincides with Mr. Verrall's view of ἐτήτυμος, ἔτυμος, put forward in his edition of the *Septem Contra Thebas*.'

Does Mr. Bury really mean that ἐτητύμως in the one clause refers to a verbal play on βοός and βωμόν in the other? That is the conclusion I have in vain attempted to avoid

But throughout the discussion he wholly omits to mention that in connexion with etymologies Aeschylus uses other words as well, as :

ὀρθῶς :

Aesch. *Theb.* 392. ὀρθῶς ἐνδίκως τ' ἐπώνυμον.
" " 814. ὀρθῶς κατ' ἐπωνυμίαν.
Soph. *fr.* 880. ὀρθῶς δ' Ὀδυσσεύς εἰμ' ἐπώνυμος κακοῖς.
Eur. *Tr.* 984. τοὔνομ' ὀρθῶς ἀφροσύνης ἄρχει θεᾶς.
" *fr.* 781. ὦ καλλιφεγγὲς Ἥλι', ὥς μ' ἀπώλεσας καὶ τόνδ'· Ἀπόλλων δ' ἐν βροτοῖς ὀρθῶς καλῇ.
Ar. *Eq.* 1082. τὴν τούτου χεῖρ' ἐποίησεν Κυλλήνην ὀρθῶς ὁτιή φησ', ἔμβαλε κυλλῇ.
" *Vesp.* 44. εἶτ' Ἀλκιβιάδης εἶπε πρός με τραυλίσας· ὁλᾷς ; Θέωλος τὴν κεφαλὴν κόλακος ἔχει. Ξ. ὀρθῶς γε τοῦτ' Ἀλκιβιάδης ἐτραύλισεν.
" *Thesm.* 1215. ὀρτῶς δὲ συβίνη 'στί· καταβινῆσι γάρ.
Hdt. iv. 52. Ὕπανις ποταμὸς . . . ῥέει ἐκ λίμνης μεγάλης . . . καλέεται δὲ ἡ λίμνη αὕτη ὀρθῶς μήτηρ Ὑπάνιος.
" " 59. Ζεὺς δὲ ὀρθότατα κατὰ γνώμην γε ἐμὴν καλεόμενος Παπαῖος.

Plato uses ὀρθῶς and ὀρθότης in this sense throughout the *Cratylus*.

So Aesch. *Ag.* 702. κῆδος ὀρθώνυμον.

ἀληθῶς :

Aesch. *Supp.* 318. Ἔπαφος ἀληθῶς ῥυσίων ἐπώνυμος.
Eur. *Ph.* 637. ἀληθῶς δ' ὄνομα Πολυνείκην πατὴρ ἔθετό σοι . . .
Ar. *Av.* 505. Π. χὤπόθ' ὁ κόκκυξ εἴποι κόκκυ, τότ' ἂν . . . τοὺς πυροὺς ἂν . . . ἐν τοῖς πεδίοις ἐθέριζον·

E. τοῦτ' ἄρ' ἐκεῖν' ἦν τοὖπος ἀληθῶς·
κόκκυ, ψωλοὶ πεδιόνδε.

Cercidas *fr.* 2. ἦς γὰρ ἀλαθέως
[Διογένης] Ζανὸς γένος οὐράνιός τε κύων.

ὡς ἀληθῶς:

Lucian i. 604, Ath. iii. 96 e, Plut. *Mor.* 34. κατ' ἀλήθειαν, Lucian iii. 97, Theophrastus *fr.* 121 (Ath. xi. 456 b).

εὐλόγως:

Aesch. *Supp.* 45. ἐπωνυμίᾳ δ' ἐπεκραίνετο μόρσιμος αἰὼν
εὐλόγως.
„ „ 258. εὐλόγως ἐπώνυμον.
„ *fr.* 6. Παλικῶν εὐλόγως μένει φάτις.
Ar. *Vesp.* 771. καὶ ταῦτα μὲν νῦν εὐλόγως, ἢν ἐξέχῃ
εἵλη, κατ' ὀρθὸν ἡλιάσει πρὸς ἥλιον.
Plat. *Cratyl.* 416 A.

κάρτα:

Aesch. *Theb.* 645. ἐπωνύμῳ δὲ κάρτα.
„ „ 923. κάρτα δ' εἴσ' ὅμαιμοι.
„ *Eum.* 90. κάρτα δ' ὢν ἐπώνυμος.
Eur. *Rhes.* 158. ἐπώνυμος μὲν κάρτα . . . Δόλων.

πρεπόντως:

Aesch. *Ag.* 692. πρεπόντως ἑλέναυς ἕλανδρος ἑλέπτολις.
so Eur. *Ion* 661. Ἴωνα δ' ὀνομάζω σε τῇ τύχῃ πρέπον.

ἐνδίκως:

Aesch. *Theb.* 392. ὀρθῶς ἐνδίκως τ' ἐπώνυμον.

None of these are open to dispute. But if we were to use Dr. Verrall's method we might discover many more. For example, if he were arguing for ἀληθής, what might we not expect him to say (since he will have not only the adverbs but also the adjectives ἔτυμος, ἐτήτυμος, to mean 'etymologically true') about

*Theb.* 927. Ἄρης ἀρὰν πατρῴαν τιθεὶς ἀλαθῆ.

where he admits that 'there is in fact a play of sound; Ares has behaved according to his appellation'?

So in other authors we find other adverbs, as:

εἰκότως:

Anaxippus *fr.* 3. B. τοῦτον οἱ φίλοι καλοῦσί σοι
νυνὶ δι' ἀνδρείαν Κεραυνόν. A. εἰκότως.
ἀβάτους ποιεῖν γὰρ τὰς τραπέζας . . .

Ath. xiv. 659 b. (οὐκ ἀπεικότως, Ath. xiv. 668 e.) Eur. *fr.* 781 (quoted above under ὀρθῶς) is thus given in sch. Eur. *Or.* 1389 ὦ . . . ἀπώλεσας· κἀκ τοῦδ' Ἀπόλλων εἰκότως κλήζῃ βροτοῖς. Antagoras *ap.* Apostol. *Cent.* v. 13 (in Max. Conf. *Serm.* xv. p. 580 δικαίως, which is used by Apostol. xi. 22).

ἀτρεκέως:

Agath. *A.P.* ix. 630. θερμὰ τάδ' ἀ. βασιλήια· τήνδε γὰρ αὐτοῖς
οἱ πρὶν ἀγασσάμενοι θῆκαν ἐπωνυμίην.

οὐ μάτην:

Alciphron i. 3. οὐ μάτην γοῦν ἀνεισιδώραν ταύτην ὀνομάζουσιν Ἀθηναῖοι ἀνεῖσαν δῶρα δι' ὧν. . .

παγκαλῶς:

Plat. *Cratyl.* 395 E; and καλῶς.

ὄντως:[1]

Aristaen. i. 13. Πανάκιον . . τὸν ὄντως ἐπώνυμον ἰατρόν.
*A. P.* ix. 609. ὄντως δὴ Χαρίτων λουτρὸν τόδε . . .

[1] ὄντως is the most prosaic word. This (or ὄντως δὴ) is used regularly in scholia as a synonym of ὀρθῶς, ἦ, ἦ μήν, ἦ που, κάρτα, etc. At Eur. *H. F.* 1352, δεῖται γὰρ ὁ θεός, εἴπερ ἔστ' ὄντως θεός, is the MS. reading; but Clem. Al. *Strom.* v. p. 249, and Plut. *Mor.* 1052 both quote the passage with the reading ὀρθῶς, which, being a word so frequently explained by ὄντως, it is hardly to be doubted is the true reading. Cf. Wilamowitz-Moellendorff on *H. F.* 58.

τῷ ὄντι:

Ath. v. 179 e, 190 f.

None of these words in itself implies truth of etymology, but with such meanings as *truly, verily, fittingly, indeed*, they mark sufficiently an etymological allusion. My argument will go to show that ἐτύμως, ἐτητύμως are used by Aeschylus with no more special meaning: indeed I shall maintain that in only one place

*Ag.* 686. τίς ποτ' ὠνόμαζεν ὧδ'
ἐς τὸ πᾶν ἐτητύμως . . . Ἑλέναν

is the word used by him with an etymological reference. Let us consider the remaining nine passages where that reference is discovered by Dr. Verrall:

*Eum.* 532. πάντι μέσῳ τὸ κράτος θεὸς ὤπασεν
ἄλλ' ἄλλᾳ δ' ἐφορεύει.
ξύμμετρον δ' ἔπος λέγω·
δυσσεβίας μὲν ὕβρις τέκος ὡς ἐτύμως,
ἐκ δ' ὑγιείας . .

Here, we are told,

> the missing point can be supplied at once. It is an apt word, says Aeschylus, that 'insolence (ὕβρις) is the child (τέκος) of impiety ὡς ἐτύμως.' Why ὡς ἐτύμως? Because insolence under another name is synonymous with τέκος, the word κόρος having both meanings. The antiquity of the ethical *etymon* is proved by the fact, that expressions derived from it are found scattered over the older poets, κόρος being sometimes the 'son' begotten of ὕβρις, sometimes the 'male' (κόρος as opposed to κόρη), who begets her; τίκτει τοι κόρος ὕβριν (Theognis), ὕβριν κόρου ματέρα (Pindar), κόρον ὕβριος υἱόν (ancient oracle attributed to Bacis). . . The meaning of ὡς ἐτύμως then is *in its truest sense, i.e.* as the name shows by a remarkable coincidence intended for the instruction of man.

In the first place, it is an assumption that the proverbial phrases connecting ὕβρις and κόρος were due to an etymon.

Secondly, Dr. Verrall helps his argument by an audacious mistranslation. Aeschylus does not say: 'It is an apt word that ὕβρις is the τέκος of impiety ὡς ἐτύμως': the Greek sentence cannot be so translated. What the Chorus do say is: 'I add a saying to match (that already quoted, *i.e.* πάντι μέσῳ κ.τ.λ.): insolence truly is the child of impiety.' Cf.

*A.P.* x. 48. Μήποτε δουλεύσασα γυνὴ δέσποινα γένοιτο ἐστὶ παροιμιακόν. τῷδε δ' ὅμοιον ἐρῶ· μήτε δίκην δικάσειεν ἀνὴρ γεγονὼς δικολέκτης,..

a useless *truly* does not satisfy the emphatic ὡς ἐτύμως, which, by its position, should contain the point of the sentence.

The reason why the Chorus add ὡς ἐτύμως is that they are quoting with approbation a familiar saying. For it is common in Greek so to introduce a proverb by some corroborative adverb signifying *truly, indeed, in fact, exactly*, or the like. Thus:

ἐτήτυμον (= ἐτητύμως), ἐτύμως:

Archil. 62. ἐτήτυμον γὰρ ξυνὸς ἀνθρώποις Ἄρης.

Antip. Sid. *A. P.* xi. 23. καὶ δὴ γὰρ ἐτήτυμον εἰς ὁδὸν ἵππος οἶνος.

Leonid. or Meleag. *A. P.* vii. 13. ἦ ῥὰ τόδ' ἔμφρων εἶπ' ἐτύμως ἁ παῖς· Βάσκανος ἔσσ', Ἀίδα.

ἀληθῶς:

Cercidas *fr.* 3. οἶκος γὰρ ἄριστος ἀλαθέως καὶ φίλος.[1]

Plat. *Cratyl.* 435 C, Aristaenet. ii. 21, Philostr. *Heroic.* 665.

ὡς ἀληθῶς:

Plat. *Laches* 197 C, Lucian i. 38, 46, 81, 413, ii. 451, Aristid. ii. p. 98, Alciphron i. 30, Ath. v. 186 f, Plut. *Mor.* 68 F, Clem. Al. *Cohort.* 64, *Paedag.* 141, 171.

ὀρθῶς:

Ar. *Lys.* 1038. κἄστ' ἐκεῖνο τοὖπος ὀρθῶς κοὐ κακῶς εἰρημένον·
οὔτε σὺν πανωλέθροισιν οὔτ' ἄνευ πανωλέθρων.

[1] Read ὁ καὶ φίλος?

Aristot. *Probl.* 30. p. $953^b$ 31.
So Theopomp. *fr.* 69. δὶς παῖδες οἱ γέροντες ὀρθῷ τῷ λόγῳ.

ἀτρεκέως :

*A. P.* ix. 459. ἀτρεκέως πάντων πολυμήχανός ἐστιν Ὀδυσσεύς.

εὐλόγως :

Lucian ii. 482. περὶ ἧς ἄν τις εὐλόγως τὸ Ὁμηρικὸν ἐκεῖνο εἴποι.

οὐ μάτην :

*A. P.* xii. 96. οὔτι μάτην θνατοῖσι φάτις τοιάδε βοᾶται ὡς οὐ πάντα θεοὶ πᾶσιν ἔδωκαν ἔχειν.

πάγχυ :

Hom. ρ. 217. νῦν μὲν δὴ μάλα πάγχυ κακὸς κακὸν ἡγηλάζει.
is apparently an instance.

ἀτεχνῶς :

Eupolis *fr.* 282. ἀτεχνῶς μὲν οὖν τὸ λεγόμενον σκύτη βλέπει.
So Plato etc.

ὄντως[1] :

Ep. Kaibel*699. ἄστατος ὄντως θνητῶν ἐστὶ βίος.
Babrius xvi. 6. λύκος χανὼν ὄντως.

[1] Plut. *Mor.* 113 E, μεῖον γὰρ ὄντως Τρωΐλος ἐδάκρυσεν ἢ Πρίαμος αὐτός, . . (Cic. *Tusc. Disp.* i. 39: non male ait Callimachus, multo saepius lacrimasse Priamum quam Troilum). Schneider (Callim. *fr.* 363) says: . . versum esse Callimachi, quem Plutarchus in suam orationem transtulerit, omnes consentiunt et post Blomfieldum Boissonadius, p. 214, Bergk, Anthol. lyr. i. n. 134=ii. n. 148, Dilthey l.l. talem fuisse putant: μεῖον ἐδάκρυσεν Τρωΐλος ἢ Πρίαμος. Sed quis non concedat praestare et retentis verbis γὰρ ὄντως (quae cur negent et ipsa esse a Callimacho profecta causam non video) et servato verborum ordine unaque inserta vocula quem saepissime versus detrimento excidisse constat, talem iambum putare a Callimacho factum esse qualem supra posuimus? [*i.e.*

μεῖον γὰρ ὄντως Τρωΐλος γ' ἐδάκρυσεν
ἢ Πρίαμος].

I cannot agree with Schneider; for it is natural to suppose ὄντως to be the adverb introducing an applied quotation. Compare instances referred to.

Lucil. *A. P.* xi. 259, Plat. *Legg.* iv. 704 A, Lucian ii. 438, Ath. vi. 270 f, xiii. 568 e, xiv. 652 f, Plut. *Mor.* 38, 62 C, 106 D, 109 F, 917 C; etc.

τῷ ὄντι:

Plat. *Laches* 196 D, *Rep.* iv. 426 E, *Theaetet.* 146 B, Polybius xxxiii. p. 1110.

That is how ὡς ἐτύμως is used in *Eum.* 535; and if it is 'useless' except with an etymological meaning, as Dr. Verrall, begging the question, calls it, so equally are these other words in all the places cited. Which it seems unwise to say.

*Supp.* 83. ὕβριν δ' ἐτύμως στυγόντες
πέλοιτ' ἂν ἔνδικοι γάμοις.

Here again

we have the same *etymon* in a slightly different form. The Danaides are imploring the gods to protect them from an enforced marriage with their cousins. When they say that the gods 'detest such insolence *as it truly is*,' the spirit which they so describe is ὁ τοῦ κόρου κόρος, the 'masculine violence' of the would-be bridegrooms, whose very name of κόρος signifies their character. It is the same ἀνδρὸς ὕβρις which according to v. 502 of our play is detested by the virgin goddess Athena.

We may be allowed to observe that when they say the gods 'detest such insolence as it truly is' they say so in remarkably bad grammar. In a sentence of this form that could only be expressed by τὴν ἐτύμως ὕβριν στ. As it is, ἐτύμως must belong to στυγόντες. But Dr. Verrall on p. 141 objects to the meaning *sincerely*. Together with this passage it will be convenient to treat

*Theb.* 902. οὐ φιλογαθής, ἐτύμως
δακρυχέων δ' ἐκ φρενός, ἃ
κλαιομένας μου μινύθει.

*truly weeping* will not pass, unless we tacitly assume that ἐτύμως, like *truly*, can mean *honestly* or *sincerely* (p. 141).
*but weeping drops which come, not in mere phrase, 'from the heart'; for my heart doth waste away as I dissolve in tears for etc.* . . Here the ἔτυμον is in the phrase ἐκ φρενός, which in common metaphorical use signified no more than *sincerely* (see *v.* 859), but is realized literally by

the violence of passionate sorrow, in which the heart seems actually to weep away and be dissolved.

I will first show how in this metaphorical sense θυμός, καρδία, ψυχή, and φρήν are used synonymously:

θυμός:

Theognis 62. μηδένα . . φίλον ποιεῦ . . ἐκ θ., ἀλλὰ δόκει μὲν πᾶσιν ἀπὸ γλώσσης φίλος εἶναι.

ἐκ θ. φιλέειν Hom. I. 343, 486 Bion viii. 2, Naumachius (Stob, *fl.* 74, 7), στέργειν Theocr. xvi. 129, Phanocles (Stob. *fl.* 64, 14), στενάχουσα Mosch. iv. 60, κλαῦσαι Philetas *fr.* 10, μέγαν ἐκ θ. κλάζοντες Ἄρη Aesch. *Ag.* 48.

καρδία:

ἐκ κ. φιλεῖν Ar. *Nub.* 86, Lucian iii. 604, ὅλας φιλέειν ἀπὸ κ. Theocr. xxiii. 4, ἀπὸ κ. φιλεῖς Marc. Anton. vii. 13, ἵλεως ἀληθῶς καὶ ἀπὸ κ. εὐχάριστος *id.* ii. 3, ἐξ αὐτῆς κ. γελᾶν Rufin. *A. P.* v. 61, ἐκ κ. σέο θυμὸς ὄμματα κοιλήνας ἐς χόλον εὐτρέπισεν *Anth. Plan.* iv. 142, ἐρεῖν τἀπὸ κ. σαφῶς Eur. *I. A.* 471, *fr.* 412, ἀκούετε, ὦ θεοί, τά γε ἀπὸ κ., φασίν, Lucian ii. 664, ἐκ κ. ἴαχον Rufin. *A. P.* v. 69.

ψυχή:

σοι ἐκ τῆς ψ. φίλος ἦν Xen. *An.* vii. 7. 43, ἀπὸ ψ. σύ με φιλεῖς Theophr. *Char.* xvii., and so commonly in prose, ἐκ ψ. τερπόμενος Nicander *A. P.* xi. 7, τὰ δ' ἐκ ψ. ἀγόρευε Pseudophocyl. 50.

φρήν:

λέξω τὸν ἐκ φ. λόγον Aesch. *Cho.* 106, μηδὲν ὑγιὲς ἐκ φρενῶν λέγοντι Eur. *fr.* 659, ἐκ φ. λιγαίνειν Aesch. *Theb.* 859, (πλεῖστον ἐξ ἐμῆς φ. στερχθείς Lyc. *Al.* 1190).

There may seem at first sight to be some colour for Dr. Verrall's view in this passage, for the physical sense of φρήν is doubtless present in the words ἃ . . . μινύθει (an expression which it might have been noted is after

Theog. 361. *ἀνδρός τοι κραδίη μινύθει μέγα πῆμα παθόντος*
*Κύρν', ἀποτινυμένου δ' αὔξεται ἐξοπίσω*).

But it must be remembered that Aeschylus' conception of *φρήν* as the seat of emotion etc. would have been always and in any case more physical than ours of the *heart* in that sense. Still more would it be so with Homer. That in

Hom. K. 9. *ὡς πυκίν' ἐν στήθεσσιν ἀνεστάχιζ' Ἀγαμέμνων*
*νειόθεν ἐκ κραδίης· τρομέοντο δέ οἱ φρένες ἐντός.*

the notion of locality is present I would readily allow; but must also feel that while to *groan from the heart* is not an unnatural expression, to *shed tears from the midriff* (*δακρυχέων ἐκ φρενός*), with insistence on the literal sense, is very far from natural. There was a proverb (to give Dr. Verrall still more odds):

Suid. *αἵματι κλαίειν: καθ' ὑπερβολήν· οὐ δάκρυσιν. ἐφ' ὧν μὴ δύναιντο πεῖσαι πάντα πράττοντες οὕτως ἔλεγον οἱ ἀρχαῖοι· οὐδ' ἂν πείσῃ αὐτὸν οὐδ' αἵματι κλαίων. λέγουσι δὲ καί· οὐδ' ἂν αἵματι στένων πείσειεν.*

for which see Leutsch and Schneidewin on Zenob. i. 34, Greg. Cypr. L i. 14, Apostol. i. 63. It is not extant in any early author, nor if it were could I think it applicable to our passage. I have shown that *ὀρθῶς* is used several times by Aeschylus of verbal truth; but I shall not on that account attempt to argue that in

Aesch. *Theb.* 858. *κλαίω στένομαι καὶ δόλος οὐδεὶς*
*μὴ 'κ φρενὸς ὀρθῶς με λιγαίνειν*

it indicates a reference to *true chest-notes* or to *ventriloquism*. Nor, because *ὄντως* is used of verbal truth, shall I urge that it is so used in

Ar. *Nub.* 858. ἀλλ' εἴπερ ἐκ τῆς καρδίας μ' ὄντως φιλεῖς.
Lucian iii. 604. εἴπερ ἐκ καρδίας μ' ὄντως φιλεῖς.

ἐκ καρδίας and ἐκ φρενός have been shown to be synonymous. Finding these phrases in four similar passages combined with ἐτύμως or ὀρθῶς or ὄντως, I shall leave Dr. Verrall to maintain that ὀρθῶς in *Theb.* 859 and ὄντως in Ar. *Nub.* 86, Lucian iii. 604, mean merely *truly, really, genuinely,* but that ἐτύμως in *Theb.* 902 means *according to the literal meaning of the phrase.* I shall hold that in these similar passages the adverbs have a common meaning, and that meaning I shall understand to be *truly, really, genuinely.* Yet this of *Theb.* 902 is called (p. 144) 'a clear and simple case' of the verbal sense.

*Supp.* 83. ὕβριν δ' ἐτύμως στυγόντες.

(which cannot grammatically bear the construction attributed by Dr. Verrall) I shall continue to interpret 'truly, genuinely hating . .' comparing

Aesch. *Supp.* 537. ἄλευσον ἀνδρῶν ὕβριν εὖ στυγήσας.

*Supp.* 742. πάτερ, φοβοῦμαι νῆες ὡς ὠκύπτεροι
ἥκουσι, μῆκος δ' οὐδὲν ἐν μέσῳ χρόνου·
περίφοβόν μ' ἔχει τάρβος ἐτητύμως
πολυδρόμου φυγᾶς ὄφελος εἴ τί μοι.
παροίχομαι, πάτερ, δείματι.

If I may trust my ear, the prominent position of ἐτητύμως demands a meaning at least more pertinent than *truly,* and this of itself satisfies me that the explanation to be sought is etymological. The speakers appear to compare themselves to animals chased and not able to escape any further. I formerly suggested that the etymon lay in περίφοβον, which, commonly meaning *very terrible,* is here to be pressed to the full etymological sense of *surrounding with terror* ; and this, I think, is true as far as it goes. But it cannot be the complete account of the matter for by the order of the words the etymon must include τάρβος. Is it not probable that this word, like the Latin equivalent *formido,* had, beside its common meaning, a technical sense in the language of hunters, *viz.* the *scare,* a line of feathers or the like with which animals were driven? This at any rate would at once permit a complete explanation: ἐτητύμως would have the same force as elsewhere, 'a περίφοβον τάρβος *truly so called,*' and would mark the allusive metaphor which τάρβος is intended to suggest.

This notion need not detain us long. It shall be enough to point out that it is absolutely condemned by the sentence itself. According to Dr. Verrall, ἐτητύμως is added to show that by περίφοβον τάρβος is meant not 'alarm' but a concrete 'scare.' But εἴ τι ὄφελός μοι, unless it is meaningless, depends upon τάρβος ἔχει με, as

Ap. Rh. iv. 1168. τοὺς . . . δεῖμ' ἔχεν εἰ τελέοιτο διάκρισις . .
Aesch. *Supp.* 76. δειμαίνουσα φίλους . . εἴ τις ἐστὶ κηδεμών.
Eur. *Med.* 186. φόβος εἰ πείσω.
„ *Heracl.* 791. φόβος γὰρ εἴ μοι ζῶσιν οὓς ἐγὼ θέλω.

It cannot depend upon it unless τάρβος has its usual meaning 'fear,' which according to Dr. Verrall it has not.

For the phrase περίφοβον τάρβος cf. *Theb.* 226 ταρβοσύνῳ φόβῳ, Eur. *H. F.* 961 ταρβοῦντες φόβῳ, Soph. *Trach.* 176 φόβῳ ταρβοῦσαν, εἰ . .

*Eum.* 491. κρίνασα δ' ἀστῶν τῶν ἐμῶν τὰ βέλτατα
ἥξω διαιρεῖν τοῦτο πρᾶγμ' ἐτητύμως.

The situation is this : Athena, having declared the cause of Orestes to be too grave for the judgment of a man, and too impure for her own interference, announces her intention to summon a jury of Athenian citizens, who decide it by division of votes. This process she describes in the citation by the words διαιρεῖν τὸ πρᾶγμα, *to divide the cause*, and to this phrase is added ἐτητύμως. Obviously the *etymon*, if there be one, must lie in the word διαιρεῖν. Can it be by accident that we are again led straight to a verbal resemblance, which the Greeks are known to have observed, and to have made the basis of a derivation, between δικάζω, *judge*, and διχάζω (=διαιρέω) *divide*? Such an accident is incredible, and we cannot but conclude that ἐτητύμως is intended to call attention to the spontaneous evidence of language in favour of *judgment* by *division*.

διακρίνειν also means to *divide, separate*, and is frequently used in the sense of *deciding, determining, judging*. If it is incredible that διαιρεῖν πρᾶγμα ἐτητύμως does not refer to an etymology, is it credible that

Pind. *P.* i. 68. διακρίνειν ἔτυμον λόγον

does not refer to the same etymology? Or why should not the etymological sense be permitted to ἀληθῶς in

*Eum.* 798. *οὐ γὰρ νενίκησθ', ἀλλ' ἰσόψηφος δίκη*
*ἐξῆλθ' ἀληθῶς, . .* ?

Now compare the following:

Plat. *Protag.* 341 C. *τὰ ὀνόματα ὀρθῶς διαιρεῖν.*
Ar. *Nub.* 742. *ὀρθῶς διαιρῶν καὶ σκοπῶν.*
„ *Plut.* 578. *οὐκ ὀρθῶς διαγιγνώσκειν.*
Hdt. i. 172. *ἀτρεκέως διακρῖναι.*

Having seen that both Aristophanes and Plato use ὀρθῶς with a verbal reference far more frequently than any other word, should we not with equal justice maintain that in *Nub.* 742 and *Protag.* 341 it marks the same verbal allusion that Dr. Verrall cannot but believe is marked in *Eum.* 492 by ἐτητύμως? But that I imagine will be maintained by no one: ὀρθῶς and ἀτρεκέως in the passages quoted will be allowed by every one to mean *truly, rightly, accurately*: and I, at least, shall consider that the same meaning belongs to διαιρεῖν ἐτητύμως in *Eum.* 492, the adverbs being synonymous in this sense, as they are in

Aesch. *Eum.* 751. *πεμπάζετ' ὀρθῶς ἐκβολὰς ψήφων.*
Lycoph. *Al.* 1470. *πάντα φράζειν κἀναπεμπάζειν λόγον ἐτητύμως.*

*Cho.* 945. *ἔμολε δ' ᾧ μέλει κρυπταδίου μάχας*
*δολιόφρων ποινά,*
*ἔθιγε δ' ἐν μάχᾳ χερὸς ἐτήτυμος*
*Διὸς κόρα (Δίκαν δέ νιν*
*προσαγορεύομεν*
*βροτοὶ τυχόντες καλῶς)*
*ὀλέθριον πνέουσ' ἐν ἐχθροῖς κότον.*

From internal evidence alone I should think it certain that this passage contained an *etymon*. I can see no other meaning in the words 'we mortals make a happy hit in calling her Δίκη.' Seeing that the daughter of Zeus here is Δίκη herself, and no one else, how can it be a 'happy hit' to call her by her only name unless that name is found to have some unexpected significance? The signification intended is clear enough :—*Upon him that loves clandestine battle hath come a crafty vengeance: the daughter of Zeus, most truly named, hath hit him in a battle of might, she whom we mortals happily call* Δίκη. It is the *spear* of Justice, cast at the guilty Aegisthus, which is in the mind of the poet, and he would connect her name with δικεῖν, *to throw.*

Both the construction and the application of vv. 945—7 are so doubtful that I can only refer to the commentators, especially to Klausen, Peile, Conington and Davies (Dr. Verrall's interpretation of ἔθιγε is new). But the question before us may be discussed apart. *Διὸς κόρα ἐτητύμως ἐστὶν ἡ Δίκη* could well refer to an etymology; not because *ἐτητύμως* in itself means 'etymologically true,' but because like many another adverb meaning *truly, really, indeed,* it is sufficient in such a sentence to point the etymological reference. But *Διὸς κόρα ἐτήτυμός ἐστιν ἡ Δίκη* could, I believe, mean no more than 'Justice is the real, genuine, daughter of Zeus.' The word is frequently used in connexion with *descent*:

Callim. *fr.* 448. *πάντες ἀφ' Ἡρακλῆος ἐτήτυμον . .*
Ap. Rhod. i. 142. *οὐ μὲν ὅ γ' ἦεν Ἄβαντος ἐτήτυμον.*
„ „ iii. 358. *εἰ δ' αὐτοῦ Κρηθῆος ἐτήτυμόν ἐστι γενέθλης.*
„ „ „ 402. *εἰ γὰρ ἐτήτυμον ἔστε θεῶν γένος.*
Archias *A. P.* ix. 343. *ἱρὸν ἀοιδοπόλων ἔτυμον γένος.*
Epigr. Kaibel 852. *Βουταδέων ἐτύμων ἐξ αἵματος.*
„ „ 874. *ταύτῃ καὶ γένος ἔσχες ἐτήτυμον, Ἡρακλεία,*
*Ἡρακλέους Φοίβου πρὸς δ' ἔτ' ἀπ' Ἰαμίδων.*

Editors quote

Soph. *Tr.* 1064. *ὦ παῖ γενοῦ μοι παῖς ἐτήτυμος γεγώς,*
*καὶ μὴ τὸ μητρὸς αἷμα πρεσβεύσῃς πλέον.*

With this notion it seems to me that a satisfactory sense may be obtained. The parentage of Δίκη is mentioned, according to Klausen, 'ut moneatur de invicta eius potentia,'

Zeus being all-conquering (*Theb.* 501, *Ag.* 173). The same, he says, is the reason that her parentage is mentioned at

*Theb.* 649. εἰ δ' ἡ Διὸς παῖς παρθένος Δίκη παρῆν
ἔργοις ἐκείνου καὶ φρεσίν, τάχ' ἂν τόδ' ἦν.

'contendit enim Eteocles pendere victoriam a Iustitia quia haec Iovis filia sit.' Conington thinks it is rather the justice of Δίκη that is thus emphasised: '. . there is force in saying that the Justice which assisted in the death of Aegisthus was the true child of Zeus, as the expression implies that the act of retribution was strictly just. So in *Theb.* 670 [657 Weckl.] Eteocles says that if Justice were to ally herself with a man like Polynices she would belie her name.' Whether it be the justice or the power of Δίκη that is thereby affirmed, I certainly agree with Klausen and Conington in believing that ἐτ. Διὸς κόρα signifies, not that she is true to her name, but that she is true to her parentage. The parenthesis does refer, I doubt not, to the aptness of her name—Δί-κα, Δι-ός (Wecklein thinks that Δι(ὸς) κ(όρ)α = Δίκα is intended): but the parenthesis is not an *epexegesis* of a preceding phrase 'truly-named'; it is a further insistence upon the descent of Δίκη from Zeus.

While, then, I see here an etymology, it is not Δίκ-η, δικ-εῖν, but Δί-κη, Δι-ός: and that etymology I consider is not marked by ἐτήτυμος.

δικεῖν serves again:

*Ag.* 177. Ζεὺς ὅστις ποτ' ἐστίν, εἰ τόδ' αὐτῷ φίλον κεκλημένῳ,
τοῦτό νιν προσεννέπω.
οὐκ ἔχω προσεικάσαι
πάντ' ἐπισταθμώμενος
πλὴν Διός, εἰ τὸ μάταν
ἀπὸ φροντίδος ἄχθος
χρὴ βαλεῖν ἐτητύμως.

. . . The order shows that ἐτητύμως is closely connected with βαλεῖν. But 'to cast truly' is an impossible phrase, unless *truly* be taken to mean *thoroughly*, which ἐτητύμως does not. Moreover, in the translation the words 'in good truth' are superfluous: in the Greek ἐτητύμως by its position is all-important. If on the contrary we seek an *etymon*, there is no difficulty in finding it. The frame of the passage shows that it must be an *etymon* upon the name Διός, and must be suggested by the word βαλεῖν. The key-word is again to be found in δι-κεῖν: the religious *etymon* to which Aeschylus alludes connected the syllable Δι- in the sacred name with ὁ δικών, and interpreted it, by the gymnastic use of δικεῖν, as a symbol of strength. . . If the passage stood alone, I should incline against an etymological reference. The general argument from the use of ἐτήτυμος elsewhere in Aeschylus turns the balance the other way.

Plausible as this may appear, I cannot see that it is warranted by any unsatisfactory sense in the usual interpretation. I consider with others the argument of the Chorus to be that Zeus being master and conqueror of all it is to Zeus they must turn if they are really to get rid of their misgivings: *I cannot guess another beside Zeus* (προσ-εικάσαι) *if I am truly to cast off the vain burden on my mind.*

*Eum.* 499. πολλὰ δ' ἔτυμα παιδότρωτα
πάθεα προσμένει τοκεῦσιν
μεταῦθις ἐν χρόνῳ.

the *etymon* should lie in παιδότρωτα, and here it is at once discoverable, for παιδότρωτον πάθος means not only 'wound struck by a child,' but also 'wound struck with the point' of the weapon, and apart from the context would be the more natural of the two.

The meaning 'point' is

from παίς, *point*, connected with παίω. See Hesychius, παιδός· ἀκμῆς. This gloss has been supposed without reason to be corrupt.

If the meaning 'etymologically true' was established for ἐτήτυμος and ἔτυμος in Aeschylus' time and one of these words had already been used by Aeschylus to mark a play on παῖς and παίς, then surely Sophocles was lucky if he escaped laughter when he wrote

ὦ παῖ, γενοῦ μοι παῖς ἐτήτυμος γεγώς, . . !

All that M. Schmidt says upon the entry in Hesych. is 'Spectat ad phrasin ἐκ παιδός.' [Cf. παῖς: . . ἄρτι ἀκμάζων]. It will be allowed that this entry is somewhat slender support for a word παὶς = *point*. Myself I do not think an etymological reference could be marked by the *adjective* ἔτυμα: by the *adverb* of course it could be. Still I must admit that I am puzzled to see the exact sense of ἔτυμα in this passage. The notion of *race, descent*, illustrated above, seems to have little [1]force here. The best meaning I can discover is 'real, downright, indisputable, without extenuating circumstances.' The editors do not help. We come at last to the passage which serves as the theme of the Excursus:

*Theb.* 81. αἰθερία κόνις με πείθει φανεῖσ'
ἄναυδος σαφὴς ἔτυμος ἄγγελος.

It will be observed that here ἔτυμος is not used exactly in the proper sense: τὸ ἔτυμον is properly the quality not of the messenger but of the message. In itself this is not remarkable; the Lexicon will show other such uses both of ἔτυμος and of similar words, such as σαφὴς or ἀληθής. But in the light of the other evidence, the slightest irregularity must excite our attention.

Dr. Verrall entirely omits to mention that twice in Homer we have this very phrase, of 'a true messenger':

Homer X. 438. οὐ γάρ οἵ τις ἐτήτυμος ἄγγελος ἐλθὼν
ἤγγειλ' ὅττι . .
*h. Cer.* 44. τῇ δ' οὔτις ἐτήτυμα μυθήσασθαι
ἤθελεν, οὔτε θεῶν οὔτε θνητῶν ἀνθρώπων,
οὐδ' οἰωνῶν τις τῇ ἐτήτυμος ἄγγελος ἦλθεν.

This Homeric use, it seems to me, is evidence much too strong to be utterly ignored: it is so strong that only the most convincing proof would persuade us that Aeschylus used the phrase in quite a different sense. Let us see what are Dr. Verrall's proofs. The ordinary rendering of ἔτυμος, he says, 'omits the chief part of the meaning, and that part which to Aeschylus justified the otherwise pointless verbosity of the description.' I shall probably have something to say another time upon multiplication of adjectives in Aeschylus: meantime it must be remembered that in a metaphor of this

[1] The argument about the father and the mother is not broached till *v.* 660.

kind, where κόνις is called ἄγγελος, it is habitual in Greek verse to add a *defining epithet*, e.g. *Theb.* 64 κῦμα χερσαῖον στρατοῦ. It could hardly be omitted with any metaphors but the few that were most familiar. What therefore to us may seem cumbrous, to Aeschylus was necessary. So

Theogn. 549. ἄγγελος ἄφθογγος πόλεμον πολύδακρυν ἐγείρει
Κύρν', ἀπὸ τηλαυγέος φαινόμενος σκοπίης.

So where Aeschylus uses the same metaphor again, he has the necessary defining epithet alone:

*Supp.* 186. ὁρῶ κόνιν, ἄναυδον ἄγγελον στρατοῦ.

σαφής, ἔτυμος (which elsewhere might be synonymous), being used together, mean 'distinct and truthful.' That is the explanation of what to Dr. Verrall seems 'pointless verbosity.' To his argument we will now return:

The question may be put thus: Does the combination κόνις-ἄγγελος admit of an etymological interpretation? If it does, the presence of ἔτυμος is sufficient to assure us that the interpretation was in the mind of the poet. But it is certain that it does admit this interpretation; for to the Greek ear the stem κον- suggested not merely 'dust,' but also an 'errand-runner' or 'servant,' as is proved by the extant words κονήτης, *a servant*, and the compound ἐγκονεῖν, both implying the previous existence of κονεῖν and κόνος.

The desired meaning 'errand-runner,' *i.e.* 'messenger,' is obtained more easily than is warranted. Of the root of κονεῖν I cannot speak: see Ebeling *Lex. Hom.* *s.v.* ἐγκονέων. But from the uses of ἐγκονεῖν it can be seen that nothing of ἀγγέλλειν is inherent in it. Dr. Verrall further thinks it probable that there was a masculine κόνις *an errand-runner*. And

From this and not from κόνις *dust*, was probably derived κονίποδες, a local name for *serfs* at Epidaurus. See the *Lex.* *s.v.*

Now, it is well known that false but obvious and apparently true etymologies of words are constantly entertained by the unlearned. It is quite likely that the old *Courts of pie-poudre* (quoted by L. and S.) did not derive their name, as was supposed, from (*Curia pedis pulverizati*) *pieds poudreux*. But with κονίποδες (see M. Schmidt on Hesych. *s.v.*) everything indicates that κόνις, the traditional, is also the true etymology—the long ῑ and the use of κονίω (which is agreed to be from κόνις), κεκονιμένος. Cf. Lucian i. 623 οὐχ ὁρᾷς δὲ καὶ τὸν Ἑρμῆν αὐτὸν ἱδρῶτι ῥεόμενον καὶ τὼ πόδε κεκονιμένον καὶ πνευστιῶντα; and Pollux vii. 86 οἱ δὲ κονίποδες λεπτὸν ὑπόδημα πρεσβυτικόν· τὸ δὲ κάττυμα κοῦφον, ὡς ἐγγὺς εἶναι τῆς κόνεως τὸν πόδα.

We have enough to see that the association between κόνις and ἄγγελος was natural to a mind studious of such things, and we know also that this association was permanent, for in the *Suppl.* (*v.* 186) the words of our passage are repeated. . . . All this being so, it may remain possible that Aeschylus described κόνις as ἔτυμος ἄγγελος, and yet did *not* mean to suggest that the very name of κόνις imported the function. But it requires a 'robust faith' to believe it.

We have been led to believe it, I think, by a method more satisfactory than faith.

The special sense of τὸ ἔτυμον, says Dr. Verrall, has since appropriated the word entirely, to the exclusion of all other meanings; and this appropriation took place so early that in the common language of Greek prose this class of words does not appear. Putting these facts together with those we have observed in Aeschylus, we are justified in the inference that already in his time the process of limitation had commenced, and had to some extent changed the colour of the word.

If so, is it not strange that in an etymological discussion Plato should never once have used this class of words?

I shall submit a different account. In poetry[1] these words are common. To Comedy they are foreign, occurring only in a passage of Aristophanes:

*Pax.* 114. ὦ πάτερ, ὦ πάτερ, ἦ ῥ' ἔτυμός γε
δώμασιν ἡμετέροις φάτις ἥκει . . ;
118. ἔστι τι τῶνδ' ἐτύμως; εἴπ', ὦ πάτερ, εἴ τι φιλεῖς με.

[1] The instances in Homer, Pindar, and the Tragedians can easily be found. Those in Hesiod occur *Op.* 10, *fr.* 108, *Theog.* 27: in Bergk's poets, Theognis 308, 713, Xenophanes *fr.* 7, Ion 4, Erinna 4, Stesich 32, Philoxenus i. 26, Pseudophocyl. 7, Archilochus 62.

*Pax* 119. TP. δοξάσαι ἔστι, κόραι· τὸ δ' ἐτήτυμον ἄχθομαι ὑμῖν.

Sch. τὸ δὲ ἦ ῥ' ἔτυμός γε εἴρηται παρὰ τὰ ἐξ Αἰόλου Εὐριπίδου (*fr.* 17)· ἆρ' ἔτυμον φάτιν ἔγνων . . ;

„ 119. καὶ τοῦτο πρὸς τὸ ἐξ Αἰόλου Εὐριπίδου (*fr.* 18) ἔπος· δοξάσαι ἔστι κόραι· τὸ δ' ἐτήτυμον οὐκ ἔχω εἰπεῖν.

From which it is plain that he is ridiculing Euripides' fondness of these words. It is easily intelligible that this might have been regarded as an affectation, for the words were exclusively poetical. In prose ἐτήτυμος is entirely unknown, and so is ἔτυμος until Aristotle, by whom it is used three times in one passage, and there in the etymological sense :

περὶ κόσμου 399$^{a}$ 14, κόσμον ἐτύμως τὸ σύμπαν ἀλλ' οὐκ ἀκοσμίαν ὀνομάσασα.

„ „ 400$^{a}$ 6, ὃν ἐτύμως καλοῦμεν οὐρανὸν μὲν ἀπὸ τοῦ ὅρον εἶναι τοῦ ἄνω . .

„ „ 401$^{a}$ 25 . . σωτήρ τε καὶ ἐλευθέριος ἐτ'μως (ὀνομάζεται Ζεύς).

From this evidence the true history of the words may be deduced with certainty. According to the Attic 'law of parsimony,' which will be understood by those who have read Dr. Rutherford's *New Phrynichus*, they were not used in prose or in Comedy because they were not needed, being merely superfluous synonyms of ὀρθὸς or ἀληθής. But later, when it had dropped out of common use, ἔτυμος was introduced again to serve in the scientific connexion of a special kind of truth.

Such is the work which in my opinion required outspoken criticism.

Any book no doubt may justly receive such criticism as it merits ; but this examination would not have been necessary had only the better understanding of Aeschylus been my concern—that is a small object which might have been attained by usual means. But when the second of these volumes appeared, constructed on the same principles as the first, it seemed to me no longer tolerable that their method should go unopposed. Much in them was indeed thought fanciful, much felt to be unsound: but their true character was not appreciated. And it would be easy to point out many whom their glitter has dazzled, fascinated, and seduced. Their influence upon such as are attracted, not repelled, can only be extremely mischievous. Such method can flourish only at the expense of its opposite; if work of this kind be admired and welcomed, scientific method must languish in disfavour; and scientific method I conceive it to be the true function of a learned University to teach and to encourage.

It has been my interest as much as possible only to repeat what was already familiar knowledge among scholars. Weary as I am and impatient of work which by its nature allows so little the proposition of what is new, I must be content with the belief that at the present moment I can best serve the cause of learning indirectly. As I have intimated, I shall go on to the *Agamemnon*, giving a full discussion of the plot. Dr. Verrall's new theory calls in any case for examination, but it could not be properly examined unless his methods first were understood.

# INDEX OF CHIEF MATTERS.

(*The numbers refer to the pages of this book.*)

# "ON EDITING AESCHYLUS."

## A REPLY

BY

A. W. VERRALL, LITT.D.

FELLOW OF TRINITY COLLEGE, CAMBRIDGE.

London:

MACMILLAN AND CO.

AND NEW YORK.

1892

*Price One Shilling net.*

# "ON EDITING AESCHYLUS."

## A REPLY

BY

A. W. VERRALL, Litt.D.
FELLOW OF TRINITY COLLEGE, CAMBRIDGE.

London:
MACMILLAN AND CO.
AND NEW YORK.
1892

# "ON EDITING AESCHYLUS."

## A REPLY.

"We parted last night in the middle of a controversy and are rageing to resume it. Where is our redoubtable antagonist?"

Mrs Mountstuart wheeled Professor Crooklyn round to accompany Vernon.

"We," she said, "are for modern English scholarship opposed to the champion of German."

"The contrary," observed Professor Crooklyn.

"Oh. We," she corrected the error serenely, "are for German scholarship, opposed to English."

"Certain editions."

"We defend certain editions."

"'Defend' is a term of imperfect application to my position, ma'am."

"My dear professor, you have in Dr Middleton a match for you in conscientious pugnacity, and you will not waste it upon me...."

Mrs Mountstuart fell back to Laetitia, saying "He pores over a little inexactitude in phrases and pecks at it like a domestic fowl."

George Meredith. *The Egoist.*

Mr Walter Headlam has recently published[1], under the title "On editing Aeschylus. A criticism," a solid pamphlet of 159 pages against my writings and me. When the book was announced, I did not expect that it would give me any reason or excuse for departing from the rule, that a review should be left, without remark, to the judgment of numbers and time, and that the author criticised has nothing to do but to correct his opinions where he sees reason, and, as occasion offers, to correct his works. I am not, I hope, so fatuous or so obstinate as to reject correction. Like all men of any candour, I am aware that I make mistakes. I supposed that Mr Headlam would note some points on which I knew that I had gone wrong, and would satisfy me that I was wrong in other places which I had not suspected. Of course I also expected to find many arguments which would not convince me. Of these last, had such been the purport and character of the book, I should have taken no notice, having never thought that public controversy between a particular pair of students, who may be in no way specially fitted to enlighten each other or to strike out truth between them, has any advantage over peaceable separate work. As to the points on which I was convinced, I might or might not have thought it desirable to make acknowledgment at once, but should probably have waited for convenient opportunities.

When the book came to my hands a fortnight ago, I saw at a glance that the tone of it was such as is now seldom used between students who merely disagree where difference is permissible. This however did not surprise or annoy me. From what I had seen of Mr Headlam in another case, I did not expect to find him in my own case a very ceremonious critic. But when I read continuously, I found, to my astonishment, that the book as a whole purported to be not a discussion of

[1] London, David Nutt, 1891.

points debateable, but an arraignment of me personally, not merely for such ignorance in elementary parts of my subject as, considering my position, might well be regarded as a moral offence, but for such wilful persistence in ignorance as in a professional writer would be nothing less than dishonest. This was another thing altogether and opened at once the question of answering.

I am not indeed afraid that these charges will be believed against me by any one well acquainted either with me or with my work, or by any competent person, who has the leisure and patience to go fully into the matter. If it were possible to create a court for such cases, Mr Headlam's statements would be actionable; and I should commence an action immediately and with confidence. I should be almost bound to do so; for whether Mr Headlam sees it or not (I think he does) his book is libellous. The question is whether, this being so, I am not now bound, for want of a court, to make some answer in print, for the credit of my position, and in consideration of the fact that among busy men mere assertion, even if not credible nor consciously believed, is apt, if not contradicted, to leave a vague impression. I have decided on the whole that I ought to answer, not without misgiving, for the whole proceeding is scandalous and unpleasant. But if there is ground for displeasure, let the blame be laid where it ought.

My critic, everywhere stern and severe, as becomes one who is demanding justice upon a criminal, is nowhere more peremptory or more confident than in his remarks upon my treatment of the pronoun *αὐτός*. In the course of my notes on the two plays of Aeschylus, which I have published as part of a complete edition of the poet, I have repeatedly made or implied a statement, which is given most fully in the note to *Theb.* 656:

> As has been observed before, the use of *αὐτός*, unless for emphasis, is very rare in Aeschylus. As unemphatic pronouns can be supplied from the context, the insertion of them is a sacrifice of force to simplicity and clearness, and alien to the weighty and sententious Aeschylean style. With the light enclitic pronouns *νιν*, *σφε* etc., this is not felt, but *αὐτός*, if needless, has an incongruous effect, and where it occurs an emphasis is to be looked for.

Mr Headlam cites from my two commentaries fifteen notes to this effect, and then continues thus (p. 57):

Now all this is due either to unverified assumption or to deliberate disregard of the evidence. The truth is stated by Dindorf (*Lex. Aesch. s. v.* αὐτός *p.* 52): αὐτός *is*, sed in casibus tantum obliquis, neque in initio sententiae, sed post unum vel plura vocabula, et plerumque in diverbiis, rarius in melicis,...

According to his list there are in Aeschylus certainly not more than thirty-one instances of αὐτός emphatic in the oblique cases, and certainly not less than 44 unemphatic. Reference to that list will save me from disproving the assertion that 'except with emphasis αὐτός is exceedingly rare in Aeschylus', as it might have saved Dr Verrall from making that assertion. Though indeed a lexicon would be of little use to the judgment that could propound such interpretations.

Let it now be carefully observed, that with the last sentence, the remark on my judgment, I have no concern whatever, and will assume that it is true, as indeed in one sense it is. It simply expresses, in language of no common asperity, the fact that Mr Headlam disagrees with me. I do not dispute this; so far as the question is one of judgment, it is no subject for polemics. The statement which I impugn is no matter of opinion but of fact. It is the false and injurious statement, that *all this is due either to unverified assumption or to deliberate disregard of the evidence,* interpreted as it is by the rest of the passage and the remark about Dindorf's *Lexicon.* Statements, or rather accusations, like this are scattered all over the book. There is nothing to indicate that Mr Headlam considers this one any weaker than the rest, nor is it. I choose it as a specimen because it is especially gross. And I say that it is a libel.

That it has one quality of a libel, that it is defamatory and injurious to my character, I need not labour to prove. It is meant to be so. If my remarks upon the use of αὐτός in Aeschylus were made negligently, the negligence is of that kind which deserves a different name. To plead an oversight would be ridiculous. The question goes to the very roots of my author's language and style. I came to it fifteen times in the two plays, and had therefore at least fifteen opportunities of reflexion. Moreover, if I was really studying Aeschylus as a whole, as I said that I was, with the intention of editing the whole, I must be finding other such opportunities frequently. The means of investigation were ready to hand. If then under these circumstances I went on making my statement, either without consulting a lexicon (*i.e.* upon an "unverified assumption"), or knowing that the lexicon was against me but resolved to ignore it (*i.e.* in "deliberate disregard of the evidence"), there is an end of my moral competence to write profitably about Aeschylus or any subject whatever. Mr Headlam's charge then is defamatory.

In the next place, it is absolutely untrue. Since there is no way of proving this except to state what I actually did, and since no one knows this fully, or well could know it, except myself, I hope I shall be excused, if I speak of my private work in a way which but for this necessity might be called obtrusive.

Doubts about the extent, to which the unemphatic *αὐτός* was used by Aeschylus and other poets, occurred to me first in the general course of my reading, and I had made many notes upon the subject. When I began to edit Aeschylus, it was necessary that, so far at least as his usage was concerned, I should go to the bottom of the matter. I read Aeschylus through, with this purpose among others in mind, completing and revising my notes on the point. I then took the list of examples in Dindorf's *Lexicon*, following here for a moment the scientific method recommended by Mr Headlam. And here I forgot to stop. If I had stopped here, it "might have saved" me from making my assertion. It might indeed. It would be a most saving and compendious method. It would save me (or any one) from making this (or any) assertion about the usage of Aeschylus. What need of it, if Dindorf's *Lexicon* is the final truth? However I went on. I examined again the examples of *αὐτός*, upwards of forty, which Dindorf classes together as unemphatic. I then took the list in Donaldson's index to Pindar (more than forty examples of the oblique cases) and spent many hours over that. I then read—for I wanted to observe several other things in connexion with *αὐτός* itself, and indices were not convenient helps—I then read, for this purpose only, the *Oedipus Tyrannus*, the *Oedipus Coloneus*, and the *Antigone*, the *Medea* and Euripides here and there, several chapters of Thucydides, and other portions of prose authors. Having done this, and not before, I wrote, as I came to the passages, the notes on the subject, about a page in all, in the *Seven against Thebes* and the *Agamemnon*. Most of what is here said I could confirm by documentary evidence and the testimony of others; for the rest I can give only my word. There is nothing to boast of. No one can do more than his duty; but I think it will be allowed that I did not do less. Upon this single subject I spent at least a week.

And here in strictness my reply to this charge, on the question of its truth, should end. To set forth my investigations, or any part of them, is not to the point; nor does it matter whether my conclusions were completely right or completely wrong. But since, though this paper is necessarily personal, I am unwilling that it should contain nothing of interest apart from my personality, I will give here briefly the rest of the statement on *αὐτός* in Aeschylus, with which I have been prepared ever since I began to edit his works. Of passages in the two plays already published I shall say nothing. All these I had certainly considered, for I printed notes on them. It will be seen that the account which follows accords with the notes and is such as any one, reading the notes, would naturally suppose me to have projected. I have used here for convenience the numeration of Dindorf's *Poetae Scenici* and *Lexicon* to Aeschylus. In my edition I use that of Wecklein.

Let us first state the question. In fully developed Greek prose the oblique cases of *αὐτός*, having practically driven out of the field some archaic rivals, are used almost as freely as the English *him, her, them, it,* and constantly without any emphasis at all. The somewhat cumbrous dissyllable, for so light a point in the sentence, is not (to my thinking) among the advantages of Greek, and the composers of Attic prose may well have sometimes regretted the general abandonment of *σφε* and *νιν*, though uniformity had carried the day. However that may be, the Attic poets show no fondness for the unemphatic *αὐτός*. They maintain the exploded enclitics. They use ellipse of the pronoun much more freely than would be convenient for prose-writers, whose first object is to be clear. They turn their sentences by preference so as not to need unemphatic pronouns. In short, from whatever motives, they manage, as compared with prose-writers, to do with very little of *αὐτός*. The poets differ slightly among themselves, and Aeschylus shows certainly not more inclination to be free with the word than others whom we should naturally match with him. It is therefore no idle enquiry, but one arising naturally out of the facts, whether, when he acts against his common inclination, he has not a motive for doing so, how far his lapses into *αὐτός* are really lapses, and how far acts of discretion. If we contrast the language of a prose-writer with that of a tragedian, even Thucydides with Euripides, no difference is more marked than the comparative rarity in the poet of sentences such as the last of these lines from Aeschylus (*Supp.* 302)

A. *τί οὖν ἔτευξεν ἄλλο δυσπότμῳ βοΐ;*
B. *βοηλάτην μυῶπα κινητήριον·*
A. *οἶστρον καλοῦσιν αὐτὸν οἱ Νείλου πέλας*[1].

Here, *prima facie*, *αὐτόν* appears to be used without any necessity at all. If it were not there, we should supply a pronoun mentally, and the meaning (it seems) would be the same. This is the "unemphatic *αὐτός*", the use of the pronoun, where by an enclitic, or by ellipse, or by turning the sentence differently, the meaning could be as well expressed without this pronoun. And the question is, how much of this use do we find in Aeschylus? I said and think that it is extremely rare.

That the classification in Dindorf, though true as far as it goes, is not exhaustive, would sufficiently appear from the fact that it includes as simply unemphatic the following case (*Pers.* 837):

*ἀλλ' αὐτὸν εὐφρόνως σὺ πράϋνον λόγοις·*
*μόνης γάρ, οἶδα, σοῦ κλύων ἀνέξεται.*

[1] The distribution of the dialogue is here immaterial. See Mr Tucker's note.

So says Darius to Atossa, requesting her to console the grief of Xerxes. Now surely we cannot say that the complexion of this sentence is precisely the same as if the poet had written *ἀλλ' εὐφρόνως σὺ πραΰνόν νιν.* The point is the special relation between the king and his mother, and this point is marked, in the most natural way, by the emphasis of the contrasted or correlated pronouns. It is Xerxes who has to be consoled; therefore Atossa, the only person to whom he will listen, must give the consolation. Both *σύ* and *αὐτόν* are emphatic, the one as much as the other: *σύ*, which is so by nature, is left to take care of itself; *αὐτόν* is reinforced by position in the sentence.

So again in *Eum.* 767, Orestes, promising that his spirit shall protect Athens against Argos, says:

> *αὐτοὶ γὰρ ἡμεῖς ὄντες ἐν τάφοις τότε*
> *τοῖς τἀμὰ παρβαίνουσι νῦν ὁρκώματα*
> *ἀμηχάνοισι πράξομεν δυσπραξίαις*
> *ὁδοὺς ἀθύμους καὶ παρόρνιθας πόρους*
> *τιθέντες, ὡς αὐτοῖσι μεταμέλῃ πόνος·*
> *ὀρθουμένων δὲ καὶ πόλιν τὴν Παλλάδος*
> *τιμῶσιν ἀεὶ τήνδε συμμάχῳ δορὶ*
> *αὐτοῖσιν ἡμεῖς ἐσμεν εὐμενέστεροι.* 774

Here, in the last line, the very position of *αὐτοῖσιν* shows that it is emphatic, and the connected emphasis of *ἡμεῖς* shows what the point is. The Athenians have bound to them, by eternal gratitude, one who is to become a chief hero ('patron-saint' is the nearest equivalent) of the Argives. So long, therefore, as they behave well to Athens, their own patron will be favourable in proportion to *them*; and if they try to assail his benefactors, *he* will use his power not against Athens but against *them*, so that *they themselves* (not Athens) shall have cause to repent of the enterprise. And this example is specially instructive, because it warns us not to be hasty in concluding that there is no point in the choice of a pronoun more weighty than usual. The structure of the verse directs us to the emphasis in *v.* 774: and when we have noted this, we can see what, if we had trained ourselves sufficiently in the habits of

Greek poetry, we should have felt before, that the weight of the pronoun is meant to tell in *v.* 771 also, although here it is not, or at least not equally, enforced by position: which is a caution not to be quick in trusting our first impressions on so delicate a matter.

Such a caution we need, for example, in another case (also classed by Dindorf, with all here mentioned, simply and without distinction as an example of "*αὐτός is*"), *Prom.* 680:

*βουκόλος δὲ γηγενὴς*
*ἄκρατος ὀργὴν Ἄργος ὡμάρτει, πυκνοῖς*
*ὄσσοις δεδορκὼς τοὺς ἐμοὺς κατὰ στίβους.*
*ἀπροσδόκητος δ' αὐτὸν αἰφνίδιος μόρος*
*τοῦ ζῆν ἀπεστέρησεν.*

Here we can of course ignore the weight, which *αὐτός*, by the mere rarity of its occurrence in poetry, should carry to the ear. But, if we do, we miss the delicacy of the expression: *ἀπροσδόκητος δ' αὐτὸν κ.τ.λ.* is contrasted with *δεδορκὼς τοὺς ἐμοὺς κατὰ στίβους*: and the point made or suggested is, that while Argus was all eyes for *Io*, he was surprised by a sudden fate which annihilated *him*.

So again in *Prom.* 306:

*δέρκου θέαμα, τόνδε τὸν Διὸς φίλον,*
*τὸν συγκαταστήσαντα τὴν τυραννίδα,*
*οἵαις ὑπ' αὐτοῦ πημοναῖσι κάμπτομαι.*

If we say that *αὐτοῦ* here is without weight, we miss the very point and pathos of the verse, which lies in this, that the *friend of Zeus* should be so *bowed with torture* by *him*, by the very Zeus whom he served: the pronoun is as plainly emphatic, as if Aeschylus had written *αὐτοῦ τοῦ Διός*. Yet even this is counted as merely one instance of "*αὐτός is.*"

So in *Eum.* 829:

*κἀγὼ πέποιθα Ζηνί, καὶ τί δεῖ λέγειν;*
*καὶ κλῇδας οἶδα δώματος μόνη θεῶν,*
*ἐν ᾧ κεραυνός ἐστιν ἐσφραγισμένος.*
*ἀλλ' οὐδὲν αὐτοῦ δεῖ· σὺ δ' εὐπειθὴς ἐμοὶ κ.τ.λ.*

It is surely not without importance to the feeling of this passage, that the poet does not use *αὐτός* habitually and constantly, as a prose-writer does. The emphasis which, owing to this parsimony, *αὐτοῦ* carries in itself, conveys exactly the meaning intended. "But there is no need of *it*." The weapon itself, the actual display of force, is not needed; it is enough, and more than enough, to hint that Athena, as is well known, could command it. Let the rebellious not wait for *her thunders*, but at once yield obediently to *her* (*αὐτοῦ—ἐμοί*).

Not less clear is it (in my opinion) that *αὐτά* has weight and significance in the following (*Prom.* 441):

> καίτοι θεοῖσι τοῖς νέοις τούτοις γέρα
> τίς ἄλλος ἢ 'γὼ παντελῶς διώρισεν;
> ἀλλ' αὐτὰ σιγῶ. καὶ γὰρ εἰδυίαισιν ἂν
> ὑμῖν λέγοιμι.

Would it have made no difference here, except to the metre, if Prometheus had said *ἀλλὰ σιγῶ τάδε*, and does he mean merely "I say nothing of them"? Surely not. In *ἀλλ' αὐτὰ σιγῶ* the pronoun, even by position, has a stress; since, metre apart, if no stress were meant, the order should be *ἀλλὰ σιγῶ αὐτά*. But *αὐτά*, 'the gifts *themselves*,' means 'the *actual* gifts,' 'the *specific* gifts,' and contributes an important quota to the sense. In English we should throw the meaning, with the emphasis, into the verb, 'But I do not *specify* the gifts.' The same thing might have been expressed a little more fully by *αὔθ' ἕκαστα*.

Again, *αὐτός* is naturally used, with the usual emphasis, when the sentence expresses an inversion of relations, a retribution in which some one is 'done by as he did,' or is treated *himself* as he proposed to treat *another*. This accounts for *Prom.* 358.

> ἐξ ὀμμάτων δ' ἤστραπτε γοργωπὸν σέλας,
> ὡς τὴν Διὸς τυραννίδ' ἐκπέρσων βίᾳ·
> ἀλλ' ἦλθεν αὐτῷ Ζηνὸς ἄγρυπνον βέλος,
> καταιβάτης κεραυνὸς ἐκπνέων φλόγα,
> ὃς αὐτὸν ἐξέπληξε κ.τ.λ.

Here the mere fact that the exceptional pronoun is used twice in a few lines is notice of some particular intention; and the intention is clear. Typhon proposed to 'storm the royalty of Zeus.' Instead of this, ἦλθεν αὐτῷ Ζηνὸς βέλος, it was the bolt of *Zeus* that descended upon *him*[1]: αὐτὸν in *v.* 360 echoes and reinforces the same idea.

Precisely similar is *Cho.* 119:

ΧΟ. τοῖς αἰτίοις νῦν τοῦ φόνου μεμνημένη—
ΗΛ. τί φῶ; δίδασκ' ἄπειρον ἐξηγουμένη.
ΧΟ. ἐλθεῖν τιν' αὐτοῖς δαίμον' ἢ βροτῶν τινὰ—
ΗΛ. πότερα δικαστὴν ἢ δικηφόρον λέγεις;
ΧΟ. ἁπλῶς τι φράζουσ', ὅστις ἀνταποκτενεῖ.

Here αὐτοῖς imports and anticipates the idea of retribution ('that an avenger, divine or human, may come to shed *their* blood'), which the speaker is afraid to put clearly, but, by the management of Electra, is led to make explicit in ἀνταποκτενεῖ.

With these passages for comparison we can see why αὐτῷ is right and desirable, even though the passage is lyric and the pronoun singularly prominent, in *Eum.* 320:

ὅστις δ' ἀλιτὼν ὥσπερ ὅδ' ἀνὴρ
χεῖρας φονίας ἐπικρύπτει,
μάρτυρες ὀρθαὶ τοῖσι θανοῦσιν
παραγιγνόμεναι πράκτορες αἵματος
αὐτῷ τελέως ἐφάνημεν.

The language is similar to that of the last example, and the point the same.

Alike in principle, though not precisely alike in form, is *Prom.* 909:

ἦ μὴν ἔτι Ζεύς, καίπερ αὐθάδη φρονῶν,
ἔσται ταπεινός· τοῖον ἐξαρτύεται
γάμον γαμεῖν, ὃς αὐτὸν ἐκ τυραννίδος
θρόνων τ' ἄϊστον ἐκβαλεῖ.

[1] *Theb.* 431 πέποιθα δ' αὐτῷ, κ.τ.λ. belongs to this class, αὐτῷ going with ἥξειν. So far I agree with Mr Headlam. I wrote my note in this sense first, but afterwards changed it (erroneously as I have long since thought) for that printed.

Here the point is that the act of *Zeus* shall have for result the expulsion of *him* from his power; and αὐτόν should no more be classed as without emphasis than αὐτός would have been, if the sentence had taken the form δι' ὃν αὐτὸς ἐκ θρόνων ἐκπεσεῖται.

Of *Pers.* 436 τοιάδ' ἐπ' αὐτοῖς (or αὐτοὺς) ἦλθε κ.τ.λ., and *Cho.* 712 ἄγ' αὐτὸν κ.τ.λ. it is needless to say anything. In each case an emphasis on the pronoun is proper, to prepare the ear for the intended sequel. In the first the antithesis is between αὐτοῖς and τοῖσδε, in the second between αὐτὸν and ὀπισθόπους 'conduct him..., and conduct his followers.'

From the nature of the case it must result that there will be examples in which the context does not determine whether the pronoun is meant to have weight or not, in which either way of reading is possible, and only a complete study of the poet's use as a whole will direct us which to prefer. Some of these I could not discuss properly without setting out the context to an inconvenient length. It will be sufficient to give one instance (*Pers.* 231), and to mention the rest.

AT. ὦ φίλοι, ποῦ τὰς Ἀθήνας φασὶν ἱδρῦσθαι χθονός;
XO. τῆλε πρὸς δυσμαῖς, ἄνακτος Ἡλίου φθινάσμασιν.
AT. ἀλλὰ μὴν ἵμειρ' ἐμὸς παῖς τήνδε θηρᾶσαι πόλιν.
XO. πᾶσα γὰρ γένοιτ' ἂν Ἑλλὰς βασιλέως ὑπήκοος.
AT. ὧδέ τις πάρεστιν αὐτοῖς ἀνδροπλήθεια στρατοῦ;
XO. καὶ στρατὸς τοιοῦτος, ἔρξας πολλὰ δὴ Μήδους κακά—
AT. καὶ τί πρὸς τούτοισιν ἄλλο; πλοῦτος ἐξαρκὴς δόμοις;
XO. ἀργύρου πηγή τις αὐτοῖς ἐστι, θησαυρὸς χθονός.

If this piece were prose, I should say that αὐτοῖς in both places had no special force, and that the meaning was simply 'they have.' Nor can it be proved that Aeschylus meant otherwise. All I can say is that, after a very careful investigation of the matter, in Aeschylus and elsewhere, I believe that, if he had not meant otherwise, he would have preferred to give his sentences another shape; that he used αὐτοῖς with consciousness, and meant, in the first place, 'Is Athens such a host *in itself?*' in the second place, 'They have a special resource *of their own.*'

The following, which are also ambiguous, I will mention only, to shew that I have not overlooked them, and believe them to fall within the general rule: *Prom.* 48, *Prom.* 454, 460, 487, *Prom.* 913, 918 (these two are connected), *Prom.* 853, *Pers.* 153, *Cho.* 1014, *Pers.* 767, 768.

In a few cases there is a question about the reading either of the line in which *αὐτός* occurs, or of the determining context, *e.g. Cho.* 883, *Prom.* 772, *Pers.* 191. None of these appear to be true exceptions.

There remain a few cases (*Pers.* 520 and *Pers.* 727 for instance) in which the use may be indistinguishable from that of ordinary prose. I will suppose these cases as many as twelve, though I think six would be too high a figure. I could suppose them twenty, and it would make no difference. It is clear that a usage, which might naturally have occurred in Aeschylus hundreds of times, if he had not regarded it as essentially prosaic and unfit for poetry unless under special circumstances, may with propriety be called 'extremely rare' in his works, if he admitted it a score of times, *a fortiori* if, as I hold, he really lapses into it not so often as once in a thousand lines.

I now return to the proper question of this paper. All the work above summarized I had gone through before I wrote upon *αὐτός* as I did; all this, and three or four times as much besides; for, as I have said, I went almost exhaustively into the usage of Pindar, and made considerable studies in other writers as well. Whether my conclusions were right or wrong is at present nothing to the purpose. I am in a position to prove that I did what I have described. The statement that what I wrote on *αὐτός* in the notes to the two plays 'is due either to unverified assumption or deliberate disregard of the evidence' is therefore absolutely untrue.

But it is not only injurious and untrue; it has also the third quality of a libel; it is, in the legal sense of the word, though in this sense only, malicious. This it would be, if it had been made merely without evidence. But there was ample evidence to the contrary, all the evidence, which, from the nature of the case, could naturally exist or be expected. My statements were limited to the usage of Aeschylus; I went far beyond Aeschylus in investigation, as seemed to be proper; but I said nothing, and meant to say nothing, about any other writer. I proposed to edit the whole of Aeschylus, and had announced this intention. I had edited two plays. On all the passages bearing on the question of αὐτός, which occur in those plays, I had written notes, whether absurd or judicious is nothing to the matter. Was it not then obvious to suppose that I was prepared to deal with the passages in other plays, when I came to them? Could anything be more perversely uncharitable than to assume that I should not, and to accuse me, on this assumption only, of 'disregarding' evidence, to the sifting of which I had given more than a week's hard work? I repeat then that Mr Headlam's statement respecting my work upon αὐτός is a complete libel; and I say that it ought never to have been published.

Of malice in the common sense, of any ill-will to me personally, I entirely acquit Mr Headlam. I believe that he would have criticized any one else, as indeed he has done before now, upon similar principles. He is a very good scholar, as this pamphlet shows, and as most of us would assume without proof from the position which he holds. If he would address himself directly to the classics and let his contemporaries alone, he would produce work, which few or none would study with more interest and pleasure than I. But for judging the work of other students there never was in the world a man more completely disqualified. The first rule for a critic, as for any other judge, is that the *onus probandi* lies always on the accusation; that you are to suppose no fault, until it is proved, and never to suppose a great fault, if to suppose a smaller will account for the facts. Mr Headlam is incapable of this equity, and his practice is the very reverse. He construes everything against the prisoner, and as strongly as possible. For him, as I have just shown, facts not cited are facts not examined, and this, however strong may be the circumstantial evidence that the examination has actually been made. For him, as I shall now show, a proposition which may be taken in an untrue sense is a proposition which was intended to bear that sense, and this without regard to the context, the position of the writer, or any other circumstance whatsoever. The following instance is typical, and is the only one, with which I shall deal in detail.

Mr Headlam charges me (p. 19—21) with ignorance of the facts about the common anapaestic dimeter. He cites these facts from familiar books, and implies truly enough, that no one, who had made serious studies in Greek tragedy, could be ignorant of them, but untruly more than enough, that I am thus ignorant. Without vanity I think I may say, that to most of my fellow-students this proposition would in itself have given some pause, that they would have examined the evidence for it with great severity, and would have preferred any other conclusion at all compatible with what I had written. Let us see then of what kind is the evidence.

In the *Seven against Thebes* is a dialogue (*vv.* 789—816) in which the text shows unusual signs of disturbance, and all commentators have suspected some more or less extensive interpolation. This dialogue concludes with a passage in anapaestic dimeters, which runs as follows:

ὦ μεγάλε Ζεῦ καὶ πολιοῦχοι
δαίμονες, οἳ δὴ Κάδμου πύργους
τούσδε ῥύεσθε,
πότερον χαίρω κἀπολολύξω
πόλεως ἀσινεῖ σωτῆρι,
ἢ τοὺς μογεροὺς καὶ δυσδαίμονας
ἀτέκνους κλαύσω πολεμάρχους;
οἳ δῆτ' ὀρθῶς κατ' ἐπωνυμίαν
καὶ πολυνεικεῖς
ὤλοντ' ἀσεβεῖ διανοίᾳ.

The conclusion at which I arrived, after an investigation as thorough as that which I have described in the case of *αὐτός*, was that almost all the dialogue is from another hand than that of Aeschylus, and that from this hand probably came the anapaests. This latter inference I based partly on the fact, that in the space of ten verses there are no less than three departures from the metrical practice of the poet, (1) the 'common' syllable at the end of *v.* 809 (*τούσδε ῥύεσθε̆*), (2) the anapaest following a dactyl (*δυσδαίμονας ἀτέκνους*), and (3) the inelegant rhythm of the verse πόλεως ἀσινεῖ σωτῆρι, compared, for instance, with ἀτέκνους κλαύσω πολεμάρχους, which is of a better type. We cannot say with certainty, in the present state of the evidence, that Aeschylus could not possibly have broken, once in a way, any one of the practices against which these verses offend. I should myself say that in these matters such an absolute *a priori* certainty could never be safely assumed. But I thought, and still think, that the conjunction of the three irregularities is highly significant. I also thought, and still think, that, when I wrote, the significance of this conjunction had been seldom or never considered. I thought so partly because the commentators, whom I had before me, called attention to the first point, but did not call attention to the others, whereas, from my point of view, the three should be noted together; and partly because in Dr Wecklein's elaborate collection of conjectures I did not find the suggestion, to which such consideration would lead, that the anapaests were part of that interpolation, which all suspected in this region of the text.

Under these circumstances I wrote as follows:

809. τούσδε ῥύεσθε̆. The original ῥύεσθαι of the MS. (corrected by the writer himself) must apparently have been merely a common slip of the pen, due to the similar sound of αι and ε. The infinitive has no construction. By the strict rule deduced from the tragedians a long syllable is required, as this anapaestic metre does not allow 'common' syllables at the division of the verses. We may of course suppose (with Dindorf) that something is lost after ῥύεσθε (*e.g.* Σπαρτῶν τε πόλιν), or that the text is otherwise corrupt. But it has not apparently been observed that we have another, less obvious but still inadmissible flaw of metre in 812, as well as the unrhythmical verse 811. My own opinion, as given above, is that, instead of assuming an unusual extent of corruption in this place, we should accept the passage as it stands for a fairly successful imitation. Athens must have contained many men capable of writing fair verse, and also quite capable of ignoring a delicate observance such as the *Synaphea*.

I take this argument to be perfectly plain and perfectly sound, as far as it goes, whatever may be held as to the strength or necessity of the conclusion. I believe that if the note were submitted to a hundred average persons of competent knowledge, and they were asked to guess what serious fault had been found with it, they would be all at a loss.

But my critic (p. 19) is not at a loss to find a monstrous fault, nor ever need be, with such divining rods as he uses here. Tearing from the context the sentence "it has not apparently been observed that we have another less obvious but still inadmissible flaw of metre in 812," and fixing particularly upon the word "inadmissible", he not only construes this as an assertion that no example, certain or doubtful, of a dactyl followed by an anapaest can be found in Aeschylus or anywhere in the Attic poets, but actually proceeds to scold me for ignorance and wilful negligence exactly as he might have done, if I had said so in so many words. He cites from Hermann and Ahrens the evidence, familiar to me and all students, which shows that in a very small number of places the rule in question is or appears to be broken by the tragedians. (Mr Headlam would apparently count *one doubtful case* in Aeschylus, and one certain case, with others doubtful, in Euripides, with whose practice, since the problem before me was the genuineness of a passage in Aeschylus, I was not at all concerned). And he draws the charitable inference that I am ignorant of this evidence and of the books in which it is stated. Upon the same principle he might have gone on to attack me about the common syllable in ῥύεσθε: for whoever declares it certain, that no Attic poet, in any part of his works, ever once broke the rule which prohibits it, says more than the evidence warrants.

But I say that it is an abuse of criticism to construe in this way, for the purpose of founding an attack, the words which I use respecting either the one rule or the other. Construed fairly, and with due regard to the tenor and purpose of the argument, my words imply nothing but what is true, that both rules are very strong rules of Aeschylean practice, so strong that to find breaches of both, together with other violations of his style and practice, within ten anapaestic verses, lays the verses open to reasonable suspicion of their origin.

But the critic has another fault to find, and finds it in the same way:

What we have here is an anapaest immediately succeeding a dactyl—a rare thing. Dr Verrall imagines it has escaped notice in this place...

Hereupon it is shown that the exception is noticed in Hermann's *Elementa Doctrinae Metricae*, and judgment is given accordingly. But where do I say that no one has recorded this exception? I am arguing that the passage is not genuine. I notice, as the commentators generally do, the breach of rule in *ῥύεσθε*. And I continue thus:

> But it has not apparently been observed that we have another, less obvious but still inadmissible flaw of metre in 812, as well as the unrhythmical verse 811. My own opinion, as given above, is that, instead of assuming an unusual extent of corruption in this place, we should accept the passage as it stands for a fairly successful imitation.

The fact of which I say that "it has not apparently been observed" is, as any one reading the note as a whole must feel and see, the fact material to my argument, the fact that the first irregularity is immediately followed by two others, so that we have three offences close together in this place. I did not mean and I did not say, with regard to any one of these irregularities in particular, that it had never been anywhere registered with other exceptions of the same class. Such notice is nothing to the purpose; because no one of the three exceptions, standing by itself in a passage otherwise unsuspicious, would afford ground for the inference to which I was leading. I thought indeed, and I still think, that the commentators (notwithstanding Hermann's *Elementa*) had been apt to overlook the collision of dactyl and anapaest; because several commentaries, which I consulted, agreed in noticing the flaw in *ῥύεσθε* and in not noticing the other, though both deserve notice, as departures from the practice of the poet, and deserve it alike. This is what I meant by the words "less obvious."

If my sentence means that no one had ever remarked the collision, then it also means that no one had ever shown dissatisfaction at the rhythm of *πόλεως ἀσινεῖ σωτῆρι*. Yet Dr Wecklein's appendix of conjectures (to which I refer incessantly and in such a way as to show that it was always under my eye) records no less than four emendations which change this rhythm and substitute one more satisfactory, and also one emendation which gets rid of the dactyl and anapaest. To these and others I allude, as might naturally be supposed, in the words "instead of assuming an unusual extent of corruption in this place," and I cite one of them, expressly as "a specimen", in the note to *v.* 811. Where then is the ground for thinking that I imagined the matter to stand otherwise than as it actually and visibly did?

Now I do not by any means say—and I ask attention to this—that in point of expression my note is perfect, or that a reasonable critic might not find something to improve. Such a critic might say—it would be a punctilious and a dubious criticism, but not unreasonable—that, for a short description of the facts or apparent facts about the dactyl and anapaest in Aeschylus, "irregular" would be a better word than "inadmissible." This, I say, is dubious, for in truth the state of the evidence forbids us to decide which word best represents the feeling of Aeschylus on the point; "inadmissible" may be too strong, "irregular" is probably too weak. Either word might be used in this context without any other inaccuracy than inevitably arises from the impossibility of saying every thing at once, and without danger of deceiving any one who did not wish to be deceived. To write "irregular" would have been no protection to me, for then some other Mr Headlam, who happened to reject the one doubtful exception in Aeschylus which this Mr Headlam allows, might have remarked, that, if I had known anything about metre, I should have written "inadmissible." Nothing less than a page of irrelevant discussion would have prevented all possibility of misunderstanding and misrepresentation. Still it may be that, if I had written "irregular," I should have erred on the better side.

Nor should I complain at all of the remark, that although from the whole of my note it may be clear enough to what I refer when I say that "it has not apparently been observed," in the sentence itself this is not so clear as it should be, and that, to be quite perspicuous, I should rather have written something like this:

> But it has not apparently been considered that, in close conjunction with this metrical flaw, we have another in 812 and an unsatisfactory verse in 811.

Neither this nor any statement, suitable to the brief limits of a note, would bring in every relevant fact or be secure from such an inquisition as that of Mr Headlam. But this would have been a better form, and something better still might doubtless be devised by a more skilful hand.

But what I have to protest against, as an abuse of criticism and an injury to writers in general, is the manner in which my critic, instead of assuming that I possess ordinary knowledge, and therefore charging me with inexact or obscure expression, prefers rather to isolate an ambiguous phrase, to fix upon it the most erroneous meaning which it will bear, and so to bring out, in place of a light objection to style, an impeachment for incredible ignorance.

Against such presumptions and such constructions no writer would be safe. But this I will add; and as it is almost the only concession which I can make to Mr Headlam, I desire to make it amply and without reserve. If there is any writer who is safe against such a method, I am certainly not that invulnerable paragon. *Humanum est*, as it was said by some Professor of imperfect Humanity, *alius aliter errare.* My readiest way of erring, as I am but too well aware, is to use, particularly in subordinate propositions and *obiter dicta*, phrases too strong or too wide for the facts. This is not due always or usually, whatever Mr Headlam may think, either to ignorance or to want of labour. I believe (I am really vexed to talk of myself; but how can I help it?) that not many writers take more pains to be informed of their subject. I have described in full one specimen of my work, and it was not an exceptional case. I do of course make blunders. But much more often an inexact or misleading phrase in my writing is the result of trying to state briefly, for the purpose of a note, the result of an investigation, which in fact cannot be so represented. I will give one example of this, a case in which (except for the tone of the criticism, which is everywhere such as, I say boldly, I do not deserve) I have nothing to object to my critic. It is I who have deceived him and have done injustice to myself.

At *Theb.* 530 occurs the phrase *Καδμείων ἕνα*, usually construed as equivalent to *Καδμείων τινά*, *a Cadmean.* I think this interpretation wrong and not agreeable to the usage of the poet, or indeed of the poets generally, respecting εἷς. The interpretation is matter of opinion, and I do not now wish to argue it. But as to the usage, to test my feeling, besides referring to two or three Lexicons, I went through the articles on εἷς in the indices to the tragedians, examining the references. This was of course no superfluity, but necessary for my purpose. In this investigation I set aside, as plainly not parallel to Καδμείων ἕνα in the sense supposed, all those cases of εἷς, in which the *one* specified is an individual named, or who could be named, and is *one* of *a fixed and permanent number*.

Thus in the *Rhesus* (393) we find παῖ τῆς μελῳδοῦ μητέρος, Μουσῶν μιᾶς, in *Rhes.* 891 Μοῦσα, συγγόνων μία, in Eur. *Hel.* 6 τῶν κατ' οἶδμα παρθένων μίαν Ψαμάθην, in *Ion* 1 Ἄτλας... θεῶν μιᾶς ἔφυσε Μαῖαν, and in *Cycl.* 21 παῖδες θεοῦ Κύκλωπες...τούτων (Κυκλώπων) ἑνός[1]. So Homer, as Mr Headlam says, writes very naturally χαρίτων μίαν Πασιθέην (*Il.* Ξ. 275); Pindar ἔγαμεν ὑψιθρόνων μίαν Νηρῄδων (*Nem.* 4. 65); Apollonius Rhodius Τερψιχόρη Μουσέων μία (4. 896). But these phrases are not parallels to Καδμείων ἕνα in the sense commonly put on those words in *Theb.* 530, *a Cadmean*, an individual not specified, nor specifiable, otherwise than as belonging to that fluctuating class. In *Rhes.* 393, for instance, Μουσῶν μιᾶς *one of the Muses*, is parallel, not to Ἀθηναίων τις *an Athenian*, but to εἷς τῶν ἀρχόντων *one of the archons*. These passages do not show that the writers were indifferent in their use of εἷς and τις (which was the point to which I was addressing myself); on the contrary the fact that several such instances occur in tragedy (whereas phrases like Καδμείων εἷς *a Cadmean* are, as I repeat, not found there) is evidence not against but in favour of the distinction between εἷς and τις for such purposes, which the

[1] As to Soph. *Ant.* 1066 τῶν σῶν αὐτὸς ἐκ σπλάγχνων ἕνα | νέκυν νεκρῶν ἀμοιβὸν ἀντιδοὺς ἔσει, I do not agree that ἕνα here means *some one;* I think that, as the rest of the sentence shows, it means strictly *one* (*for one*), and that to write τινά would have spoiled the expression. Ap. Rhod. 4, 1016 is parallel to Eur. *Med.* 945, Ar. *Eq.* 1300 to Soph. *Ant.* 269. Ar. *Vesp.* 1165 belongs to the class above discussed. As to *Ion* 1 see note there.

tragedians appear to have felt. In *Rhes.* 393, if the author had written Μουσῶν τινός, he would have changed the colour of his expression, as it seems to me, and changed it very much for the worse. And on the other hand, in *Theb.* 530, if Aeschylus had meant what he has been thought to mean, he should and would have written, not *φῶτα* Καδμείων *ἕνα,* but *φῶτα* Καδμεῖον, or *φῶτα,* Καδμείων *τινα.*

In the course of the investigation I noticed particularly that in several places, where εἷς might at first sight seem simply equivalent to τις *some one,* it is really equivalent to *quivis, any one,* and essential to the meaning intended. Mr Headlam allows that this is possible in all the cases I cite and others, though he does not agree; but of our disagreement another time, or not now. Having then completed my work, I put into my note the following parenthesis:

(It should be observed that εἷς is not found as a mere equivalent for τις: in the apparent examples it generally signifies nearly *quivis* 'any one, equal to one, merely one'; see Eur. *Med.* 945, *Or.* 264, *Bacch.* 917, Soph. *El.* 1342. In Soph. *Ant.* 269 λέγει τις εἷς ὃς πάντας κ.τ.λ. there is an antithesis between εἷς and πάντας, and so elsewhere.)

Now, to the substance of this statement, so far as the purpose of my note is concerned, I do not allow that any exception can be taken. But to the form of it two exceptions may be taken. In the first place, for "not found" I should perhaps have written "not found in authors comparable on such a point with Aeschylus," because I had not, and have not, ascertained precisely what are the limits in other Greek. I cannot think this a serious matter, because any one reading the parenthesis with the context (Mr Headlam takes it out, drops the marks of parenthesis, and considers it as a principal and separate statement) would see that I was thinking and speaking only of writers, whose use in such matters can be held to warrant a conclusion about Aeschylus. I could scarcely be bound to maintain for instance, that εἷς and τις were not used indifferently by Dion Cassius or Eustathius. The second exception is more important. I said nothing about such examples as Μουσῶν μιᾶς simply because I did not think them "*apparent* examples" of εἷς for τις: I thought it apparent that they were not such.

But, as I fully admit, this is not so apparent, that I could afford to leave it unexplained. That much is proved enough by the fact that Mr Headlam, a reader more than competent, did not see how I meant to dispose of these cases; and if he had called on me to explain myself further, he would have been perfectly in his right. Whether under all the circumstances it was judicious or considerate to conclude peremptorily that, because the critic saw no explanation, therefore I could have no explanation to give, or whether it was fair to collect a number, not very large, of such incomplete or imperfect statements, and to use them as secondary evidence in support of the charge that I do not know the elements of my subject and have taken no pains to learn them, are questions which I must leave to the judgment of the reader.

I do not see reason for going further into the details of Mr Headlam's book. A large part of it deals with matters of opinion, matters which according to my notions should never have been introduced into the body of an accusation, matters which I do not intend to discuss with any one who has taken the tone of an accuser. For instance, it is not to any person in the temper of Mr Headlam that I shall address myself, if I wish to defend further my suggested emendation of *Theb.* 1002 *τέθνηκεν οἷσπερ ὀρνέοις θνῄσκειν καλόν* (for *τέθνηκεν οὗπερ τοῖς νέοις*), based upon a note in the scholia. Mr Headlam gives three pages to this, but touches the base of my argument only in one sentence (p. 94), "The schol. refers to the line of Homer only as the most famous praise of fight in defence of one's country. The quotation is so familiar that there is no need for him to finish it." I, as well as Mr Headlam, know something about the scholia to Aeschylus; and I do not consider his explanation adequate. Of the judgment shown in my emendation Mr Headlam speaks in his invariable tone of contempt. I shall say only this. There are a few living Englishmen who, having achieved the feat, now very difficult, of suggesting a correction of Aeschylus both new and valuable, have a right to speak on such a matter. One of these is unquestionably Mr A. E. Housman. Mr Housman has declared in print that my emendation seems to him "highly probable." This does not prove that I am right; but it does prove that the style assumed by Mr Headlam, here and elsewhere, is unfit for the subject and the persons concerned.

To form an opinion on Mr Headlam's accusation, it is necessary first to abstract all that large part of his 159 pages which deals with matter of opinion, and is distinguished in no way, except the asperity, from the common staple of discussion. All this, be it right or wrong, might have appeared just as well in the periodicals, and affords no reason or excuse for a hostile pamphlet. The not very large residue, if carefully examined in the light of the cases considered above, would support the conclusion that in several places, not many but all too many, I have written too briefly, too obscurely, or in such a way as might naturally mislead. This kind of fault is, I believe, inevitable in long, elaborate, and fatiguing work. I know that I could easily show examples of it in the works of others; and at any rate I am well aware that my own is not exceptionally free from it, but indeed quite otherwise. What Mr Headlam has done is to collect these faults, to construe and misconstrue them with pertinacious iniquity, to swell the apparent bulk of them with matter not relevant to an accusation, and to tack them to one or two statements, like that concerning my investigation of *αὐτός*, which, if they were true, would be really incriminating. But these incriminating statements are untrue; and it is untrue altogether that I do not know my subject, that I have neglected the means of information, or that I practise any other method than the one only scientific method which Mr Headlam, truly if somewhat ostentatiously, himself professes.

About the usefulness or propriety of such books as Mr Headlam's, elaborate works consisting entirely of attack and adverse criticism on a particular writer, I have myself a decided opinion. I think that they never, literally *never*, ought to be published or composed; and that it is practically impossible for such books to be just either to the subject or to the writer of them. No one, without injury to his temper and judgment, can dwell for laborious weeks and months upon that which, with or without reason, he dislikes and despises. Mr Headlam dislikes my writings. I can see plainly enough that I am not likely to give pleasure or instruction to him. In the various constitution of minds this case will sometimes happen, without any particular fault on either side. He does not allow, and doubtless therefore he does not find, any substantial merit in me at all. This I sincerely regret; for I see much merit in him. But this being so, why can he not burn his copies of my volumes, buy no more, and work at the classics himself with the help of such writers as he finds to be helpful?

Mr Headlam, as I gather from his conclusion, would as a general rule think it undesirable that the expression of opinions about literature should take the form of his pamphlet. But he holds that my writings are a peculiar case, an insidious danger which calls for an exceptional remedy. "It would be easy to point out many whom their glitter has dazzled, fascinated, and seduced." I have not myself observed this crowd of obsequious victims. I should have said that I have received at least my share of contradiction. The truth I take to be this. Mr Headlam has noticed with displeasure that my works have been praised, and heartily praised, by many who are very unlikely to err with me, whose humanity errs, when it errs, in other and opposite ways. He draws the conclusion that these persons are under some glamour or spell, which prevents them from discerning that I am an impostor. My own explanation is different, simpler, and certainly kinder to every one concerned. It is that my writings, though they have doubtless faults of their own, have also merits of their own, and have rendered to many some not very common services. For the sake of these services, generous people, thinking perhaps that merit of any kind is not too common, and perhaps not sharing, for various reasons, the fear of Mr Headlam that I shall make too many go and do likewise, have forgiven me when I go wrong and will, I hope, continue to treat me as my efforts shall seem to deserve.

TRINITY COLLEGE, CAMBRIDGE,
*Jan.* 30, 1892.

For EU product safety concerns, contact us at Calle de José Abascal, 56–1°,
28003 Madrid, Spain or eugpsr@cambridge.org.

www.ingramcontent.com/pod-product-compliance
Ingram Content Group UK Ltd.
Pitfield, Milton Keynes, MK11 3LW, UK
UKHW012346130625
459647UK00009B/563

* 9 7 8 1 1 0 8 0 0 9 6 4 5 *